Neo-Nationalism

"Erikur Bergmann's new book reveals the connections between nationalism, populism, authoritarian drifts, conspiracy theories, and fake news, providing valuable insights into the decline of democracy around the world and especially in Western democracies."
—Professor Susanna Cafaro, *University of Salento, Italy*

"This excellent book is timely and important. It highlights the need to consider the historical context and evolution of nativist forms of populism to fully understand their implications for our own time. It also reminds us that these implications are potentially so dire as to overturn our current word order, not by evolving it but by disrupting it."
—Lone Sorensen, *University of Huddersfield, UK*

Eirikur Bergmann

Neo-Nationalism

The Rise of Nativist Populism

Eirikur Bergmann
Centre for European Studies
Bifröst University
Reykjavik, Iceland

ISBN 978-3-030-41772-7   ISBN 978-3-030-41773-4 (eBook)
https://doi.org/10.1007/978-3-030-41773-4

© The Editor(s) (if applicable) and The Author(s), under exclusive licence to Springer Nature Switzerland AG 2020
This work is subject to copyright. All rights are solely and exclusively licensed by the Publisher, whether the whole or part of the material is concerned, specifically the rights of translation, reprinting, reuse of illustrations, recitation, broadcasting, reproduction on microfilms or in any other physical way, and transmission or information storage and retrieval, electronic adaptation, computer software, or by similar or dissimilar methodology now known or hereafter developed.
The use of general descriptive names, registered names, trademarks, service marks, etc. in this publication does not imply, even in the absence of a specific statement, that such names are exempt from the relevant protective laws and regulations and therefore free for general use.
The publisher, the authors and the editors are safe to assume that the advice and information in this book are believed to be true and accurate at the date of publication. Neither the publisher nor the authors or the editors give a warranty, expressed or implied, with respect to the material contained herein or for any errors or omissions that may have been made. The publisher remains neutral with regard to jurisdictional claims in published maps and institutional affiliations.

Cover credit: Collage by eStudio Calamar

This Palgrave Macmillan imprint is published by the registered company Springer Nature Switzerland AG.
The registered company address is: Gewerbestrasse 11, 6330 Cham, Switzerland

For Hrafnhildur

Preface and Acknowledgments

When travelling with my family on a ferry from Tarifa in Spain to Tangier in Morocco, in the summer of 2018, we encountered a group of African refugees who were being taken to shore by armed guards who had been patrolling the area out at sea. Upon returning three days later we saw the refugees still held captured under armed guard on a boat in the harbour—before being returned back across the Strait of Gibraltar. We, however, sailed right through and easily re-entered Spain on our European passports. I remember the difficulty of trying to explain this situation to my twelve-year-old daughter, who couldn't contemplate the calamity she was witnessing. This book is partially an attempt to explain the politics that over the last half-century resulted in this state of affairs.

Over the last two decades I have studied both nationalism and populism and published several books and articles on the separate phenomena. Although the two should not be conflated, the current era has seen the convergence of both populism and nationalism. In previous publications I have developed the concept of *nationalist* populism. However, when dealing with politics that primarily point to dangerous outsiders, my focus here is on the *nativist* kind, which I maintain has turned into a separate *Neo-Nationalism* spreading across Europe and America.

This research has benefitted from interactions with many colleagues in several academic fields, for example in the EU-funded COST action, *Comparative Analysis of Conspiracy Theories (COMPACT)*. I thank all my colleagues in the network for thought-provoking discussions and for exposing me to some of the most pristine research in the fields of both populism and nationalism studies. I owe special thanks to the network leaders, Professors Peter Knight and Michael Butter.

The research also benefitted from the research fund of Bifröst University.

Several colleagues gracefully gave up their time to read over different parts of the manuscript. For that I am in dept to Professors Michael Butter, Susanna Cafaro and David Farrell, as well as to Drs Christian De Cock, Heather McRobbie, Lone Sorensen and Ilya Yabolokov. All provided me with important feedback. I am thankful for their excellent suggestions. Any mistakes found in the text are, though, solely my own responsibility. I thank my publishers at Palgrave Macmillan, Ambra Finotello and Anne-Kathrin Birchley-Brun, for flawless co-operation, and for all their valuable help.

I would also like to thank my family for tolerating me through some of the more trying times of the drafting process. Especially I thank my partner in life, Aino Freyja Järvelä, for all her support. I thank our children, Sólrún Rós, Einar Sigurður, Hrafnhildur and Ægir Bergmann—as well as our grand-daughter, Dagný Birna, who was born during the writing process.

Contents

Introduction: The Rise of Nativist Populism	1
Understanding Nativist Populism	29
The First Wave: The Oil Crisis and the New Nationalists	53
The Second Wave: The Collapse of Communism and 9/11	83
The Third Wave: The International Financial Crisis and Refugees	131
Conclusions: The Neo-Nationalist Order	209
Index	221

ACRONYMS

AfD	*Alternative für Deutschland* (Alternative for Germany)
BNP	British National Party
CDA	Critical Discourse Analysis
CIA	Central Intelligence Agency of the United States
DDF	*Den Danske Forening* (The Danish Association)
DDR	German Democratic Republic
DF	*Dansk Folkeparti* (Danish Peoples Party)
EC	European Community
EEA	European Economic Area agreement
EFTA	European Free Trade Association
EP	European Parliament
EU	European Union
FN	*Front National* (National Front of France, later National Rally)
FPÖ	*Freiheitliche Partei Österreichs* (Freedom Party of Austria)
FrP	*Fremskrittspartiet* (Progress Party of Norway) / *Fremskridtspartiet* (Progress Party of Denmark)
IMF	International Monetary Fund
ISIS	Islamic State, terrorist organization
LN	*Lega Nord* (Northern League of Italy)
M5S	Five Star movement of Italy
MEP	Member of the European Parliament
MP	Member of Parliament
MSI	*Movimento Sociale Italiano* (Italian Social Movement)
NATO	North Atlantic Treaty Organization
ND	*Nouvelle Droite* (New Right of France)
NGO	Non-Governmental Organization
NHS	National Health Service (of the United Kingdom)

NSA	National Security Agency
OEEC	Organization for Economic Co-operation in Europe
OPEC	Organization or the Petroleum Exporting countries
OSCE	Organization for Security and Co-operation in Europe
ÖVP	*Österreichische Volkspartei* (Austrian Peoples Party)
PEDIGA	Patriotic Europeans against the Islamization of the Occident
PM	Prime Minister
PS	*Perussuomalaiset* (The True party, later The Finns Party)
RAF	*Rote Armee Fraktion* (Red Army Faction)
RT	Russia Today TV station
SD	*Sverigedemocraterna* (Sweden Democrats*)*
SMP	*Suomen Maasedun Puolue* (The Finnish Agrarian Party)
UFO	Unidentified Flying Object
UK	United Kingdom
UKIP	United Kingdom Independence Party
UN	United Nations
US	United States of America
VB	*Vlaams Bloc/Vlaams Belang* (The Flemish Bloc in Belgium)
VVD	*Partij voor de Vrijheied* (Freedom Party of the Netherlands)
WB	World Bank
WHO	The World Health OrganiZation

Introduction: The Rise of Nativist Populism

On the eve of 9 November 1989 the Berlin Wall came tumbling down. During a press briefing that night, the spokesman for the Politburo of the Socialist Unity Party in the German Democratic Republic (DDR), Gunther Schabowski, announced a plan to open the gates to the West. After delivering the statement, Schabowski found himself pressured on the question of when the policy would be put in place. He fumbled for a while, before finally replying: 'as far as I know—effective immediately, without delay'.

Schabowski had not been involved in the preparations. Only just minutes prior to the press conference had he been handed a note on the change, but he did not know that the plan was first to take effect the following day, so as to prepare for orderly implementation. For instance, the border guards had not been properly informed.

The regulation had only been agreed few hours earlier, in response to mounting pressure which was building after Hungary had begun to dismantle its border infrastructure with Austria. Many East Germans had been fleeing over to the West via that route, in ever increasing numbers. However, several of them were being detained and forcibly returned by Hungarian authorities, leading to large scale public protests within the DDR. Starting on Monday nights in front of the St Nicholas church in Leipzig, and soon also in Dresden, the crowds were calling for the gates to be opened. Gradually the protest spread around the country, eventually accumulating in large numbers on and around Alexander Platz in Berlin. Their chant grew louder; 'Wir wollen raus!' (We want out!)

© The Author(s) 2020
E. Bergmann, *Neo-Nationalism*,
https://doi.org/10.1007/978-3-030-41773-4_1

Schabowski's hesitant reply, which we later learned was premature, marked the end of the Cold War system. After the announcement on TV, the crowds immediately rushed to the Bornholmer Strasse crossing. Others ran down Unter den Linden—the majestic boulevard leading from Alexander Platz to where the Wall surrounded the landmark Brandenburg Gate. There they started to tear the wall down, initially—quite literally—just with their bare hands. The border guards had not been warned of the avalanche of protestors arriving, but luckily, they did not open fire with their fully loaded firearms. Change was in the air. Through the night *Ossis* and *Wessis* were embracing and dancing together on top of the wall, celebrating their sudden-found unity. The following day saw the dawn of a new political order.

I myself was standing in the living room at home in eastern Reykjavik, watching these dramatic events on TV. Barely twenty years old, I struggled to understand the meaning of the moment. Still, I remember it dawning on me that history was unfolding before our eyes, and that this was indeed pivotal.

Although the writing on the wall for the eventual downfall of the communist regimes was perhaps becoming increasingly apparent, and that the DDR and even the entire Eastern bloc was not sustainable, the fall of the Wall was surprisingly sudden to most people. The swiftness of it reminds us of how established political systems that we grow used to, and even start to take for granted, can come to an end—sometimes quite rapidly as was the case with the Berlin Wall and the communist structure in Eastern Europe. It can be useful to bear that lesson in mind when mapping the progression of nativist populism over the last half century—which is the aim of this book. Before delving into the meaning of nativist populism, I first turn to briefly discussing the liberal democratic order of our time.

Liberal Democracy

The end of the Cold War prompted many people to contemplate the nature of the coming political order in the West. One of the most influential intellectuals was the American political scientist Francis Fukuyama (1992). In his book, *The End of History and the Last Man*, he argued that the Western order of liberal democracy, reaching across the Atlantic from North America to Western Europe, would prevail for the foreseeable future. He wrote that we might not only be witnessing the end of the

Cold War, an identifiable period in political history, 'but the end of history as such: that is, the end point of mankind's ideological evolution and the universalization of Western liberal democracy as the final form of human government' (Fukuyama 1989).

Fukuyama firmly believed in the resilience of democracy, which, he claimed, had since the French Revolution proven to be a superior system of government. With alternatives out of the way after the collapse of communism the period of dialectic contrasts and ideological conflicts, such as those identified by Friedrich Hegel and Karl Marx, was, he argued, over. In using the term 'the end of history' Fukuyama was not arguing that events would stop occurring, but that politics would predominantly be conducted within the framework of liberal democracy, that is, within the parameters of representative democratic governance in an open and free market economy.

For the West, the end of the Second World War marked the foundation of a new world order. Although the outer parameters of the post-war era were framed by the global Cold War system, the West united internally around a new political construction: the liberal democracy of independent states within a vast international architecture. This new order was to replace the fallen model of insulated sovereign nation-states, which in two world wars had left Europe in ruins. The new post-war order was partially to be regulated by international law and external authorities that in some instances overreached internal national autonomy. An era of unprecedented level of international integration emerged.

Cross-border institutions included the Organization for Economic Co-operation in Europe (OEEC), the Bretton Woods agreement establishing the World Bank (WB), and the International Monetary Fund (IMF). In 1949, both the United Nations (UN) and North Atlantic Treaty Organization (NATO) were founded. The European integration process began in the early 1950s, leading to the supra-national European Union (EU) of today. From the outset, the integration process was a conscious attempt to intertwine interests across borders in Europe so tightly that any military invasion would only hurt one's own interests.

In the following three decades, these institutions, firmly tying cross-border co-operation into a joint international framework, contributed to the increased prosperity and rapid economic growth which the region enjoyed until the Oil Crisis hit in the early 1970s.

New World Order(s)

The significance of this change to the international system was perhaps of a similar magnitude to the Westphalian order of sovereign states that was established after the end of the Thirty Year's War in the seventeenth century. The peace agreements signed in the cities of Osnabrück and Munster in Westphalia in 1648 instated a new principle of international law, a mutual recognition of each state having exclusive sovereignty within own territory. This created the system of independent and sovereign states, refusing all rights of external state interference across borders.

Instead of continuing intra-continental conquests, European countries embarked on expansions elsewhere, leading to much further colonialization than before. In the following decades and centuries, Europeans were conquering the world. Much later, as I will explore in this book, this endeavour would result in massive migration from the colonies to the West. Finally, by the outbreak of the Great War in 1914, this Westphalian order had collapsed.

It can be argued that the institutional framework instated after the end of the Second World War in 1945 similarly created a new international order. Again, after another thirty years of conflict—between 1914 and 1945—a neoteric state order was to replace the fallen one.

As I will discuss further in the following chapter, the new post-Second World War system rested no longer solely on a principle of insular sovereign states, but—vitally for the story told on these pages—a new international institutional architecture was added to it. This change, instead, turned states interdependent. Sovereignty, as such—as a concept—gained an outer layer. It no longer solely revolved around a monopoly of internal authority, but also rested on a right that only independent states enjoyed, that of participating in international operations and pooling their sovereignty in shared institutions.

Shared Values

In the post-Second World War era, nationalism and nativism had not only come to be considered a discredited ideology, but such sentiments were even widely and firmly held in contempt. Nationalism was in this era equated with racism, and world leaders were adamant in insulating contemporary society from its toxic nature. The very term itself came to be understood as being pejorative. To be called a nationalist was a synonym for being racist and even being sympathetic to fascism and Nazism.

The system built after the devastations of fascism and Nazism was based on several broadly shared liberal values. In addition to increased systemic cross-border state co-operation and pooling of sovereignty, as I have already mentioned, they also included, for example: the rule of law, firm division of power, free trade across borders, respect for human rights, wide reaching civil rights, unbiased and professional administration, and a free and independent media. These were some of the basic rules of Western liberal democracies, respected across the political spectrum, from left to right. Politics, thus, did not challenge this commonly accepted frame. Rather, political adversaries campaigned for advancing their policies firmly within these parameters. In other words, these were the outer limits of partisan pursuits.

The new post-war order thus not only rested on democracy as such, but also on liberal rights, that is, civil liberties and human rights. The system relied equally on both these pillars. The liberal aspect was built in to protect individuals and minorities from oppression from the majority. Liberal democracy therefore not only insists on majority rule, but, equally—and indispensably—on minority protection. The system actively and persistently counters collectiveness. In its essence, it instead celebrates human diversity.

Migration

The post-war order brought escalated decolonialization. It was no longer deemed moral for the West to control a vast colonial system around the globe. However, Europe was at the same time in need of workers to help resurrect its economies—including the physical work of rebuilding the continent out of ruins. Most of the countries on the Western side of the Iron Curtain thus welcomed large number of foreign labourers.

In the 1960s migrants were flocking to Europe from places like Turkey, India, Pakistan, northern Africa and the Caribbean. Many came from far away colonies—former and present—of the respective European countries, bringing with them a new cultural flavour to the continent. As I will analyse further in the following chapter, collectively this was a liberal internationalist and, indeed, a multicultural response to the devastations of war caused by nationalism.

Europe came late to the game of mass migration. Rather, it had previously been a continent of emigration. A vital part of the national identity in the United States, on the other hand, was in being a nation of immigrants, mainly from Europe. Correspondingly to that fact, the US had until recently operated a relatively liberal immigration policy.

With the fall of the Berlin Wall, Francis Fukuyama thought that the system of liberal democracy within a shared international architecture, that had proved to be so prosperous for the West, would simply be exported to replace the communist system in Eastern Europe—that is, the end of history. For a while that was indeed how it seemed. Despite serious troubles such as the Yugoslavian War, the 1990s were in many respects the heydays of liberal globalization. Several scholars started to predict the end of the nation-state. German philosopher Jürgen Habermas (1998) for instance wrote an influential essay outlining a post-national constellation of Europe.

Illiberal Democracy

Three decades on, however, we now know that the story was not to be that rosy or that simple. The promise of 1989, of ever-increasing and globally spreading liberal democracy, did not materialize. Despite the multicultural and integrationist response to devastations of the two world wars, nationalism was still always an undercurrent in the post-war years, though perhaps mostly dormant at first.

Over the years that have passed since this auspicious outlook for the future was presented by Fukuyama and many others in wake of the downfall of the Berlin Wall, populist political parties have emerged in many parts of the continent. Several of them were established to contest precisely that same post-war liberal order as Fukuyama predicted would finally prevail.

As for example Yascha Mounk (2018) has pointed out, one of the defining features of the populist political actors discussed in this book is found in their disrespect for this shared framework of the liberal democratic post-war order. Many of them have based their entire claim to power precisely on their willingness to undermine core norms of liberal democracy.

It is exactly in their willingness to dispose of these shared democratic values where populists most clearly depart from mainstream parties and break away from the status quo. Indeed, much of their appeal comes from challenging the established post-war system—in fighting against what they brand as being the establishment.

Put more simply, these can be seen as challenges to what we deem being proper and professional politics. Cas Mudde and Cristóbal Kaltwasser (2017) view this conjuncture as a 'illiberal democratic response to undemocratic liberalism'. Mounk (2018) furthermore labels this stream of thought as a bifurcation of liberal democracy, giving way to two new regime forms: illiberal democracy—democracy without rights; and undemocratic liberalism—rights without democracy.

An illustrative example of this change—when shared rules of political conduct are being contested—is found in an ongoing move away from merely seeing political opponents as adversaries who are competing within a level playing field and according to shared rules. Instead, opponents are increasingly being turned into enemies. As political theorist and former leader of the Liberal party of Canada, Michael Ignatieff (2013), wrote, 'an adversary is someone you want to defeat. An enemy is someone you have to destroy.'

In voicing their willingness to dismiss these formerly universal democratic values in the post-war era, the populists often accuse the establishment of betraying the people into the hands of foreigners.

The Populist Rise

In the summer of 2019, the ship *Sea Watch* docked in Italy after having rescued to safety forty Africans out of the sea near Libya. Its young captain, Carola Rakete, did not receive a hero's welcome for her humanitarian efforts. Instead, she was brought to jail where she would await trial for bringing illegal migrants to port. In a stream of angry tweets, Italy's nativist populist Interior Minister, Matteo Salvini, called Rakete a pirate and an outlaw. It is telling for how far from the liberal democratic promise of upholding human dignity, irrespective of colour or kind, the world had gone, that Rakete was but one of several humanitarian workers that faced similar hostility for the crime of rescuing people. In effect, Rakete and other rescuers were incarcerated for humanitarianism.

As I will discuss at length throughout this book, populist politics have evolved in varying ways across the different areas in Europe. For instance, they have progressed very differently from north to south, and panned out almost poles apart in old Western Europe and the former communist East.

The first prominent post-world-war movements tapping into nationalist thought in Western Europe had arisen in opposition to over-taxation and multiculturalism in the wake of the OPEC Oil Crisis in the 1970s. In France, the colourful demagogue Jean-Marie Le Pen founded the National Front (*Front National*—FN) in 1972, aiming to unify a variety of French nationalist movements. The party was constructed directly in opposition to postwar multiculturalism and immigration.

Meanwhile a somewhat different kind of right-wing populism was simmering underneath the surface in Denmark and in Norway. Protesting against rising tax levels, the Danish and Norwegian Progress Parties promoted anarcho-liberalism and campaigned against the increased economic and bureaucratic burden on the ordinary man. They argued against wide scope social services, immigration and cosy consensus politics in these corporatist social-democratic welfare states.

Prior to that, exclusionist and highly nationalist parties had existed in the Alp countries: the Swiss Peoples Party and the Austrian Freedom Party. In Finland an agrarian populist party had been established in 1959. Still, it was only after the Oil Crisis in the early 1970s that a significant wave of nativist populism arose in Europe.

The National Front in France and the Progressive Parties in the Nordic countries were not established around the traditional right-wing neo-liberal rhetoric, but rather they were a new populist version of it, where charismatic leaders positioned themselves alongside the blue-collar public and against the political elite. These movements offered an alternative voice to the mainstream in politics, tapping into the fears of the ordinary public. A vital component of their rhetoric was to accuse the ruling elite of having abandoned these ordinary folk.

Over in America, the so-called Neoconservatives were around the same time gaining ground within the Republican Party. In opposition to the social-liberal tide of the late 1960s and early 1970s the Christian right wanted to revert back to protection of more orthodox family values at home, and a more aggressive approach abroad.

Prior to the collapse of communism, in the wake of the downfall of the Berlin Wall in 1989, right-wing populism was kept firmly on the fringe of European politics. For example, the National Front was in its early years isolated far out on the periphery of French politics,

When Fukuyama was predicting the longevity and universality of Western liberal democracy, there was still no indication of the later surge of rogue nativist populist actors in Western politics, as was to occur in the coming years and decades, which has accumulated into the Neo-Nationalism analysed in this book.

Prevalence

Much of the early literature on populist parties predicted their rapid demise. The opposite has proved to be true. Since the late 1990s, populist parties who contest core norms of liberal democracy have been on the rise, and their support in Europe has more than tripled over the past two decades. The National Front (now the National Rally) has, for instance, increasingly gained influence and remained a force to be reckoned with—often even dominating the discourse in French politics.

Populists had graduated to power in at least a dozen European countries, and such parties were in power in all of the four largest democracies in the world: India, the United States, Indonesia and Brazil. Yascha Mounk and Jordan Kyle (2018) calculated that forty-six populist leaders had reached power in thirty-three democracies since 1990. Their study found that populists in power were prone to erode democratic norms and to make changes within constitutions for their own benefits, for instance by reducing checks and balances, removing term limits and gerrymandering constituencies. Populists in power were also found liable to limit both academic and press freedoms.

Populists have also become more skilful in holding on to power. A study published by the British daily the *Guardian* found that the number of populists in politics had more than doubled since the early 2000s (Lewis et al. 2019). Freedom House, the independent US-based watchdog monitoring the state of democracy and civil liberties around the world, concluded that democracy was in decline, and that more countries were moving away from democracy than stepping towards it.[1] The same applied to citizens' views. Fewer in the West were now found to agree with the statement that it was important to live in a democracy. And more people supported strongmen-leaders than before. A report published by the Bertelsmann Stiftung in Germany found that restrictions on political freedom were increasing, and that world governments were rather curtailing democratic norms and practices than strengthening them (Schwarz 2018).

One of the first country leaders of this nature was the flamboyant neoliberal, and at least semi-populist, Silvio Berlusconi, who brought his Forza Italia to take control of Rome in 1994. His focus on controlling the media proved successful and was later mirrored by others, in what was branded the *Berlusconization* of politics.[2] Donald Trump was for instance later to adopt many of his qualities.

In Austria, Jörg Haider was also turning the Freedom Party in a sharp populist direction, eventually landing in government. This he did by tapping into the fears and emotions of the ordinary public, while avoiding the more intellectual debates. With active and systematic help from the tabloid media he set his sights on the domestic elite, who he argued were betraying the people into the hands of an external threat. This mounting threat, he found, stemmed from foreign migrants entering Austria in increased numbers at the time.

The *Guardian* found that populist parties had surged from barely bagging 7 per cent of the vote on average in nation-wide elections in the late 1990s, to winning one-quarter of the vote by 2018 (Lewis et al. 2018). Already in the 1990s, nativist populism was, however, taking a new form in many European capitals.

Transmission

Recent years and decades have seen the renaissance of nationalism in the West. Contrary to Fukuyama's predictions, nativist populism was only to grow stronger and spread further. Its transmission was further fuelled by the emergence of the 24-hour broadcast news media. In addition to that the proliferation of online media, especially social media, windswept the gate-keeping role of mainstream media of the twentieth century. Populist rhetoric spiked once again in the wake of the financial crisis starting in 2008. It also snowballed south, often taken on a more leftist form.

The era of conspiratorial populists has furthermore led to the emergence of what has been branded post-truth politics, where the overflow of information drowns out facts and public discourse appeals rather to emotions and personal belief (Bergmann 2018).

Society is now flooded with an avalanche of indiscriminate information, under which people cannot easily separate facts from fabrications. This opens up a space for misinformation to thrive, leaving democratic societies vulnerable to manipulation. As result, modern media has brought increased polarization, which has proved to be rather favourable to the rhetorical style of populist communicators.

In 2014, right-wing populist parties won a record number of votes in the European Parliament (EP) elections. In the 2019 vote they increased further. The period in between is when Neo-Nationalists really came to dictate much of the political agenda in the West. The year 2016 brought a double shock, with the Brexit vote in the UK and the election of Donald Trump to the White House in Washington.

Interestingly, Donald Trump found success on a completely inverse platform to the promise of liberal democracy. The wings that allowed him to take off and dominate American politics were weaved out of material made by first, the so-called Neoconservatives, and later, the Tea Party. Contradictory to tearing down barricades, Trump was indeed largely elected on a promise of building new ones. In 1987, US President Ronald Reagan had in his famous speech in Berlin called on Soviet Union chairman, Mikhail Gorbachev, to 'tear down this wall!' Just shy of three decades later, Donald Trump—who, it is worth noting, claimed to adore Reagan—promised to build a brand-new wall, running along the entire US border with Mexico. Converse to Reagan in Berlin, the crowds at Trump rallies in the US chanted, 'build that wall!'

It was a telling moment for this political turn when Victor Orbán of Hungary said in celebration of Trump's victory that it marked America's transition from a 'liberal non-democracy' to a 'real democracy'.

In 2017 Marine Le Pen, who had succeeded her father as leader of the National Front, competed against Emmanuel Macron in the run-off to the French presidency, where she won a staggering one-third of the vote. Later that year, the anti-immigrant Alternative for Germany surged in the federal elections to the German *Bundestag*. Their support came on the canopy of the migration crisis of 2015 in the wake of the Syrian War. This was the first time that an anti-immigrant and far-right populist party found real a foothold in post-war Germany, where such sentiments had been forcefully suppressed after the devastations of Nazism.

In 2018, two populist parties took Rome by storm and united in a short-lived coalition. That was the first time that populists fully controlled government in one of the six founding member states of the European Union. On canopy of the Coronavirus Crisis of 2020 several nativist populist leaders in government took steps to advance their authority domestically, such as in Russia, Hungary and in Poland. Russia used the opportunity to implement a controversial massive facial-recognition system, and authoritarian government of China also enhanced surveillance of its citizens.

Pathological or Practical

Populism can be a complicated concept to comprehend. When Richard Hofstadter (1964) published his landmark book, *The Paranoid Style in American Politics*, the term populism—or what constituted being a populist—had not yet gained the same connotations it later contained in contemporary political studies. Still, present day populism can at least partially be fitted into his framework. As Noam Gidron and Bart Bonikowski

(2013) point out, Hofstadter's analysis of the paranoid style in American politics, 'characterized by heated exaggeration, suspiciousness and apocalyptic conspiratorial worldview' can also shed light on the 'properties of populist politics as a discursive style'. In a somewhat similar vein, British scholar Margaret Canovan (1981) saw populism as 'the shadow of democracy'.

In Hofstadter's view, populism was merely one of many other conspiratorial fantasies emanating from the political far-right at the time. He saw the radical-right as standing psychologically outside the frame of normal democratic politics. In this regard, populism has often been explained as a sort of pathology in post-war Western societies, some sort of delusion and deviation from normal politics.

This view, however, does not always hold up in empirical testing. As will become evident in the following discussion, the spread of populism in contemporary Europe has proved to be much broader and reached further into the mainstream than can simply be dismissed or marginalized as paranoid and/or delusional. As such, populism is neither necessarily always pathological.

In fact, populism can in certain situations be seen as a sensible worldview of the deprived and powerless who are faced with a dominating capitalist order aligned against them. Populist leaders claim that politics have become increasingly alien to the people, for instance when insisting that the professionalization of politics has turned governance into a trade that ordinary folks are in effect barred from.

In that regard, populism can be viewed as a legitimate strategy in the campaign for winning back lost authority from an overtly powerful elite. Thus, populism can be a useful tool in delegitimizing established authority and power relations. In some sense, populism is thus also partly a call against professional politics. And thus, perhaps rather a call for the re-amateurization of politics.

However, one of the main weaknesses of populism is found in its notion of capturing the 'will of the people'. 'The people', as such, do not possess a cohesive will. Human societies are usually not very homogeneous. Rather, they are much more diverse and do not usually display a cohesive and unified will of the people. Still, in a performative act, populists tend to create into being such a cohesive 'will of the people'.

Into the Mainstream

Although nativist populist movements have been established as a significant part of European politics since the 1970s, their reach has altered over time and across the continent. Initially, these were mostly white Christian men upholding conservative family values. Gradually however, women have become more prominent in many nativist populist movements than before, for example, Marine Le Pen in France, Pia Kjærsgaard in Denmark, Siv Jensen in Norway and Frauke Perry in Germany. These are, thus, no longer only angry white men. Angry white women are also rising to leadership roles within populist parties throughout Europe.

Over the years, populist parties have moved from the fringes of Western politics and found foothold firmly within the established political systems. Furthermore, after decades of marginalization in the wake of the Second World War, mainstream parties started in the 1990s gradually to abandon their adversarial stance against the populists, and in many cases instead adopted a strategy of accommodation. Formerly discredited and ridiculed parties have not only become accepted but have to a large extent emerged to dominate the political discourse. Rhetoric that was widely rejected and condemned in the wake of the Second World War has gradually crept back into the public debate.

In a process of normalization, nationalist, xenophobic and outright racist rhetorics are no longer necessarily treated as taboo, but have instead found widescale backing. Mainstream centre-right parties have for instance been found to be increasingly susceptible to views that previously were only held on the radical-right, such as of continuously adopting ever-stricter immigration policies.

Cas Mudde (2016) maintains that the populist radical-right constitutes a radicalization of mainstream views, that key aspects of the populist radical-right are now being shared by the mainstream. Indeed, recent years have seen the infiltration of populism into the mainstream in many countries, to the extent that it has become increasingly difficult to disentangle the two.

Populism has been deeply integrated into contemporary democratic politics. Populist rhetoric is no longer only a tool of powerless protestors and no longer merely a symptom of a crisis of democracy or crisis of faith in democracy. Rather, it is being firmly woven into democratic societies, which as result, are in many ways being dominated by the populist rhetoric.

The use of the term, *populism*, spiked in 2016, in the wake of the Brexit vote in the UK and the election of Donald Trump in America, to become one of the most common in political discussions. In many ways, populism was becoming a defining element of the politics of our time. This is illustrated by the fact that the Cambridge Dictionary chose it as the word of the year in 2017.[3]

The process of normalization of populist politics occurs, for example, when mainstream parties follow suit in the wake of the populists, and in their quest for winning back lost supporters, themselves start to abandon the once-shared values of Western democracies. This, in turn, serves to erode the once-shared liberal democratic norms of the West.

Although often veiled, contemporary nativist populism can be traced from the fascism of a previous era. At the present time, even discredited authoritarian leaders of the past such as Benito Mussolini and Joseph Stalin are again being glorified. And notorious policies that had for a long time been collectively canned—such as religious and racial segregation—are rising to the surface again. Jörg Haider of Austria's Freedom Party, for instance, dismissed much of the discussion around Austria's Nazi past. 'Our soldiers were not criminals', he said to a group of Second World War veterans, 'at most, they were victims'.[4] Likewise, the leader of the Italian Lega, Matteo Salvini, openly voiced his admiration of Mussolini. And in Russia, President Vladimir Putin has repeatedly acted to resurrect Stalin's reputation.

In many Western countries, aggression against Muslims has been normalized to the extent that even many heads of state frequently uphold a rhetoric of anti-Muslim fear-mongering. The previously discredited and marginalized conspiratorial scare-mongering populism of rogue actors that were firmly placed on the periphery has graduated to become the core message spread from the very power centres themselves—for instance from the Kremlin in Moscow, the Sándor president palace of Budapest and the Oval office in Washington. When mapping the evolution of nativist populism, it is difficult to overestimate the significance of this change.

Varieties of Populism

Right-wing populism is by now well established in European politics, and the literature on populism and extremism is vast and far-reaching. In fact, more academic studies have focused on far-right populism than on any other political party family combined (Mudde 2016). The phenomena have been studied from a plethora of different approaches, such as political science, communication studies, historical analysis, social psychology, political economy and democratic theory.

However, framing what constitutes populist politics and populist political movements can be a daunting task. As I will discuss further in the following chapter, definitions on the phenomena have been quite fleeting in the social sciences. Not only can populism be understood as either an ideology or a rhetorical style, but these are often quite different groupings holding a variety of positions which can be changeable from country to country. Most often they are constructed around respective national interests, and can also be contradictory across borders. And the different actors are sometimes at odds with each other. After the 2014 European Parliament elections, UKIP in Britain for example, refused to co-operate with the French National Front which they accused of being racist. A similar problem arose again around the EP 2019 election, when several populist actors attempted to unite the far-right in a cross-border alliance.

Many of the populist movements held neo-liberal economic policies, while some were mostly concerned with protecting the welfare system from immigrant infiltration—for the benefit of the ethnic population. This was for example the case in Scandinavia, where interestingly, populist movements in the 1970s had started out being neo-liberal. Modest versions of populist movements existed. Some were primarily nationalist. They could be far-right or what can be called extreme far-right, sometimes even a militant version denouncing democracy. Others were ultra-nationalist. There were those of a more neo-fascist nature, mostly found in Eastern Europe, but also in Greece and other Western European countries, such as in Sweden.

Then there were also left-wing versions. In the wake of the Financial Crisis that began in 2008, such parties for example found success in Greece (Syriza) and in Spain (Podemos). The fundamental difference between the two is that while the right was preoccupied with the interests of the ordinary public, the left was particularly concerned with the socially underprivileged. Both however unite in criticism of the political elite, for example in the European Union.

More militant versions of populism have also existed around the world, across the political spectrum from left to right. Many of the most notorious have been in South America.

OTHER ERAS AND AREAS

Most of these parties turned their gaze against diversity and social heterogeneity, the post-war internationalized architecture, and primarily opposed the increased migration that had followed. In some sense, this can entail a nostalgic wish for bringing back the collapsed Westphalian order of insulated sovereign states; a glorification of simpler times, when sovereign states were not constrained by international treaties and institutions.

However, neither nationalism nor populism were limited to Europe or the West. Indeed, versions of nativist populism have thrived around the world, for instance in Latin America, the Middle East and Africa.

In the 1890s, the People's Party of the United States (also known as the Populist Party), rallied farmers and workers against the elite. Many other populist parties followed in the US, for instance the Progressive Party founded in 1912 and led by Theodore Roosevelt, who later became US President.

Populism as such should not be conflated with extremism, although many extremist groups have applied populist means. Levitsky and Ziblatt (2018) note that around 800 extreme-right groups existed in the US in the 1930s alone. In 1938, the American diplomat and influential strategist George Kennan, for example, suggested that in line with trends in Europe, the US should turn to authoritarian rule. He suggested that voting rights should be withdrawn from all American women, immigrants and Afro-Americans. The aviation legend Charles Lindbergh sympathized with Nazi Germany. Famously he upheld the slogan 'America First'—later adopted by Donald Trump who forcefully applied it in the 2016 presidential election.

Although fascist regimes survived the Second World War in southern Europe—Spain under Francisco Franco and Portugal under António Salazar—populism was in those years generally more prominent in South America than in the West, where it developed much later. In many respects, the interwar fascism in Europe travelled to Latin America where it merged with anti-liberal and anti-communist ideology. It can be argued that the first modern post-war populists to find success were the Argentinian Peronists from 1946. The three-times Argentinian President Juan Peron built his movement on the intellectual fascism that had been prominent in the country for the previous two decades. As elsewhere, Argentinian fascists had denounced democracy. Peron's political creation was however a hybrid structure, merging corporatism with authoritative democracy.

Peronism rejected both capitalism and communism. Known as the 'three flags', it rested on the trinity of social justice, economic independence and political sovereignty. The corporatist state was to be the powerful mediator between the conflicting interests of capital and workers. Federico Finchelstein (2017) describes Peron's regime as a 'postfascist, authoritarian, and antiliberal version of democracy'.

Many movements have since been based on a similar approach. Among actors of that ilk was for example Alberto Fujimori who served as the President of Peru in the last decade of the twentieth century. Accused of widespread corruption and severe human rights violations, Fujimori fled to Japan after seceding power in 2000.

In 2019 the far-right populist Jair Bolsonaro was inaugurated as President of Brazil after having tapped into a similar heritage of Latin American populism. When assuming office his new Foreign Minister Ernesto Araujo said that his country would abandon globalism. Science denialism was apparent amongst many populist leaders during the Coronavirus Crisis of 2020. Bolsonaro was amongst several strongman leaders who dismissed warnings of scientists regarding impact of the disease.

On the left side of the populist spectrum, many countries in Latin America have also fallen into the hands of the radical left, such as in Venezuela and in Bolivia. Hugo Chávez's Bolivarian Revolution in Venezuela rose to power on a promise to a deprived public: that of resurrecting the destitute many against the oppression of the privileged few. Several years after coming to power in the late 1990s, Chávez rewrote the constitution and consolidated authority into his own hands. Democracy was replaced with authoritarianism and the Venezuelan economy deteriorated, leading to vast impoverishment and large-scale economic emigration.

THE EROSION OF DEMOCRACY

Many examples exist of democracy dying out accompanying the rise of populists or other kinds of authoritarian actors. Most obvious is where that occurs via *coups d'état*, such as when General Augusto Pinochet ousted Salvador Allende's democratic socialist government in Chile on 11 September 1973. Military coups have occurred in countries like Turkey, Greece, Thailand, Argentina, Brazil and Uruguay. Then there are the communist revolutions, such as when Fidel Castro seized control of quasi-democratic Cuba in 1959. During the Cold War these were indeed the most common causes of the demise of democratic states.

Democracies have also come to an end after authoritarian leaders were freely elected. The most notorious examples of dictators abandoning the very democratic process that brought them to power are for instance Adolf Hitler in Germany and Benito Mussolini in Italy. Both were facilitated by mainstream collaborators who thought they could tame the demagogues once in office. The opposite proved to be true. Hitler used the *Reichstag* fire in 1933 to kill off democracy in Germany.

Traditionally, these political outsiders emerge on a canopy of a popular movement that elevates them to power. Still, in most cases they never enjoyed majority support. As Levitsky and Ziblatt (2018) note, there was for instance never any evidence of majority support for authoritarianism in Germany and Italy in the 1920s. In other words, even though the mainstream is usually in a position to stem their surge, there are instances when polarization has gone so far as in tempting mainstream actors to rather collaborate with the demagogues, than in reaching across the traditional dividing lines in domestic politics. In doing so, there are instances where mainstream actors have unwittingly facilitated the demise of democracy.

Levitsky and Ziblatt (2018) however, also list many cases during the interwar years where such an authoritarian surge was stemmed, such as in Belgium, Britain, Costa Rica and Finland. These are examples of countries where the mainstream was able to unite across political dividing lines against challenges waged from demagogues.

INCREMENTAL UNADMITTED AUTHORITARIANISM

A subtler and less noticeable version of the erosion of democracy is the more recent phenomena of incremental authoritarianism. This is when liberal rights are submerged more slowly, such as in Russia and to a lesser extent also in Hungary and Poland. Here, the leaders often don't even acknowledge the gradual change; rather, they take to redefining what democracy really means.

This is democracy only in name. While arguing that the liberal democratic system is rigged for the benefit of the elite, a populist leader can insist that his actions, effectively eroding democracy, are instead being made in order to return power to the people. As I will illustrate further in the following chapter, the populist leader then commonly starts equating his own policies with the will of the people.

As I will also explore further throughout this book, this kind of change often occurs in the wake of a crisis. Social and economic catastrophes can open up a space for re-examining the foundations of political systems. This is what is sometimes referred to as a constitutional moment. Populists have proved to be especially capable in exploiting such situations for their own political gain. In addition, they have furthermore proved prone to discursively manufacture a sense of crisis among the public.

In Venezuela for instance, Hugo Chávez was able to rally support against what he called the corrupt governing elite in Caracas, promising to enrich the poor and, indeed, to replace what he called the infected and fraudulent Venezuelan democracy with a more 'authentic' democratic representation of the people. Chávez's Bolivarian revolution indeed started out on a democratic footing and there was never any popular call for autocracy. However, after pushing through his constitutional changes, which for example eliminated term limits for the president, Chávez took to dismantling liberal media, rolling back civil rights and oppressing political opposition. In 2017, Chávez's successor Nicolas Maduro took the definitive step of absorbing the power of Congress, completing the turn of Venezuela into a widely recognized autocracy.

This was a similar move to Alberto Fujimori, who however operated on the other side of the political spectrum. Via a televised address in April 1992, he killed of Congress and dissolved the Peruvian constitution.

More often though, this kind of subversion of democracy leads to more hybrid structures than the now full-blown dictatorship in Venezuela. During the Coronavirus Crisis of 2020 the prime minister of Hungary, Viktor Orbán, used the opportunity for a power grab when rushing emergency legislation through parliament, which, in effect, gave him powers to rule by decree. The legislation threatened to erode what was left of liberal democracy within the country.

Democracy in Name

In the modern version, these states commonly still bear a resemblance to democracies. Although institutions and rules of law are habitually presented as corrupt and preventing the populist leader from realizing the will of the people, democratic conventions are often rather circumvented than abolished.

The authorities still call people to the polls, the media continues broadcasting news, and some political opposition is still allowed. The domestic dissidence is however often quite contained, as has for instance been evident in Russia where political actions that might not be to the Kremlin's liking are closely monitored. The media is controlled, and elections are effectively rigged.

Some of these tribulations became evident to me when serving as an OSCE (Organization for Security and Co-operation in Europe) election observer in the Russian 2012 presidential election. Based in a rural area outside of Kazan in the Russian state of Tatarstan, I witnessed how the electoral process was arranged—not only by a few deviations from conventional practices, but rather in its entirety. Here are some examples. First, viable candidates that realistically could have contested Vladimir Putin had been disqualified and thus prevented from even entering the race. Secondly, voters could not be sure of the secrecy of their ballot. Web cameras had for instance been installed around the voting stations and it wasn't all that clear what they were recording. The rules forbade folding the long ballot paper sheet. And as the ballot boxes themselves were semi-transparent, the ballot sheets could in some instance be read after submission.

On top of this, we encountered representatives of Putin's party roaming around the voting stations. A few times I witnessed voters not so discreetly baring their ballot sheet to an official-looking person standing on the sidelines. In one polling station we witnessed a stern-looking man sitting in the entrance near the ballot box, scribbling something down on a piece of paper when voters passed him. We asked our driver to find out who that person was. He turned out to be a foreman in a local factory, making sure that his employees correctly cast their votes. The list of discrepancies from proper voting practices we encountered was long.

Vladimir Putin also took a page out of the playbook of some South American leaders, mentioned above, when changing the Russian constitution for his own benefit, bypassing clear term limits. Both Hungary and Poland have also entered on a journey down a similar road. How far they will go remains to be seen. In these cases, leaders have often started out respecting democratic norms, only to abandon them later. Such was the case with Victor Orbán and Fidesz in Hungary, and in Turkey as well. The consolidation of power is most commonly justified by casting opponents as posing an existential threat to society, whom they vow to protect.

In these cases, democracies die more with a whisper than with a bang, by incremental erosion of the norms that are necessary to underpin democracy. There is no single act that kills it off. No *coup d'état*, no armies on the streets. No one necessarily notices the time of death. In fact, as will become evident when several of these cases are discussed in the following chapters, many of the acts taken to subvert democracy are in name meant to improve it.

The Transformation of Party Politics

Alongside the rise of populism, political party systems in Europe have been in transformation. The surge of right-wing populist is only a part of the story. Similar to the media becoming much more fragmented and polarized over the recent years, politics has also followed such a path. Election results in Europe over the past two to three decades have been increasingly volatile. This indicates a much broader pattern of societal fragmentation than is illustrated by the populist rise. The mainstream right in European politics has also become more radical, and the same has recently started to occur on the political left. Central parties have found diminished support. This process has brought the gradual demise of the centre-left/centre-right duopoly that dominated Western liberal democracies in the post-war era.

In an attempt to stem the electoral tide towards populist parties, many mainstream parties responded by following suit in a more radical and/or populist direction, reverting to partially adopting some of the populist rhetoric, thus shifting the general political discourse in the populist direction and widening what was considered acceptable in public debate. Progression of this kind has, for example, occurred in Austria, Denmark and in the Netherlands.

This trend has been especially evident within social democratic parties, who have seen support moving over to the populists. In fact, centre-left parties have lost out the most with the populist uprising. Many of their supporters have accused traditional social democratic leaders of being in bed with the capitalists. In some regard, the populist rise can be viewed as a response to the ideological convergence of mainstream social democrats and mainstream economically liberal parties. In other words, this evolution can be viewed as a protest against the 'end of history' where all mainstream parties have come to resemble one another. Cleverly, for instance, the National Front in France branded the convergence of the centre-left Socialist Party (PS) and the centre-right Union for Popular Movement (UMP) as UMPS. This indicated that both parties were indeed one and the same. As result, social democrats were relegated to diminished roles even in many of their traditional strongholds, such as in France, Denmark, Italy, Germany and in the Netherlands.

The links between the leadership of social democratic parties in Europe and their traditional blue-collar supporters started to fray back in the 1990s. Instead of focusing most forcefully on progressing the economic prosperity of the working class, many social democratic leaders instead became increasingly preoccupied with newer and more sophisticated political tasks, such as international integration, gender equality, professional administrative practices, democratic innovations, fine arts and higher education, as well as with environment protection. As result, many of the traditional working-class voters on the left felt politically alienated, which allowed populists from both left and right to sneak past and fill the vacuum.

More recently, this same turn was occurring within traditional right-wing conservative parties, such as in the UK. The rise of first UKIP and later the Brexit Party led the Conservative Party to become much more Eurosceptic than before, leading to the Brexit endeavour which I will discuss later in this book.

More generally, this change is also illustrated by the increased fragmentation of party systems and greater volatility in many Western states. Governments now change more frequently than before. The centrifugal nature of this trend has led to a transformation in European party politics, where centre parties were largely losing to the periphery on both sides.

Distant and Aloof

Although populism is increasingly being entangled into the mainstream, that does not dissolve the need for framing the phenomena. Irrespective of frames and competing definitions, however, populist nationalism commonly entails a nostalgic longing for bringing back the glory days of the post-war nation-state. It can thus partially be seen as a call for national restoration—if you will, a return to the nation. Ruth Wodak (2015) calls this the renationalizing of nativist tendencies. In other words, the story told on these pages, the contemporary rise of nativist populism, is one of Neo-Nationalism—which I will return to discussing further in the following chapter when examining the contemporary convergence of the otherwise distinct phenomena of populism and nationalism.

In the wake of the Second World War, the system of nation-states within a shared international architecture brought the promise of ever-increasing prosperity. Indeed, the post-war era was a period of spectacular growth and far-reaching welfare systems were instated around Western Europe. However, with growing globalization it has become increasingly difficult for governments to make good on that promise. Countries have become embedded in the same system. This has led to the gradual waning of the nation-state, a decline in national authority.

Surely, globalization of the economy has enriched many, and even brought wide economic gain to large swaths of perhaps most populations. However, while the wealth of the richest has skyrocketed, globalization has also brought increased inequalities. This has led to distrust within society and a growing feeling among many people of their lives increasingly being dictated by a detached and aloof elite, who are no longer listening to the ordinary person. A feeling of being left behind in fast-moving contemporary society while others might be prospering has fuelled support for political actors that position themselves against the globalized liberal democratic system.

The control of public authority has to an increased extent shifted to domestic non-governmental actors such as specialists, media and financial elites. Special interest has become increasingly stronger in many Western countries, often hiding behind armies of lobbyists and public relations people who guard their interests.

Politicians and public officials often become captives of these immense special interest actors, who in many cases fund their political campaigns. In addition to that, politicians have seen their influence on unelected public bodies, such as independent agencies and central banks—and, of course, on global corporations and supra-national institutions. Then there are globalized social media conglomerates, like *Facebook* and *Twitter*, who seem to be regulated by no one.

Critiques of this change have pointed to governments becoming captured by internal and external constraints which prevent them from offering a viable and plausible future for their lower-income citizens. These critics argue that governments are no longer in control of capital, which flows across border from the nation-states—for example into booming offshore zones. This, they maintain, is causing national decay.

In positioning themselves against this convulsion of national politics, one of the Neo-Nationalists' claims to power is, then, calling for the resurgence of the nation-state, and, indeed, to free governance from the constraints of this globalized state system.

The weakness of the internationalized capital system becomes most evident in crisis, when those feeling left out from the benefits of boom-periods find themselves in further dire straits. Austerity, such as the severe measures that were instated widely in Europe in the wake of the Financial Crisis starting in 2008, brings fury against governments. Suddenly, authorities find themselves accused of not guarding their people, and, as result—thus also by default—betraying the very people they should be serving. This kind of feeling was mounting again in several countries during the Coronavirus Crisis of 2020.

In some sense then, we are dealing with a revolt of the underclasses who have become disillusioned with mainstream politics. This is the uprising of those who feel left out in the new liberal, high-tech and internationally connected economy. In some respect this is the roar of those who have grown frustrated with being silenced and sidelined within society.

In this situation, all sorts of chauvinists and other mischievous figures can rally support. Often they point to scapegoats, such as immigrants, who in turn become victims of irrational rage. This sort of politics thus brings a call for reaffirming borders, kicking out migrants, building walls—then a longing for strongmen leaders to guide the ordinary people out of a bad situation. Ironically, the rise of nativist populism brought the globalization of nationalism.

Anti-immigration

In this book I argue that contemporary nativist populism has travelled in waves, rising on the canopy of crisis. The first wave arose in the wake of the Oil Crisis of the early 1970s, and the second after the collapse of communism. The third wave rose most clearly in opposition to migration—mainly against Muslims settling in the West. Shortly after the terrorist attack in Nice on Bastille day 2016 Marion Maréchal Le-Pen, a prominent member of the National Front and a niece of the leader Marine Le-Pen, crystallized this message when she said: 'Either we kill Islamism, or it will kill us.' She added that those who choose the status quo 'become complicit with our enemies' (qtd in Riddell 2016).

Surely, this response was spurred by mass migration from North-Africa and the Middle East to Europe. Still, there was not necessarily a correlation between actual social developments and the level of support for populist parties. Among countries where these kinds of parties have found greatest support are for instance the more wealthy Switzerland and Austria. Denmark is another example of a highly successful radical-right populist party flourishing in a rich welfare state. In Britain, interestingly, many of the areas most heavily subsidized by the EU largely voted to leave in the 2016 Brexit elections.

Furthermore, both the True Finns and the Dutch Freedom Party grew stronger while immigration levels were falling in Finland and in the Netherlands. And although being almost untouched by the Refugee

Crisis, and even also seeing economic growth at the time, populist parties were on the rise in the Czech Republic. The anti-immigrant former businessman Andrej Babis, who led the ANO party to victory, became Prime Minister. Some of the most hardened rhetoric against Muslim migration has been heard in countries where Muslims are low in number, such as in Hungary and Poland.

Many further examples exist of such discrepancies. Unlike what might have been expected, support for Donald Trump among ethnic whites was, for instance, not greater in areas with higher levels of immigration, such as in Chicago, Los Angeles and New York. Neither did the Alternative for Germany find much support in the most diverse parts of Berlin. Nor did the National Front do especially well in the most motley parts of Paris or Marseille. In fact, the contrary was true.

This suggests that actual situations around the state of the economy, immigration or other social aspects are not necessarily the main explanatory factors around the rise of nativist populism, like many have insisted. But perhaps, rather, that mere political rhetorics might here also be at play, a discourse that can mobilize anxieties and anger from certain demographics that feel left behind. As both Wodak (2015) and Mounk (2018) have argued, fear of an imagined grim future might explain as much as disenchantment with the actual living reality. In fact, as will become evident on these pages, a perceived bad situation in society compared to others is key to understanding support for nativist populist parties.

The Aim and Frame of the Book

This book maps the rebirth of nationalism in Europe and America since the Second World War, which has taken on a populist form. As I mentioned above, populism has already been vastly studied. The main contribution of this study is in separating nativist populism from other kinds within the populist family. Based on the approach of Critical Discourse Analysis (CDA), developed by for example Ruth Wodak and Norman Fairclough (2013), I will highlight discursive manipulations and structural inequities. The surge of populist politics examined in this book has indeed brought back the importance of dialectic observation, examining populism as countering mainstream politics.

The book furthermore offers two other main academic contributions. The former is a novel way of framing three waves of nativist populism in the post-war era, each examined in a separate chapter. Each wave occurred in the wake of crisis or major social change, and each grew stronger than the one before. All are identifiable by their own qualities and characteristics, which are analysed here. Another contribution is in identifying ten common qualities of nativist populism.

In essence, this book provides a broad overview of modern political history in Europe and in America. It covers some of the most contested phenomena in contemporary politics, focusing on nationalism, populism and right-wing extremism. Perhaps most vitally the book documents a turn away from liberal democracy established in the post-war era, and towards more authoritative illiberal modes of democracy. In some cases, such as in Hungary, Poland and Russia, authorities have already moved away from many democratic principles. Collectively, I refer to this overall trend as a turn to Neo-Nationalism.

Structure

The book is divided into six chapters. Following this Introduction, the next chapter will lay out how the Neo-Nationalism of contemporary nativist populists should be understood. In mapping their historical evolution through three waves and identifying common qualities, the book provides a context for studying the rise of nativist populists. Each of the three subsequent chapters examines one of the three waves in the post-war era.

The First Wave rose in opposition to over-taxation and multiculturalism in the wake of the Oil Crisis in the 1970s—bringing forth for instance the National Front in France and the Progress Parties in Scandinavia. The chapter furthermore explores the foundations of the post-war liberal democratic order, which nativist populists have been contesting.

The Second Wave grew out of resentment in Western Europe against workers from the eastern regions of the continent flocking over the former Iron Curtain after the collapse of the Berlin Wall in 1989. A spike within this wave occurred in the wake of the terrorist attacks in the US on 11 September 2001. This wave for instance brought Silvio Berlusconi to power in Italy, Jörg Haider to prominence in Austria, and laid the ground for the renewed rise in nationalist sentiments around Eastern Europe as well as in America.

The Third Wave was brewing in the wake of the International Financial Crisis that began in 2008. This wave brought for example Donald Trump, Brexit and illiberal democracy to Eastern Europe as well as populists to power in Italy. A fundamental shift occurred in the third wave with the heightening refugee crisis in 2015. Nationalist sentiments were again awakening with the Coronavirus Crisis of 2020. Whether it will lead to rise of a fourth wave of nativist populism remains to be seen.

The closing chapter traces the progression of nativist populism over these three waves, constituting a rise of contemporary Neo-Nationalism, which largely is defining our times.

Notes

1. Freedom House. 2018, 16 January. 'Democracy in Crisis: Freedom House Releases Freedom in the World 2018'.
2. *The Economist*. 2009. 'The Berlusconisation of Italy'.
3. Cambridge Dictionary's Word of the Year (2017).
4. *BBC* news. 2002, 2 February. 'Jörg Haider: Key quotes'.

References

Bergmann, E. (2018). *Conspiracy & Populism: The Politics of Misinformation*. London: Palgrave Macmillan.

Cambridge Dictionary's Word of the Year 2017. (2017, November 29). About Words—Cambridge Dictionaries Online Blog. Retrieved January 2, 2019, from dictionaryblog.cambridge.org.

Canovan, M. (1981). *Populism*. San Diego: Harcourt.

Finchelstein, F. (2017). *From Fascism to Populism in History*. University of California Press.

Fukuyama, F. (1989). The End of History? *The National Interest, 16*, 3–18.

Fukuyama, F. (1992). *The End of History and the Last Man*. New York, NY: Simon and Schuster.

Gidron, N., & Bonikowski, B. (2013). *Varieties of Populism: Literature Review and Research Agenda*. Working Paper Series, Weatherhead Center for International Affairs, Harvard University, No. 13(0004).

Habermas, J. (1998). *The Postnational Constellation*. Boston: MIT Press.

Hofstadter, R. (1964). *The Paranoid Style in American Politics*. New York: Vintage Books.

Ignatieff, M. (2013). *The Lesser Evil: Political Ethics in an Age of Terror*. Princeton University Press.

Jörg Haider: Key Quotes. (2002, Summer). *BBC News*. Retrieved January 4, 2019, from news.bbc.co.uk.

Levitsky, S., & Ziblatt, D. (2018). *How Democracies Die*. New York: Crown.

Lewis, P., Clarke, S., Barr, C., Kommenda, N., & Holder, J. (2018, November). Revealed: One in Four Europeans Vote Populist.
Lewis, P., Barr, C., Clarke, S., Voce, A., Levett, C., Gutiérrez, P., & Gutiérrez, P. (2019, March). Revealed: The Rise and Rise of Populist Rhetoric. *The Guardian*. London.
Mounk, Y. (2018). *The People Vs. Democracy: Why Our Freedom Is in Danger and How to Save It*. Harvard University Press.
Mounk, Y. M., & Kyle, J. (2018, December 26). What Populists Do to Democracies. *The Atlantic*. Retrieved October 2, 2019, from theatlantic.com.
Mudde, C. (2016). The Study of Populist Radical Right Parties: Towards a Fourth Wave. *C-REX Working Paper Series*, *1*, 1–23.
Mudde, C., & Kaltwasser, C. R. (2017). *Populism: A Very Short Introduction*. Oxford University Press.
Riddell, M. (2016, July 23). *Exclusive Interview with France's Youngest and Most Controversial MP: Marion Maréchal-Le Pen on Brexit, the Nice Attack, Gay Marriage and Her Aunt Marine*. London: The Telegraph.
Schwarz, R. (2018). *Democracy under Pressure: Polarization and Repression Are Increasing Worldwide* (p. a). Brussels: Bertelsmann Stiftung.
The Berlusconisation of Italy. (2009, April 30). *The Economist*.
Wodak, R. (2015). *The Politics of Fear: What Right-Wing Populist Discourses Mean*. New York: Sage.
Wodak, R., & Fairclough, N. (2013). *Critical Discourse Analysis*. London: Sage.

Understanding Nativist Populism

The recent surge of populist parties has brought back nationalism as a central element in European and American politics. However, understanding the phenomena can be a daunting task. Nationalism has many faces and its factions can be compartmentalized into many different categories. The relationship between nationalism and democracy has furthermore been precarious through history, and, thus, complex to analyse. Growing out of the Enlightenment and Romanticism, nationalism initially coincided with demands for democracy in the eighteenth century. In its most elementary form, it was the demand that nations had an inherent right to establish sovereign states, governed by the people.

Nationalism was thus a fundamental component of the struggle for democracy against absolutist monarchs in Europe, for example leading to the French Revolution. In that spirit, the heroic endeavours of the French national army during the Prussian invasion of 1792 were praised in their national freedom song, the *Marseillaise*. After the revolutions of 1848, nationalists saw democracy as part of the struggle for national independence. Nationalism is thus the ideology that synthesizes the social-cultural entity of the nation with the political entity of the state.

Nationalism spread rapidly through Europe and found its way into many of the European foreign colonies. In this regard, nationalism was the struggle against oppression, often forged in defiance of colonial powers. This was, for example, instrumental in Palestine, Lithuania, Cuba, Iraq and China. Nationalism also fuelled many separatist movements, such as in Catalonia and the Basque region in Spain, Quebec in Canada and the Scottish movement in the UK.

As I discussed in the Introduction to this book, the Westphalia peace agreement, signed in 1648—ending the Thirty Years' War—gave birth to the international system of independent nation-states. For the most part of human history, people had, however, lived in other polities.

Nationalism has proven to be a resilient ideology and the nation-state, as a political entity, emerged as the underlying source for legitimacy of the global order. The nation-state is still the principal actor in international relations. Despite the internationalization of the political system, no other political order has emerged as a real alternative to the system of nation-states, which also has framed political identities in each of them. Identifying one's uniqueness is thus built into the very nature of nation-states, finding justification for its very existence by emphasizing what sets it apart from others.

As will become clear in the coming discussion, precisely this notion has proved to be a vital ingredient in the winning formula of contemporary nativist populist parties in Europe; they are staunchly nationalist. Before attempting to frame nativist populism more firmly, which I return to later in this chapter, I first take to discussing two underlying elements: nationalism and fascism.

NATIONS AND NATIONALISM

Generally, nationalism departs from polarizing ideologies such as liberalism, anarchism, feminism, socialism and conservatism by its nature of encompassing the entire native population—this is a catch-all political approach. It can take on several forms and function across the political spectrum. Nationalism brings forth a feeling of belonging and discursively creates a common identity around the inner group. It emphasizes uniqueness and intra homogeneity, while often ignoring internal diversity. It sharpens the contrast between those who belong to the group and others who are alien to it. Benedict Anderson (1983) argues that this might explain why some people are willing to 'die for the nation'. And although nationalism was condemned in the wake of the Second World War, it has always survived. It is a feeling that often resides deep within people, not always completely consciously.

The rise of nationalism also brings the underlying concept of *nation* back into focus, which is even more challenging, and perhaps one of the most nuanced in social sciences. Indeed, scholars have for centuries been struggling to define what exactly constitutes a nation. A nation is closely linked to the idea of a heartland, a sort of a family that we belong to by birth.

In the late eighteenth century, the German philosopher Johann Gottfried von Herder (1784) maintained that a nation was in a way an extension of family. He wrote that nations were almost a natural phenomenon. He claimed that strong links existed between nature and nation; that traditions and habits in society emerged over a long period of time in a relationship between nature and the nation. Furthermore, he said the cultural essences of nations were kept in their languages. It was thus languages that really set nations apart. In this understanding, the nation survives the individual, and the mortal person lives on as part of the nation's history.

The French intellectual Ernest Renan (1882), disputed Herder's naturalist approach and claimed that nations were not natural, but rather culturally constructed. In his view, a nation was similar to a soul, a spiritual principle, some sort of a moral conscience—this is for instance the way that Vladimir Putin describes the Russian nation. Providing perhaps the only fully comprehensive definition to date, Renan said that distinguishable groups of people were a nation simply if they considered themselves to be one: 'a nation is a daily plebiscite', he claimed. This, however, is far too general to be useful.

In addition to Renan's definition, some identities and qualities can be listed which nations often share. Among these can be a separate land, shared history, common language, ethnic origin, religion and other cultural elements. One problem with these sorts of criteria listing definitions is that exceptions can always be found.

However, in this regard nations are perhaps not naturally, or only culturally, but also historically constructed. Nations rise, they can die out, and new ones can emerge. Most often, nations share a common understanding of their history, and unify around a myth of the past which continues to be reproduced.

Nations can be constructed in various ways. The German philosopher Friedrich Meinecke (1908), developed the concepts of *Kultur*-nation and *Staats*-nation to distinguish between the different sorts of nationalism in Germany and in France. On the one side there were nations like the Germans who build their nationhood on a common cultural heritage. On the other were nations like France, which more often were constructed by a common political history and based on a constitution. This could be simplified by saying that in Germany the nation had created the state, while in France the state had manufactured the nation.

Discursive Constructs

Contemporary scholars such as Ernest Gellner (1983) and Anthony Smith (2002) view nations as social creations and are, thus, in contrast to Herder's naturalist view. Still, Smith maintained that nations were much more firmly rooted than Renan claimed. According to Smith, nations—or ethnises more broadly—are 'named units of population with common ancestry myths and historical memories, elements of shared culture, some link to a historic territory and some measure of solidarity, at least among their elites'. Smith maintains that nations are logical and modern depictions of a deeply rooted common history and culture. He saw the nation as a 'sacred communion' of the citizens.

Benedict Anderson (1983) famously described nations as imagined communities. Gellner (1983) furthermore claimed that nations were created within the social relations of peoples of a similar culture. Nationalism, he claimed, was 'primarily a principle which held that the political and national unit should be congruent'. He saw the nation as superseding previous subgroupings, and thus being the most important social construction of contemporary time.

Eric Hobsbawm (1990) built on Gellner and claimed that nations were indeed creations of nationalism; without nationalism there were no nations. Similar to Renan, he considered 'any sufficiently large body of people whose members regard themselves as members of a "nation"' to be such. He emphasized that even though nations were created from above, it was necessary to study nationalism from the view below, that is, 'in terms of the assumptions, hopes, needs, longing and interests of ordinary people', who were the objects of the nationalistic message.

For the purpose of this book, irrespective of whether Renan's, Smith's, Gellner's or indeed Hobsbawm's approaches are applied, nations can be seen as products of a common social understanding of those who belong to the national group. Similarly, Ruth Wodak (2015) views nations as perceptual constructs, arguing that they are 'mental communities', that people accept belonging to. Nations are also most often a social and cultural creation of a distinguishable group of people who unite around a common understanding of their shared history.

Nationalism is thus in its essence a fictional invention, expressing an imagined will of a discursively created nation. As will become evident in the following three chapters, it is precisely into this social creation that contemporary nativist populists tap when constructing their discourse and framing their political message. In doing so they tend to exaggerate the distinctions between their own nation and others while overemphasizing internal homogeneity, often treating the nation as a single body.

Fascism

Fascism emerges when political nationalism leads to authoritarianism, economic isolation and political extremism, based on viewing one's own nationality as above that of others. This sort of militant internal political nationalism can for instance be traced to the writings of Italian intellectual Giuseppe Mazzini (1862) in the mid-nineteenth century, who claimed that the highest level of freedom was not of individuals but the collective freedom of the nation. To reach higher freedom, he wrote, the individual surrenders his freedom over to the state. Since then, political nationalism has travelled different routes, most notoriously emerging into fascism in Italy in the 1920s, and Nazi Germany in the 1930s.

In practice, fascism was conceived from the crisis of liberalism in the wake of the First World War. Liberal democracy stood accused of having failed to bring about peace and prosperity. Max Ascoli and Arthur Feiler (1938) wrote that 'fascism was the product of democratic decay'. With democracy in disarray, both the political left and the right took to authoritarianism—communism on the left and fascism on the right.

Born in Italy, the word fascism derives from *fascio*, literally a bundle of rods strapped together forming an a stronger whole. Initially these were united bands of militarist nationalists declaring war on socialism. Travelling from the trenches of the war, fascism fused radical nationalism with the glorification of strength and violence as an answer to the crisis of liberal democracy. The interwar fascism, causing much of the pain Europe suffered in the twentieth century, was largely born out of the Great Depression of 1929.

Fascism was to a certain degree a dialectic response against the Enlightenment and early European liberalism that spread in the wake of the French Revolutions. Ernst Nolte (1966) for instance defined it as a simultaneous reaction against liberalism and Marxism. Fascists dismissed the era of political plurality that had existed prior to the outbreak of the

Great War, denouncing democracy, freedom, tolerance and the liberal rights of the Enlightenment. Fascism was a counterattack against these principles of the French revolution, and instead found progress in consolidating authority into the hands of a strong leader who would unify the nation against its external enemies.

The fascist rhetorical platform did not rest on a coherent political philosophy. Rather, it rejected compromise and harboured contempt for established society and the intellectual elite. While emphasizing their own leaders' mystical relationship with the ordinary public, most of these movements were chauvinistic, anti-capitalist and advocated voluntary and violent actions against both socialist and bourgeois enemies.

Their anti-capitalist rhetoric was however, always very selective. Despite rhetorically siding with the working class, fascist regimes in government never did much to denounce capitalists, rather, they dissolved labour unions and banned strikes. Similarly, they criticized the bourgeoisie for lack of loyalty to the nation rather than for exploiting workers. In place of dismantling the capitalist order, in accordance with the argumentation, the interwar fascists offered instead a corporatist component to it, promoting the syndication of private capital and state within a dictatorial order.

The (Infallible) Interpreter

Fascism always had a populist side to it. One of its central features is found in the claim that the leader is able to represent the people in a more thorough way than can be done in a representative liberal democracy. In fascism, the leader becomes the (infallible) interpreter of the true will of the people. He becomes the sacred source of the nation's desires. In many ways, fascism became a political religion with the leader positioned as prophet, who is worshipped by his followers.

Many of the contemporary populist movements do tap into similar mixtures of nationalism (rhetorical) anti-capitalism and an emphasis on voluntary actions against elites as fascists did in the interwar years. After the devastations of the Second World War, post-war far-right populists have, though, tended to camouflage their origins, dressing their politics differently, as I will discuss in the following chapters. Accordingly, the post-war nativist populists have largely moved away from this previous anti-democratic fascism. Most often they also refrain from openly referring to Mussolini's fascism or Hitler's Nazism. Still, as I discussed in the

Introduction to this book, there are notable exemptions to that rule—such as Jörg Haider referring positively to Adolf Hitler and Matteo Salvini to Mussolini.

In his book, *Ur-Fascism*, Italian writer Umberto Eco (1995), who was born in Mussolini's fascist Italy, warned that fascism could come back under the most innocent of guises. 'Our duty is to uncover it and to point our finger at any of its new instances—every day, in every part of the world.'

Robert Paxton (2004) similarly warned that this became an alibi for onlookers, and that fascism, was often overlooked in contemporary societies, most importantly in Western Europe, where he claimed fascists had always found the most fertile ground.

Framing Populism

Although not as notorious as fascism, *populism* is neither a neutral analytical concept. Unlike those who proudly identify themselves as socialists, conservatives, liberals, feminists, anarchists or even nationalists, people usually don't refer to themselves as being populists. Rather, populism is a pejorative label slapped onto other people's explanations that are perceived to be unfounded. It has commonly been used to belittle or marginalize rival explanations. The examiner must therfore be careful when applying it to his subjects.

The word *populism* stems from the Latin word *populus*, simply meaning *the people*. Correspondingly, the ancient population of Rome was referred to as *Populus Romanus*. The concept clearly corresponds to the *Nation*—*Volk* in German, *Folk* in Scandinavian languages. It relates to the public and stands directly in contrast to the elite.

Politics that relate first and foremost to the people have, of course, existed through the centuries. In itself, that is nothing new. Another key point is that populism as such does not contain either left or right leanings. Populist politics can tilt either way. Instead, at its core, the concept rather relates to the quest of bringing forth the *pure* will of *the people*. One of the first populist parties harnessing this essence was the American Peoples Party in the US in the 1890s, which sought to align farmers and workers and willingly described itself as populist.

In his influential book *The Populist Zeitgeist*, American-based Dutch scholar Cas Mudde (2004) describes populism as a 'thin-centred ideology' separating society into two homogenous and antagonistic groups: 'the pure people' versus 'the corrupt elite', emphasizing the 'general will' of the people. Mudde (2016) furthermore explains how 'the people' are then interpreted as a homogeneous moral entity.

According to this approach, the main aim of politics should be to realize the will *of* the people, rather than the elite being allowed to impose its will *on* the people. The domestic elite is here identified as a single actor. The elite is then accused of siding with international actors against the nation and the people. Here, the people are almost seen as sacred and being unassailable. As populism is a 'thin ideology', Mudde argues that it can be combined with a 'host ideology', such as nationalism, liberalism or socialism.

This is in line with what I discussed above; that populism exists in many different forms. As Margaret Canovan (1981) maintained, each trait is rooted in its own social and historical context. Populist politics is thus a broad church, and populism as such does not fit into one particular ideology. It is not a well-squared set of rational policies. Although scholars might differ on many aspects related to populist politics, most of them unite in recognizing their emphasis on the people versus the elite. As is the case with nationalists more broadly, any populist movement aims to mobilize the masses. Its appeal is to the people, rather than the elite. Indeed, like in nationalism as was discussed above, populist movements are catch-all rather than class-based.

For populists, the people are always in a central position—a kind of heartland to be protected against both external threats and domestic traitors. As Ruth Wodak (2015) argues, populists endorse a nativist notion of belonging, presenting themselves as servants in the interests of the internal nation.

Anti-politics

A characterizing feature of populists is thus in positioning themselves as outsiders and casting their domestic opponents as an elite establishment. This was the position of the European fascists in the interwar years, as well as of the Latin American autocrats in the post-war years. And this has also been the position of contemporary populists in the West. The Le Pens, Farage, Wilders, Orbán, Trump and Salvini all positioned themselves as outsiders.

In comprehending the rise of populism, one has to understand the growing feeling among many people of being left behind in a fast-moving contemporary society, while others might be prospering. A sense of relative deprivation is thus key to understand the appeal of nativist populism.

Despite their different manifestations across time and regions, populist politicians unite in a *Manichean* worldview, in which societies are seen as divided between evil elites who are in control of the pure people. According to this binary viewpoint, the pure people are unaware of the malignant parasitic forces exploiting not only their naivety but also their inherited goodness. Populists generally split society into two, *the people* versus the elite/external *others*. The 'others'—whoever they are at any given time, domestic or foreign—are thus excluded from the *demos*. In this intolerant *people* vs *anti-people* binary, an exclusion of *others* is a vital component.

Although many other elements can be identified, the two central elements to populism are people-centrism and anti-elitism. This is the process of delegitimizing opponents and positioning them as enemies of the people. Alberto Fujimori of Peru linked his adversaries with drug trafficking and terrorism. Hugo Chávez of Venezuela equated his rivals with 'rancid pigs'. Silvio Berlusconi dismissed the judge's ruling against him in Italy as being communist. Like Rafael Correa of Ecuador, who called the media a 'grave political enemy', so did US President Donald Trump when branding the media as 'the enemy of the people'. Recep Tayyip Erdoğan in Turkey went even further when accusing journalists of propagating terrorism.

Politics is here cast as a dualistic struggle between the people and the undeserving and self-serving political class. As Daniele Albertazzi and Duncan McDonnel (2007) put it, populists 'pit a virtuous and homogenous people against a set of elites and dangerous "others" who are depicted as depriving the sovereign people of their property and rights'.

In their politics, populists thus tend to exploit a growing feeling among many in Western societies of being deprived and betrayed by the elite. In Kirk Hawkins' (2003) analysis, populists view politics as a struggle between good and evil, a discourse that counters 'the people' against the 'elite'. Ideologically, right-wing nativist populism is thus defined on the sociocultural dimension, rather than on the socio-economic axis.

As previously discussed, populists are prone to apply a rhetoric that undermines liberal democratic norms. This can be viewed as the practice of operating what can be branded anti-politics. Correspondingly, Andreas Schedler (1996) identified populism primarily with a broad array of anti-attitudes: anti-elite, anti-establishment, anti-modern, anti-urban, anti-industrial, anti-state, anti-foreign, anti-intellectual and anti-minority sentiments. Taken collectively, populists are perhaps most simply 'naysayers' who resist change, as German scholar Hans Georg Betz (2001) claimed. In effect, they strive to stop modernization and social change.

Nativism

As already discussed, both nationalism and populism invoke 'the people', but they do so in different ways. The former traditionally encompasses the entire demos while the latter designates a narrower internal pure people against the corrupted elite. Recent years have seen the synergy of the two—or perhaps rather the entangling. In the following chapters I will document how populist movements have become increasingly ethnonationalist, and, indeed, nativist. American scholar John Higham (1955) defined nativism as an 'opposition to an internal minority on the grounds of its foreignness'. This is precisely the politics of contemporary nativist populists. Their nativism has mainly been sharpened in opposing the 'others' in society, primarily in protecting the native population against an influx of immigrants. Therefore, it is beneficial to identify the specifically *nativist populism*, the politics which separates outgroups from those who are considered as constituting 'the people'.

As discussed above, scholars have struggled with defining this phenomenon. Many have focused on the right-wing aspect of populism, mainly when dealing with extremist movements. Others have viewed them as primarily nationalist or even autocratic. Good arguments have been presented for each classification.

In previous books (see Bergmann 2017, 2018), I have applied the concept of *nationalist* populism. Roger Eatwell and Matthew Goodwin (2018) similarly use the term 'national populism', the ideology of prioritizing 'the culture and interest of the nation', while promising to 'give voice to people who feel that they have been neglected, even held in contempt, by distant and often corrupt elites'.

However, when dealing with political movements that have primarily found success in opposition to migrants and external influences, my focus here is on the *nativist* kind. In this book I maintain that the convergence of *nativism* and *populism* has turned into a separate *Neo-Nationalism* spreading across Europe and America. This has brought a new demand for reinforcing barriers between countries. In other words, this populist and nativist kind of contemporary nationalism, entangled with new kinds of communicative tools and tactics emerging in what has been branded 'post-truth' politics, distinguishes modern-day nationalism from that of former times, which was discussed above. Therefore, the term *Neo-Nationalism* can be of benefit to understanding more broadly the phenomenon largely defining political developments.

This comeback of nationalism, now by way of nativist populism, can be seen as the return to the *People* ('Volk'/'Folk') that are in dire need of protection from an aggressive *Other*. As I will discuss in the following chapters this sort of identity narrative has been increasingly constructed in both European and American politics. Nativist populist movements reject the existing political consensus and combine anti-elitism with opposition against external threats. Vital for understanding the phenomena, the nativist othering can also be applied to the elite, which are also placed as an external (foreign in the understanding of Higham) threat to the people. As I will explore in the following three chapters, this rhetoric is then usually enhanced by crisis. This was the case in the post-Oil Crisis era, the post-1989 era, and in the wake of the Financial Crisis of 2008.

One element of the populist rhetoric is reducing complex problems and vast social developments down to simple solutions, such as the ousting of foreigners. *Their* infiltration into *Our* inherently good society is blamed for the present bad domestic situation, and also for the even bleaker future outlook. Thus, the solution is simple and clear cut: The cleansing of the external parasites.

Here, the process of 'othering' is vital to the populist rhetoric. The enemy must be clearly identifiable. For that, identifying stereotypes comes in handy. For instance: Jews are parasites; Muslims are infiltrating the West and staging a hostile takeover; Roma people are dirty; cultural Marxists are traitors; international institutions are undermining national authority; humanitarian organizations are preventing us from defending ourselves against these malicious elements.

Cultural Separatism

One aspect separating post-war nativist populism from interwar fascism is that biological racism was replaced with cultural xenophobia. In this transformation, arguments based on a racial hierarchy were replaced with an ethno-pluralist doctrine of 'equal but separate' (Rydgren 2005). Although humans were now considered biologically equal, culture still separated nations, which formed closed communities bounded by a common cultural identity. Claims for the superiority of Europeans and the Western world now thus relied on history rather than biology—often on an implicit but firmly underlying premise that Europeans were culturally superior.

Correspondingly, contemporary nativism, which here is under examination, does not necessarily revolve around race, but rather around culture. Well-integrated migrants with an established history in society can over time be considered a part of the native population. In other words, they become part of 'us' against 'other' external migrants. This is vital for understanding nativist populism. Importantly, the nativism of the Neo-Nationalists does not necessarily exclude descendants of immigrants that have been incorporated into the domestic demos.

Similar to biological racism, cultural racism constructs closed and bounded cultural groups and, as Karen Wren (2001) explains, 'conveniently legitimates the exclusion of "others" on the basis that they are culturally different'. As I will discuss later in this book, the French new-right think tank *Nouvelle-Droite* developed this doctrine, based on a philosophical claim that nations had a right to cultural differences (McCulloch 2006). Swedish scholar Jens Rydgren (2007) points to how radical-right populists create an ethno-nationalist myth of the past, bringing their politics to revolve around reinstating the glory of their golden age.

Norwegian scholar Anders Jupskås (2015) furthermore claims that aggressive racist nationalism has been replaced by a defensive nationalism promoting a mono-cultural society within the borders of the nation-state. The new racist discourse thus relies on a nativist separation of 'us' who belong to the cultural entity, from 'others' who are not part of the nationhood and do not belong to it. In this identity-based political discourse, a myth around the history of the 'pure nation' is conversely created in order to legitimate the populist agenda.

The nation-state creation in Europe is within this discourse seen as a natural construction around cultural entities developing naturally. This proved to be a widely successful political framing. Cultural racism has found a foothold in Europe since the 1970s, specifically in opposing the cultural infiltration of 'others' who are deemed as not belonging to 'our' cultural entity.

The new-right discussed throughout this book surely taps into a nationalism of earlier periods but applies it in a less violent way; perhaps in what Michael Billig (1995) referred to as 'banal nationalism'—the everyday display of the nation in the public domain. Here, national pride and loyalty are reaffirmed in everyday routines in society. These can be monuments and other reminders of national heroes, the flying of flags, national holidays and celebrations, and so on.

Referring to Renan discussed earlier, this is the constant reproduction of the nation as a cohesive entity, which as a result begs protection. The counter-effect is the exclusion of 'others' such as immigrants, which perhaps was the very foundation of nativism in contemporary politics. In other words, nativist populists are culturally xenophobic.

SIMPLE SOLUTIONS

As mentioned above, one of the main elements in populism is offering simple solutions to address complex problems. Whether it is Alexander Gauland in Germany, the Le Pens in France, Nigel Farage in the UK, Geert Wilders in the Netherlands or Donald Trump in the US, they all insist that solutions to the most pressing problems of ordinary people in society are much more straightforward than the establishment makes them out to be: If only immigration could be stopped, all would be better in France; exiting the European Union brings glory back to Britain; banning burqas and the Koran returns the cosy hippie ambience back to the streets of Amsterdam; only a grand and shiny border wall can keep Americans safe from Mexican immigrants.

As the populist message is based on offering straightforward solutions to often quite tortuous issues, they simultaneously accuse the mainstream authorities of distorting the will of the people, and of hiding their true agenda; as otherwise they would of course simply implement the easily applied solution.

Yascha Mounk (2018) identifies two types of accusations here. Either authorities are corrupt, or they are working on behalf of outside interests. The specifically nativist populists tend to focus on the latter, insisting that the domestic authority is not loyal to the people, but is in bed with foreign aggressors. This then crystallizes the populist message: With ousting the elite from power and implementing the simple solution Britain/France/Russia/America/will become great again.

After coming into power, populists have often found themselves in trouble when they cannot implement the simple remedy to the malignant condition. Think of Brexit or stopping immigration to America. A similar tactic is then often applied against domestic institutions, that are not under control of the populist authority. They are blamed for preventing the leader from implementing the will of the people and accused of betrayal, be they the state-run media not toeing the populist line, independent courts, elections councils, ethical watchdogs or the military refusing to implement illiberal orders. Think for example of Boris Johnson and the British Parliament and Supreme Court attempting to stop Brexit, or of Donald Trump and the Deep State apparatus in Washington. In these sorts of situations, all sorts of conspiracy theories become a useful tool in shifting the viewpoint and agenda.

The next step for the authoritarian populists is bypassing disobedient public institutions, sometimes through rewriting the constitution and consolidating power in the hands of the leader, such as in Venezuela, Hungary and indeed in Russia. In America Donald Trump promoted a national emergency to bypass Congress in order to build his border wall.

Style and Content

Populism can furthermore be seen as a style, or a technique, of political mobilization and communication. The main method is in constructing fear among the public and in pointing to scapegoats that are blamed for ruining—or threatening to ruin—our (inherently good) society. However, as for instance Ruth Wodak (2015) argues, radical-right populism is not only a form of rhetoric. Rather, it also contains specific and identifiable contents. Both style and substance are thus interlinked in populist politics.

As will become evident over the following three chapters, the fear that they instate is, for instance, of a specific and identifiable kind. It consists of several core aspects, such as losing jobs to immigrants, and of migrants undermining the welfare state to the detriment of the vulnerable and the elderly among the native population. Furthermore, the rhetoric usually points to the increasing powerlessness of the nation-state in protecting the intranational public. It warns against the erosion of values and the demise of traditions and native culture.

These are actually some of the main forms of the populist appeal, and, as I mentioned in the Introduction to this book, it would be mistaken to dismiss all these concerns as unfounded. In fact, they might easily have some merit. Still, the way these concerns are articulated is often quite populistic.

One communicational aspect comes with the use of all kinds of rhetorical fallacies. Of course, rhetorical fallacies have been used in political debates throughout the centuries, when politicians attempt to mislead the discussion for their own gain. Studies have found that populists have been more prone than mainstream politicians to apply informal fallacies in their rhetoric (Blassnig et al. 2019).

These can be of several kinds. They might include *ad hominem* arguments such as personal attacks rather than tackling arguments put forth by opponents. Donald Trump for example added negative nicknames to his opponents, such as 'Crooked' Hillary, 'Little' Marco and 'Lying' Ted. *False cause* is another version, when wrongly attempting to create causal links between separate acts. *Faulty analogy* is when comparing things that are only partly compatible. A *straw man* is created when misrepresenting the argument of one's opponent. A *red herring* is the deviation from the topic at hand by pointing to something else that might only be loosely related to the issue.

As will come to light in the following chapters, these and many other rhetorical fallacies are often used to derail the discussion and steer it into directions that better serve the interests of the operator.

Four-Step Rhetorical Formulation

One aspect of the populist rhetorical style entails dramatization—being deliberately provocative in order to draw attention and promote polarization. This can be done by breaking publicly accepted norms such as in dismissing an entire religion as a 'dangerous totalitarian ideology', as Geert Wilders of the Netherlands did when denouncing Islam.[1] This process of eroding norms generates tension for the purpose of rallying support for the party—in opposing the 'other' or/and the 'establishment'.

Central to their appeal is how they put the spanner in the works of the establishment. This can be understood as the politics of disruption, protesting against scripted political performance. Lone Sorensen (2018) documents how populists instead tend to claim authenticity by exposing the professionally calculated and scripted performance of the elite. The norm-breaking provocations of populist actors thus contradicts the mainstream, and, in doing so projects some kind of authenticity. It also generally triggers protest from the mainstream. In turn, the populists are then able to exploit that response by complaining of ill treatment by the 'politically correct' mainstream—an interlinked established authority in politics, academia and media. In the new landscape of digital media this kind of communication now spreads much further than before and allows the populist actor to weaponize with visibility. This dynamic can be structured into a four-step rhetorical formulation, by in which populists come to dominate the political agenda (Wodak 2015).

First comes the scandalous act or comment of the populist, for instance a racist comment against a Muslim. That triggers a push-back from mainstream actors opposing the racist comment. The third step is then for the populist to claim victimhood and/or deflecting by pointing to others, even equating the comment in question with something entirely different. The final step is going on the offensive and dramatizing the cycle with exaggerations, emphasizing the right to free speech and accusing those that countered the initial comment of silencing and oppression. As can be seen in the following three chapters, it is through this rhetorical pattern that populists have been able to set the agenda.

The ever hungry 24-hour rolling news media and the modern online media are widely exploited for transmitting the scandalous message of the populists. In fact, the new media became an instant bedfellow with populism, as both benefitted from one other. The new media provided the populists with the oxygen of attention that they desperately needed to succeed. Because of audience interest, the media in fact became obsessed with the norm-breaking behaviour of many populists. In the new media environment, sensational stories travel much faster and further than the more serious and traditional news. In fact, as I will return to discussing in a later chapter, fake news is shared far more often on social media than mainstream news.

THE FÜHRER PRINCIPLE

As was the case with fascism, populist movements have usually only found success when led by charismatic leaders. They are more leader-driven than based on a clear party structure. One of their main forms of appeal is in positioning their leader as the saviour of the ordinary people. In the case of the nativist populist, this comes more specifically in the form of saving the people from an external threat and the traitorous elite.

Democracy is here usually viewed very narrowly, often simply intertwined with the will of the leader, who—as I discussed above—becomes the interpreter of the people. Not only is a fictional single desire attributed to the entire *demos*, but the leader is also seen to understand the true will of the people even more clearly than the public might do themselves. As Frederico Finchelstein (2017) writes, 'populism replaces representation with the transfer of authority to the leader'.

Many examples of this can be mentioned. In 2017, Marine Le Pen ran her presidential campaign on the slogan 'Au nom du peuple', meaning in the name of the people. In 1988 her father Jean-Marie Le Pen had run on a slogan 'Le Pen, le peuple', meaning Le Pen, the people. Donald Trump toed a similar line when claiming before the 2016 presidential election: 'I am your voice.' Pegida in Germany insisted 'Wir sind das Volk', meaning we are the people. Perhaps this idea is not in a completely separate category from the claims made by Louis XIV, the absolutist king of France, who in the late eighteenth century famously—and ever so arrogantly—insisted that he, personally, was the state: '*L'Etat, c'est moi*'.

Many similarities can also be drawn between populist politics and celebrity culture. The populist leader often approaches the public in a way similar to pop stars, applying the same frontstage techniques in drawing attention, for instance, appearing in tabloids rather than in the mainstream well-regarded and sophisticated broadsheet media outlets. Perhaps this is similar to the way pop culture challenged the fine arts in the latter half of the twentieth century—in effect obfuscating much of the so-called (and sometimes imagined) high society. Akin to rock stars, the populist leader rather appeals to the public, than to sophisticated high society.

Intolerant Democracy

What sets contemporary right-wing nativist populists apart from earlier fascist and Nazi versions—discussed above—who favoured authoritarian leadership, is that most of them now accept democracy and parliamentarianism, at least in name. They are thus more anti-elite than anti-system.

However, although contemporary nativist populism clearly parts from pre-war fascism, mainly in rejecting political violence and accepting enforcing the democratic will of the people, it still taps into the same ideological source; in both instances for example, always attributing a single (invented) will to the *demos*. This collectivist approach clearly contradicts the pluralist values of liberal democracy.

In fascism, Umberto Eco (1995) wrote, individuals have no rights. Instead, 'the People is conceived as a quality, a monolithic entity expressing the Common Will'. Eco said that 'The People is only a theatrical fiction', and since large groups of people don't usually share a common will, the leader becomes their interpreter. This same fascist element has filtered over to contemporary nativist populism. 'We no longer need the Piazza Venezia in Rome or the Nuremberg Stadium', Eco wrote. 'There is in our future a TV or Internet populism, in which the emotional response of a selected group of citizens can be presented and accepted as the Voice of the People.'

This homogenizing element of a cohesive people promotes intolerance within democracy. It is an illiberal form of democracy, rejecting diversity and stripping away its inhered emphasis on individual rights and the separation of power. This is democracy without liberal rights. Therefore, it might be mistaken to think of modern populism as void of authoritarian tendencies.

However, populists do depart from neo-fascists and neo-Nazis when aiming to reshape and redefine democracy, rather than dismissing it altogether. As discussed, the relationship between populism and democracy is both murky and ambivalent; democracy is diminished to being understood as the majoritarian will as interpreted by the leader.

A Winning Formula

In the late 1990s Herbert Kitschelt (1997) introduced what he called the 'winning formula' of right-wing populism, in combining neo-liberal politics with authoritarianism and a policy of anti-immigration. In addition to Kitschelt's formula, another aspect for the success of nativist populists is also found in the way that they are able to combine a powerful message of imminent external threat with an aggressive style of communication, speaking on behalf of the ordinary man against the corrupt elite.

I thus maintain that the winning formula is furthermore and also found in the dual processes of instating fear and scapegoating. First fear is created and then blame is attributed. Fear is used to legitimize policies of protecting the people, of putting up barriers, closing borders, ousting immigrants, exiting international institution, emasculating the elite, and so on.

Not only are these policies *justified* by the emanating threat, but it indeed becomes the *duty* of authorities, the populists argue, to protect the ordinary public by instating them.

Three Waves

Similar to fascism in the interwar years, which was at least partly born out of the Great Depression of 1929, the post-war nativist populist movements have also tended to surge in the wake of crises. In the late 1980s, professor of politics Klaus von Beyme (1988), identified three waves of extreme-right politics since 1945: First the nostalgic wave of fascism that arose in Germany and Italy before soon dying out; secondly, the anti-tax wave in the 1950s and 1960s, mostly found in France; and finally a more pan-European trend appearing in the 1980s.

Benjamin Moffitt (2016) also separated different forms of populism over time, between early and new populism. The earlier version included the Latin American movements lasting from the 1930s to the 1960s, and the McCarthyism of the 1950s. The latter kind of populism, Moffitt maintains, started in the late 1980s and early 1990s and included for instance Jean-Marie Le Pen of France, Jörg Haider of Austria and Umberto Bossi of Italy.

For understanding specifically nativist populism in the post-war era up until 2020, which is my intention in this book, a different categorization of three main waves of populism is here more useful. As was mentioned above, the first arose in the wake of the Oil Crisis in the 1970s. The second wave grew out of resentment in Western Europe against workers from the Eastern part of the continent flocking over the former Iron Curtain after the collapse of the Berlin Wall in 1989. A sudden spike within this wave occurred in the wake of the terrorist attacks in the US on 11 September 2001. Finally, the third wave was brewing in the wake of the international financial crisis starting in 2008, reaching new heights on the canopy of the 2015 refugee crisis.

As will become evident when analysing these waves in the following chapters, each is identified by their own qualities. The first wave rose rather on an anti-tax and a neo-liberal notion, instead of being based on hardcore nationalism. At first sight this might seem a bit paradoxical, as initially most populists of the first wave were positioned much further out on the fringe in politics than those finding support in the third wave. However, although many of them resorted to rogue demagoguery, their aim was initially mainly against big government and the corrupt domestic political elite. Nationalistic sentiments rose more clearly to the surface during the second wave, when populist parties were refocused and opposed multiculturalism and immigration. In the third wave, nativist populists became much more mainstream and were by that time firmly centred against mainly Muslim immigration. During the Coronavirus Crisis of 2020 nativist populists around the world reverted to renewed nationalist responses, elevating the likelihood of another rise of Neo-Nationalism, which I will discuss later in the book.

In the following chapters I will further trace this progression of populist parties across the different parts of the European continent as well as in America. Despite the varying evolutions across regions and time, and their varied aspects—all examined further in the following chapters—most of these parties have been quite distinct from the interwar fascist versions. As I mentioned above, these newer waves of nativist populism depart from earlier fascist movements in that contemporary nativist populists do not denounce democracy. Rather, their sights are set against the liberal aspects of the post-war Western democratic order. Secondly, and equally important, is that biological racism was replaced with cultural racism. For this reason, I maintain that post-war nationalism should be understood as a novel populist version, that is, as Neo-Nationalism.

Common Qualities

Whichever viewpoint we choose from the differing definitions discussed above, some similarities can still be identified, which might help in framing the phenomena. Here, however, the focus is firmly on those that can be understood as specifically *nativist* populist. Despite their variations, nativist populist parties have many qualities in common, as will be explored.

In my previous research analysing nationalism in the Nordic countries (2017), and far-right conspiracy theories in Europe (2018), I have developed a scheme identifying ten common qualities of nativist populism. In the following chapters I will build on that framework in mapping the progression of populist movements in Europe and across the Atlantic over the three waves here identified.

First of all, the populists here analysed are nationalist and nativist. Within a nostalgic framework, they are prone to apply myths in order to bring people together within common and cohesive national boundaries.

Secondly, they are exclusionary. They create a division between 'us' who belong to society and 'them' who should not belong to it. Who *they* are can be, for example, immigrants, asylum-seekers, ethnic or religious minorities, even the domestic political elite. The others are discursively turned into enemies of us, threatening our identity and culture or exploiting and ruining the welfare state 'we' have built. Others are here clearly distinguished from the ethnic natives, *us*. This often results in open xenophobia and racism. In Western Europe, this is most often aimed against

Muslims, for example, in Austria, Denmark, France and the Netherlands, while in Eastern Europe the targets are often Roma people or even Jews, as was the case in earlier times. Perhaps most obviously, they campaign against multiculturalism and strive to stem the flow of immigration.

Thirdly, populist movements often revolve around a strong charismatic leader. Most often they rely on what they claim to be a special relationship between the leader and the ordinary public. Particularly, the leader is often seen to understand the burdens of the ordinary public, which, vitally for the story, is being overlooked by the established political elite. The populist leader, on the other hand, usually claims to know how to solve the people's problems. As result, the leader becomes the interpreter of the will of the people.

This brings forward the fourth shared characteristic. Populists are anti-intellectual and anti-elitist. This is often the case even though their leaders themselves often tend to come from the same privileged background as the elite they are fighting against. Still, they claim to be advocates of the nation, and seek to speak in its name. In doing so they differentiate between honest ordinary people and the corrupt elite and discursively turn them into two homogeneous and antagonistic groups. One of their main successes recently has been in criticizing the consensus politics of the corrupt political elite.

Five, the message for solving the ordinary public's most pressing problems tend to be simple; these are straightforward solutions to meet complex national interests. Often they call for mobilizing answers, such as the cleansing of foreign parasites.

Six, populism is more moralistic than practical. They tend to speak to emotions rather than to reason and to avoid intellectual debate. Populists are often not bothered by contradictions, for example, simultaneously promoting economic liberalism and the lowering of taxes, while also promising increased welfare services and easy implementation of high cost policies.

Seven, while often claiming to be economically liberal, populists are more usually protectionist of national production from international competition, especially in the field of agriculture. Often, they exploit a lack of confidence, for example in the wake of a crisis. They voice the dissatisfaction of those losing out to increased globalization and rapid social change.

Eight, populist parties are usually authoritarian and social conservatives; they believe in a strictly ordered society and are rather defined on socio-cultural aspects than on the socio-economic scale. Nativist populists are thus not necessary positioned on the classical economic right. They emphasize family values and law and order, often claiming that the system protects criminals rather than their victims among the ordinary public. Another aspect here is that they disproportionally bring attention to crimes conducted by alien forces, such as migrants.

Ninth, their understanding of democracy is illiberal. They claim to be able to interpret the will of the people. Correspondingly, they have contempt for traditional gatekeepers, such as specialists and mainstream media. Instead they attempt to appeal directly to the people, through their own media, social media and public events, rallies—and so on.

Finally, in international relations populists are usually suspicious of multilateral institutions. In Europe they are most often staunchly Eurosceptic. Some only talk about stemming further integration, while others strive to push back Europeanization and even abolish the European Union.

A THREEFOLD CLAIM FOR THE PEOPLE

Taken collectively, nativist populists put forth a threefold claim in their support of *the people*:

- *First*, they tend discursively to create an external threat to the nation.
- *Second*, they accuse the domestic elite of betraying the people, often even of siding with the external aggressors.
- *Third*, they position themselves as the true defenders of the 'pure people' they vow to protect, against both the elite and these malignant outsiders, that is, against those that they themselves have discursively created.

In the following three chapters I will apply this model when analysing the political discourse of contemporary nativist populists—the Neo-Nationalists of our time.

NOTE

1. *Breitbart.com*. 2017, 28 February. 'Geert Wilders: Islam Is Not a Religion, It's a Totalitarian Ideology'.

References

Albertazzi, D., & McDonnell, D. (2007). *Twenty-First Century Populism: The Spectre of Western European Democracy.* London: Palgrave Macmillan.
Anderson, B. (1983). *Imagined Communities: Reflections on the Origin and Spread of Nationalism* (Rev. ed.). London and New York: Verso.
Ascoli, M., & Feiler, A. (1938). *Fascism for Whom?* (1st Unknown ed.). W. W. Norton & Company.
Bergmann, E. (2017). *Nordic Nationalism and Right-Wing Populist Politics: Imperial Relationships and National Sentiments.* London and New York: Palgrave Macmillan.
Bergmann, E. (2018). *Conspiracy & Populism: The Politics of Misinformation.* London: Palgrave Macmillan.
Betz, H. G. (2001). Exclusionary Populism in Austria, Italy and Switzerland. *International Journal, 53*(3), 393–420.
von Beyme, K. (1988). *Right-Wing Extremism in Western Europe.* London and New York: Routledge.
Billig, M. (1995). *Banal Nationalism.* London: Sage.
Blassnig, S., Büchel, F., Ernst, N., & Engesser, S. (2019). Populism and Informal Fallacies: An Analysis of Right-Wing Populist Rhetoric in Election Campaigns. *Argumentation, 33*(1), 107–136.
Canovan, M. (1981). *Populism.* San Diego: Harcourt.
Eatwell, R., & Goodwin, M. (2018). *National Populism: The Revolt Against Liberal Democracy.* Penguin UK.
Eco, U. (1995, June 22). Ur-Fascism. *The New York Review of Books.*
Finchelstein, F. (2017). *From Fascism to Populism in History.* University of California Press.
Gellner, E. (1983). *Nations and Nationalism.* Ithaca: Cornell University Press.
Hawkins, K. (2003). Populism in Venezuela: The Rise of Chavismo. *Third World Quarterly, 24*(6), 1137–1160.
von Herder, J. G. (1784). *Ideen zur Philosophie der Geschiche der Menschheit.*
Higham, J. (1955). *Strangers in the Land: Patterns of American Nativism, 1860–1925* (Rev. ed.). New Brunswick, NJ: Rutgers University Press.
Hobsbawm, E. (1990). *Nations and Nationalism since 1780: Programme, Myth, Reality.* Cambridge: Cambridge University Press.
Jupskås, A. R. (2015). *The Persistence of Populism. The Norwegian Progress Party 1973–2009.* Oslo: University of Oslo.
Kitschelt, H. (1997). *The Radical Right in Western Europe: A Comparative Analysis.* University of Michigan Press.
Mazzini, G. (1862). *The Duties of Man.* Chapman & Hall.
McCulloch, T. (2006). The Nouvelle Droite in the 1980s and 1990s: Ideology and Entryism, the Relationship with the Front National. *French Politics, 4*(2), 158–178.

Meinecke, F. (1908). *Cosmopolitanism and the National State*. Princeton: Princeton University Press.

Moffitt, B. (2016). *The Global Rise of Populism: Performance, Political Style, and Representation*. Stanford University Press.

Mounk, Y. (2018). The People Vs. Democracy: Why Our Freedom is in Danger and how to Save it. Harvard University Press.

Mudde, C. (2004). The Populist Zeitgeist. *Government and Opposition*, 39(4), 541–563.

Mudde, C. (2016). *On Extremism and Democracy in Europe* (Vol. 34). Routledge.

Nolte, E. (1966). *Three Faces of Fascism: Action Francaise, Italian Fascism, National Socialism* (1st ed.). Henry Holt & Company, Inc.

Paxton, R. (2004). *The Anatomy of Fascism*. London: Penguin Books.

Renan, E. (1882). *Qu'est-ce qu'une nation?* Presented at the Paris: Sorbonne. Paris: Sorbonne.

Rydgren, J. (2005). Is Extreme Right-Wing Populism Contagious? Explaining the Emergence of a New Party Family. *European Journal of Political Research*, 44(3), 413–437.

Rydgren, J. (2007). The Sociology of the Radical Right. *Annual Review of Sociology*, 33, 241–262.

Schedler, A. (1996). Anti-Political-Establishment Parties. *Party Politics*, 2(3), 291–312.

Smith, A. D. (2002). *Nations and Nationalism in the Global Era*. Cambridge: Polity Press.

Sorensen, L. (2018). Populist Communication in the New Media Environment: A Cross-Regional Comparative Perspective. *Palgrave Communications*, 4(1), 1–12.

Wodak, R. (2015). *The Politics of Fear: What Right-Wing Populist Discourses Mean*. New York: Sage.

Wren, K. (2001). Cultural Racism: Something Rotten in the State of Denmark? *Social and Cultural Geography* 2(2), 141–162.

The First Wave: The Oil Crisis and the New Nationalists

The first wave of contemporary nativist populism rose initially in the wake of the OPEC Oil Crisis which hit the Western world hard in the early 1970s. The crisis led to economic hardship, for example to a spike in unemployment. Jean-Marie Le Pen of France was one of the first demagogues to challenge the mainstream post-war political system of compromise and cohesion when founding the National Front in 1972. In addition to neo-liberal and anti-elite emphasis he constructed the party directly in opposition to post-war multiculturalism and immigration, mostly from Muslim countries.

Prior to Le Pen rushing onto the scene, populists in both Austria and in Switzerland had gained significant support, even based on the fascist heritage of the interwar years. In Finland, an agrarian populist party survived for a while in the wake of the Second World War. It was though, rather in Denmark and in Norway where right-wing populists found a real foothold in the Nordic region. Protesting against rising tax levels, the Danish and Norwegian Progress Parties followed in Le Pen's wake, promoted anarcho-liberalism and campaigned against increased economic and bureaucratic burdens on the ordinary man. They argued against wide-scope social services, immigration and cosy consensus politics in these corporatist social democratic welfare states.

This was not the regular right-wing neo-liberal rhetoric, but rather a new populist version, where charismatic leaders positioned themselves alongside the blue-collar public and against the political elite. As I will illustrate in this chapter, the Nordic populist parties started out being fiscally libertarian before becoming more middle ground on economic policy while turning even more hostile towards immigration.

At the time, nativist populism was also brewing across the Atlantic. The red-bait tactics of Senator Joseph McCarthy were clearly of a populist nature. A real rise of nativist populism in the US was marked by neo-liberal factions of the Republican Party merging with social conservative evangelicals from the Democratic Party, leading to the Neoconservative movement—the Neocons—emerging as political force in America.

Initially, the anti-tax neo-liberal populists in Europe were securely kept out on the fringe. First, they were widely dismissed by the mainstream, and then discredited—by other parties and the mass media alike. Generally, they were viewed as being a nuisance, and not really taken seriously. Throughout the 1970s their wins were very modest. But already in the 1980s, however, populist parties were finding a firmer foothold in many Western countries.

The 1980s were also a time when skinheads emerged on the streets of many European capitals. Disgruntled youths were violently marching against immigrants, for example in Britain, Germany, Italy and through Scandinavia. Revelling in fascist symbols such as Nazi tattoos, wearing swastikas and playing loud white-pride rock music, helped in dismissing these actors as rogue demagogues. Only later did nativist populists disguise their neo-fascist nature for a more sophisticated façade.

In this chapter I will map the first wave of political populism that arose in Europe in the post-war era. Throughout this era, populist parties were largely kept out on the periphery, only coming to prominence in the new millennium.

Before exploring these and some other examples further, it is first necessary to quickly sketch out the political environment they were facing—and opposing—in the post-World War II era.

The New Post-War Order

The two world wars not only left the European continent in ruins, causing the death of many millions of people in the world's most horrendous conflicts, it also led to the formation of a profoundly transformed post-war international order. The old system of insular independent states was uprooted. Several autocratic empires and regional powers disappeared.

For instance, the Austro-Hungarian Empire, Prussia, the Ottoman Empire, Tsarist Russia—all were gone by the end of World War I.

Eric Hobsbawm (1994) famously described the twentieth century as the Age of Extremes. A trinity of contradictory ideologies clashed: Fascism, Socialism and Liberal Democracy. After World War II, fascism was discredited and largely rendered illicit. Communism and liberal democracy were then left to compete for dominance across the Iron Curtain, which separated Europe in the Cold War that followed.

On the Western side, liberal democracy was re-emerging, now under a new international architecture. As I discussed in the Introduction, the values of liberal democracy grew to become the framework defining politics in the West. As a universally accepted frame, politics were conducted within the boundaries drawn around a shared understanding of what the limits of liberal democracy allowed. With the previous polarization between fascist and communists gone, all major players in Western politics—from left to right—united around protecting the parameters of liberal parliamentary democracy. In place of ideological conflict that had defined previous eras, mainstream politicians now strived for consensus and the forming of coalitions across political dividing lines.

Although several autocratic regimes still survived into the latter half of the twentieth century, the general direction was firmly set towards liberal democracy. When the Estado Novo regime of António de Oliveira Salazar was overthrown in Portugal in the Carnation revolution of 1974, and after the death of General Francisco Franco of Spain in 1975, democracy spread down the Iberian Peninsula. After several failed attempts, Greece also returned to democracy when the military seceded power in 1974. Largely, these dictatorial regimes in southern Europe were viewed as remnants of days already gone by—that they had only by a mistake of history lived far past their expiration date.

And as I discussed in the Introduction to this book, central and eastern Europe then saw a wide-scale transition to democracy in wake of the collapse of the Berlin Wall in 1989—which I turn to discussing more closely in the next chapter.

International Institutional Architecture

After the Red Army and the Allied forces reached each other in Germany, when defeating the Third Reich and ending World War II, neither superpower, the Soviet Union nor the United States, seceded their influence in

Europe. Instead, a new dividing line was drawn between the liberal democratic West and the communist East, for which Winston Churchill coined the term 'the Iron Curtain'.

One of the defining features of the liberal democratic system raised on the Western side was the construction of a new international institutional order, which was to bind nation-states together within a common architecture. This new nation-state system rested on three pillars: democracy, liberal rights and international co-operation. The United States forsaking its previously held policy of isolation was a central force in the success of the new order. This time around, the US did not leave Europe to sort out its own problems, as it had done after World War I. Instead, Washington firmly applied a new policy of engagement and active international co-operation. With the Cold War looming, and the ghost of communism running wild, America wanted to demonstrate and cement its full commitment to the democratic countries of Western Europe.

The United States became the leading force in the West, largely steering the build-up of the new international institutional architecture. The US also led a more global endeavour of removing barriers to trade. As I will discuss later in this book, these long-held policies of the US were being reversed after Donald Trump came to power.

The generous Marshall Aid Plan of 1947—named after the US Secretary of State, George Marshall—was offered to rebuild infrastructure in Europe following the devastating war. A key aim was to keep Europe committed to both capitalism and liberal democracy. The Bretton Woods agreement established the World Bank and the International Monetary Fund. The United Nations was then invested with power to issue resolutions considered equal to international law, while NATO was to bind the security interests of European and American allies together through a firm collective military commitment on defence. The World Health Organization (WHO) was established in 1948.

Perhaps the most important endeavour to constrain rampant nationalism was the European economic integration process, developing into the supra-national European Union of today. The process was initiated precisely to intertwine interests across borders so tightly that any military invasion would only hurt one's own interests. In response to the Great Depression of 1929 nations-states had competed to put up massive barriers to trade against each other. One of the main aims behind building the vast post-war international architecture was rolling back the economic nationalism of previous times.

Many of the main thinkers behind the integration process saw it as an answer to the toxic nationalism that had devastated the continent. Among them was, for instance, the Italian thinker Altiero Spinelli who had been incarcerated by the Mussolini regime in a prison on top of a cliff rock out at sea called St Stephano, near the island of Ventotene of Italy's Mediterranean coast.

When visiting the prison sometime in the late last century, I remember climbing the steep and narrow path from where our boat had landed. The natural beauty and peaceful calm of the place struck me when reaching to the top of the rock. So did the apparent cruelty of Mussolini's regime. After visiting the cell where Spinelli had been held, I was taken to the prison's torture room. Creative minds of the fascist regime had clearly been given full artistic freedom in crafting some of the most original instruments designed to cause maximum pain to humans. One specimen on exhibit was a bed made of metal rails. We were taught how the prisoners had been strapped down to it by their wrists and ankles. In the middle of the metal bed was a large hole so that anyone strapped in it would have to struggle not to fall into it, which in addition to increased pain threatened to break their spine. While contemplating all of this I remember feeling the burning Mediterranean sun on my neck. In the ceiling of the oval torture room was a large hole, adding to the agony of anyone strapped to the metal rail bed positioned right under it.

Although Altiero Spinelli might perhaps not himself have endured much physical hardship while held on the rock, it is palpable that the place must have left a lasting mark on him. In captivity he wrote the so-called Ventotene manifesto, published in 1941, which questioned the supremacy of nation-states in the international system. Spinelli argued that unleashed and absolute sovereign nation-states were prone to aggression and dominance, leading to wars. Instead he called for the establishment of a true European federation of states, as an 'instrument for achieving international unity'.

Others followed suit, for instance Jean Monet, a French businessman and advisor to foreign minister Robert Schumann. In a speech to the French National Liberation Committee in 1943 he said that there would be no peace in Europe if the states were reconstituted on the basis of national sovereignty. Even Winston Churchill, the victorious Prime Minister of war-time Britain, called for the establishment of a United States of Europe.

Although the dream of a European federation was never realized, the EU was set afloat with significant supra-national qualities. The following years saw fast and far-reaching economic surges. Unemployment was largely over, and the post-war economy was booming. Many of these post-war thinkers envisioned the abolition of borders in Europe. Since its initiation, the European integration process had indeed gradually but continuously brought down barriers between European states, one brick at a time.

As I will discuss later in this book, it was only in the new century that voices calling for the reversal of this trend rose to prominence.

Nations on the Move

Contrary to the autocratic empires of the past, which often were not necessarily framed around a specific nation, the new post-war liberal democracies found their legitimacy in the idea of the nation-state. In the interwar years, they often rested on an exclusionary idea around the nation, leading to antagonism in ethnic relations and internal oppression of minority groups. Although the notorious actions of the Nazi state were of course far more profound, such strokes were still not limited only to fascist regimes. For instance, France deported tens of thousands Algerian workers in 1919, proclaiming them as being unassimilable.

Forty million people lost their lives in the Second World War. Another eleven million found themselves displaced in its wake. In conjunction with this crisis of displaced people, and due to the economic demand for workers, the post-war years thus saw the simultaneous trends of revitalizing the nation-state and liberalizing the movement of peoples between countries.

This mass movement of deposed people later proved to be a recipe for the cultural clash discussed throughout this book. However, in the first two decades of the post-war era, immigrants were welcomed to Western Europe.

Alongside migration marking modern times, the mainstream media and the political class largely celebrated the emergence of multicultural societies. Europe's door not only stood wide open, but states like France, West Germany and the UK even set up active recruitment offices in Africa and elsewhere. The fact of the matter is that these migrants, who later were increasingly viewed as being a burden, were actively recruited from overseas.

Here we should, however, clearly remember that even though a few millions of people were coming to Western Europe in the wake of the war, their number was still dwarfed by the many tens of millions that had left the continent to the Americas in the nineteenth and early twentieth centuries. Until the relatively modest influx in the post-war years, Europe had for centuries rather been a continent of emigration, than one of immigration. And although the outflow of previous times was being reversed, their numbers were far from making up for all those that Europe had previously lost.

Putting Down Roots

Despite the general and wide-reaching celebration of foreign workers, there were still many who warned that crude nationalists could stir up suspicions around them. Exploiting peoples' fear of migrants—which in many ways defines contemporary politics in the West—is not much of a novelty. Playing on polarization is a persistent and ongoing act in politics. However, although migration was perhaps nothing new, the sudden influx of foreigners came unannounced. And even though fascism and Nazism were widely delegitimized, racism had never been eradicated from Europe's soil. For instance, on the door to many lodging houses in the UK at the time, a placard still read: 'No Blacks, Irish or dogs' (qtd in Frawley 2011).

Many countries operated racial separation. Factories in the UK were for instance thirsting for labour and the government operated a scheme called *European Volunteer Workers*. The programme prioritized white people from the Baltics and emphasized keeping out Jews. Another example was when the Icelandic authorities allowed the American army to open up a base on the island on the condition of excluding people of colour from serving there.

In general, there was never any long-term assimilation plan around this massive immigration in the wake of the war. Governments were rather just muddling through on a day-to-day basis. In fact, the migrants and refugees were initially mostly treated as guest workers. Soon, however, we came to realize that many of them were putting down roots, and that they were not at all intent on leaving. Instead, immigrants would often cluster in cheaper areas, leading to the formation of immigrant ghettos in many European cities.

The Post-War Economic Boom

In the post-war era, constant economic growth was gradually being taken for granted. For a quarter of a century the Western economies saw an almost unhindered boom. Many took this as simply being the way of modern times, brought by free trade and social welfare. A new social contract was slowly being cemented, tightly combining capitalism and the welfare state within a democratic order. This Keynesian economic model was widely accepted.

In this new order, the state was all-embracing and much more present in people's lives than it had been before. The British post-war Labour Party Prime Minister, Clement Attlee, for instance insisted that the main task of his government was in laying the foundations of the welfare state.

Mark Mazower (2009) argues that the very term, *welfare state*, the idea of an all-encompassing social authority, had been deliberately contrived in opposition to Hitler's Nazism. Indeed, British PM Attlee positioned the welfare state in opposition to Nazism of previous times and placed it as a far better alternative to Stalin's Soviet Union. In fact, it was the West's answer to both.

In the post-war era, the liberal democratic welfare state of the West was equated with constant economic growth, full employment, financial freedom, population growth, higher education and better health services. In short, a society of ever-increasing prosperity. This novel post-war creation completely contradicted the previous crisis-ridden societies of political extremes.

Among other novelties was the emergence of the mass media reaching the majority of people at the same time. This was the high time of broadsheet newspapers and linear TV. The new and professional media positively reported on the perceived prosperity, and it was firmly a part of the new mainstream establishment. Furthermore, this was the time when globalization really took off, not only in cross-border trade and culture, but also with the new mass tourism. People were on the move in record numbers. Now, not only as refugees and migrants, but with the leisure economy taking off, also as tourists.

Early Extremism

Although people on the move were relatively well-received in most places in the post-war years, there were always exceptions. Several extremist views and movements existed out on the fringes. In Italy, for instance, fascism never fully perished. In contrast to Germany where Nazism was almost entirely uprooted in the wake of the war, authoritarian nationalism never completely left Rome or Milan. For instance, the government of Fernando Tambroni in 1960 openly relied on support from neo-fascist parliamentary groups.

At the same time, extreme leftist movements were also running rogue in Italy. Such associations were causing mayhem in Germany as well. In politics, the pendulum sometimes tends to swing from one extreme to the other. In wake of the devastations left by fascism and Nazism, many young people in Western Europe turned to the far left. And some of those movements did turn to violence.

Among the most notorious were the Red Armies in Germany and in Italy. The *Rote Armee Fraktion* (RAF) in West Germany, led by Andreas Baader and Ulrike Meinhof—the so-called Baader–Meinhof gang—aggressively turned against their parent's generation, who they accused of having moved from one kind of fascism to another. One of the movement's main thinkers, Rudi Dutschke, described the new post-war order as aggressive and fascist consumerism. The Baader–Meinhof group took to urban terrorism in a violent 'anti-imperial' struggle.

Dissatisfaction was surely growing among the youth in West Berlin, Rome and Paris. The left was rapidly fragmenting, and polarization was increasing. With the Vietnam War raging, the cleavage between generations was expanding. With it, the moral leadership of the US, which it had gained in the post-war era—for example via the Marshall Aid Plan discussed above—was fast evaporating.

The student youth protests of 1968, which for instance almost caused Paris to grind to a halt, marked a cultural turn. Change was in the air. But it turned out to be one not so anticipated by many at the time. The initial major revolt against the liberal post-war order stemmed from the political left. However, it was the challenge waged from the political right, emerging in the wake of the economic slowdown of the early 1970s, that was having greater political impact on the turn towards the nativist populism examined in this book. In place of increased tolerance and freedom promoted by the left-wing and socio-liberal 1968 movement, we later learned that the tide was, indeed, turning in another direction, which I turn to discussing next.

The Oil Crisis of 1972

The post-war golden age of full employment and constant growth came to an abrupt halt with the so-called Oil Crisis that hit the Western world in 1972. The crisis brought a renewed clash between capital and labour and tested the resilience of the very social fabric that Western nations had been firmly weaving together in the preceding two decades.

While inflation was on the rise, purchasing power was plummeting. For the first time in a long while, unemployment was up. Poverty was again baring its ugly head. These new times were defined by increasing economic uncertainty. Countries that had enjoyed extensive growth fell into recession and prolonged stagflation. Long lasting mass unemployment seemed unavoidable. For the first time in a quarter of a century, Western societies were moving backward, not forward.

The economic crisis took most people by surprise. Many had come to believe that economic hardship was a thing of the past—something to read about in history books, not to suffer from in reality. Instantly, thus, governments were blamed for losing their guard.

The crisis opened up a space to re-examine the social contract that had combined capitalism with wide scale welfare, which the nation-state operated and guaranteed for all. For the first time, the post-war Keynesian political consensus of the West was being challenged. Economic liberalism was instead coming back in vogue, taking on the form which has been branded as neo-liberalism.

The economic and political evolvement of the late 1960s and early 1970s shattered many people's trust in the political establishment. This was occurring simultaneously on both sides of the Atlantic. Protests were occurring in Paris and in San Francisco. The Vietnam War, The Watergate scandal and the economic downturn all played their part.

In the wake of the war, far-right parties had been completely marginalized and firmly kept on the fringe in Western politics. Germany had gone so far as banning neo-Nazi parties. The early 1970s crisis, then, brought renewed polarization. It was shattering the once-held consensus. The Age of Extremes was, perhaps, not completely over.

Polarization Anew

In wake of the crisis, the political right was heading further out on that spectrum. The political left, was, however, not necessarily following suit. But it did suffer less support, and was, as a result, gradually being deemed irrelevant in modern day politics.

The rosy promise of previous times, of a prosperous future for all, had suddenly evaporated. Someone had to be blamed. Many started to point a finger to foreigners, for stealing jobs and burdening the welfare system. Simultaneously, government and the elite were accused of having abandoned the people, of having betrayed those that they had been trusted with protecting.

It was in this socio-economic climate that political parties were first formed on a nativist populistic base in the post-war era. In France, Denmark and Norway, for example, in rallying support from those that felt left out, populist leaders started to simultaneously blame both migrants and the elite. The elite was held liable for having deserted those that precipitously found themselves unemployed and living in deprived areas. And what was even worse, because of mass migration they would now be without a future.

This was the economic climate that brought Margaret Thatcher to power in the UK in 1979 on a neo-liberal platform. Her government brought monetarism, deregulation, lower taxes and started to dismantle the welfare state. Over in America, President Ronald Reagan was setting out on a similar voyage. In this era, with Adam Smith's liberal economic theory back in vogue, Keynesian economic theory was being thrown out like last year's fashions.

Paradoxically, however, Thatcherian neo-liberalism also had an authoritarian side to it. While emphasizing privatization, the government consolidated power into the hands of Whitehall, for instance extracting competences from local authorities. Family values and an emphasis on tradition were also brought back to prominence. In combining economic liberalism with social conservatism, this can be seen as a Hobbesian intertwining of competition and compliance. In a way, Thatcherism was a non-populist version of the same right-wing trend of the time, which here is under examination. It portrayed the same push-back against the welfare state as was the case with right-wing nativist populist actors in France, Italy, Denmark, Norway and elsewhere.

THE CULTURAL TURN

Yet another depiction of this time of economic decay and cultural decadence was illuminating on the pop culture scene, with the emergence of the punk-rock movement. In their punk anthem, *God Save the Queen*, the Sex Pistols shouted: 'Don't be told what you need/There's no future/No future/No future for you.' In many ways, this is the feeling that laid the foundation for the coming rise of nativist populism.

Racial tensions were once again increasing. Neo-Nazis were seen protesting on the streets in many countries. Increased racist attacks followed and ideas of racial purification programmes were resurfacing. For instance, in a quest for protecting the Christian values of Europe, sixteen university professors in West Germany signed a declaration in 1982, calling for returning all migrants to their home countries (Mazower 2009).

Many felt that the way of life they had become used to during the growth years was being threatened. As result, economic nationalism of the interwar era was resurfacing, now via a populist plea of the radical-right. European governments responded with increasing restriction on immigration and on foreign workers already in the country. With increased preference given to the domestic population, foreigners were now even expected to leave. Discrimination was furthermore on the rise. In a short span of time, migrants went from being considered assets, to being viewed a burden. In many countries, immigration policies were being reversed, from emphasizing recruitment to encouraging return. In other words, this initial wave of post-war nativist populism resulted from prolonged economic crisis and rose in conjunction with concerns around mass migration.

This was also a time of gradual rehabilitation of some of the previously condemned figures of Nazi Germany. In her review on Leni Riefenstahl's photographic book titled *The Last of the Nuba*, Susan Sontag (1975) identifies the insidious rehabilitation of fascist views. Sontag wrote that the 'purification of Leni Riefenstahl's reputation of its Nazi dross' had for a while been gathering momentum.

However—and this should be stated very firmly—while racism was surely somewhat on the rise, so was anti-racism. Opposition against *Apartheid* in South-Africa was for example rising around the world at the time. Although the rough right-wing extremism surely found new-fangled ground, it never reached much mainstream support in this era. And even though state sponsored welfare was perhaps being contested, the democratic order remained unchallenged.

In the following sections, I will sketch out how the first wave of nativist populism rose in Western Europe in the wake of the Oil Crisis of 1972. The phenomena evolved in various ways in the different countries. While it is relatively recent in countries like Sweden, Germany and the United Kingdom, such parties have survived for almost a half century in France, Italy, Denmark, Norway and in the Alpine countries.

THE NATIONAL FRONT

Jean-Marie Le Pen is perhaps the archetypical Neo-Nationalist of the first wave. Never hiding his rogue demagogue nature, he founded the French National Front (*Front National*) in October 1972, which grew to become one of the most influential far-right parties in Europe. The party synthesized many and diverse nationalist and far-right groupings that at the time had been operating far out on the fringe in French politics.

Jean-Marie-Le Pen had for example been an activist for the so-called Poujade movement in the 1950s, named after a shopkeeper, Pierre Poujade, who rallied small businessmen against the establishment and high taxation. Another prominent group was New Order (*Ordre Nouvau*). Initially the Algerian War was the main unifying factor of these otherwise fragmented groups, especially dissatisfaction with President Charles de Gaulle seceding French control in northern Africa. In 2018, the National Front was renamed *Rassemblement National*, National Rally in English.

Throughout the first decade of its existence the party was not only struggling for relevance, but also for its mere survival. Because of its blatant nationalism and flirtation with both fascism and anti-Semitism, the FN was easily dismissed by its opponents. That started to change in the 1980s. Together with initial purging exercises when expelling some of the most notorious neo-Nazi actors from the party, and at the same time attracting more traditional Catholic members, it was finding renewed legitimacy. Still, it was their fierce criticism of immigration, and of the governments bad handling of the economic crisis, that kept Le Pen's party gradually growing, finding initial significant success in the 1983 municipal elections.

Its first real electoral breakthrough came in the following year, when Le Pen secured a seat in the European Parliament, winning a full tenth of the vote. In the first round of the 1988 presidential election, Le Pen received 14 per cent of the vote.[1] Equating himself with the ordinary people his slogan was simple; 'Le Pen, le peuple', meaning, Le Pen, the people. From then on, the party became a force to reckoned with in French politics, at times even dominating the political debate.

The vast influence of the Socialist Party under President François Mitterrand, and its lenient immigration policy, played to the advantage of the FN. In fiercely opposing the government, the FN was able to position itself as a more credible alternative on the right than before. Still, because of the electoral system, their representation in the National Assembly was limited.

The party positioned itself alongside the ordinary man and against the elite. It firmly opposed migrant workers settling in France. They furthermore set out to stem globalization and external influences. The National Front opposed the European Union from the outset and campaigned both against the Euro and France entering the Schengen border scheme. The view on the US was more ambiguous. Although the party was surely quite critical of the overall Americanization of French society, Jean-Marie Le Pen clearly identified with US President Ronald Reagan, who came to power in 1981. In fact, he saw himself as being a kind of a French version of the American President.

Antagonism

Substance of policy was not the only source of success for the FN. Its combative and antagonistic style was also of significance. A charismatic demagogue, Jean-Marie Le Pen was prone to put forward views that were largely viewed as scandalous. This brought nationwide attention to his politics. By deliberately causing outrage in the mainstream media, he mastered the populist style of playing on provocations. As I discussed in the previous chapter, this style was later to become a unifying trademark of populist politicians. Many decades later Donald Trump adopted the same style.

Several French scholars such as Cuminal et al. (1997), Guland (2000) and Jamin (2009), note how the National Front was prone to weave conspiracy theories into their political discourse. In doing so they rhetorically aligned the corrupt governing elite in Paris with the alleged conspirators, and the pure people with the unknowing, that is, the victimized.

With entangling populism and conspiracy theories, the FN was able to attack the domestic establishment, though without seeking to overthrow the democratic system—which was vital for withholding its credibility. Rather, the party advocated ousting of the elite and instating an ameliorated democratic system of the common people and for the common people.

Positioning themselves as outsiders in French politics the FN accused the elite of being corrupt and collectively engaging in covert cross-party manipulations. Skilfully the FN also accused the mainstream of being accomplices of the foreign conspirators and, thus, of betraying the ordinary people in France into the hands of external evil.

Prior to the collapse of the Berlin Wall the FN mainly set out to unravel a global communist conspiracy, which they argued was for example concocted via the United Nations—where communists were allegedly manipulating events behind the scenes. The party also warned against communists infiltrating many other international organizations, including the European Community and even NATO—sometimes in league with Jews—which were seen as facades for a communist led New World Order. On these grounds, the FN opposed the internationalization of France, and was on that platform able to accuse the domestic elite of being entangled with a global cabal of evildoers.

Over time, this anti-communist rhetoric evolved and gradually changed, until the FN primarily set out to fight against Islamist infiltration—which I will return to discussing further in the following two chapters.

The discourse of the FN clearly followed the three-level rhetoric of nativist populism, identified in the previous chapter; discursively creating an external threat, pointing out internal traitors, and then offering to protect people from both. An interesting shift can also be detected, in who was placed as the external threat. First, it was the communists, later the migrants. The role of traitor, however, remained constant. The domestic Parisian elite was persistently accused of betraying the people; first, into the hands of communist, and later to Muslim migrants. Throughout the period, Le Pen perpetually positioned himself as the protector of the people.

Ethno-Nationalism

Ideologically, the National Front tapped into a political philosophy developed within a far-right think-tank and a political movement established in the late 1960s, called the *Nouvelle Droite* (ND), meaning New Right. Like elsewhere in Europe, the French extreme-right had been driven underground in the wake of World War II. Still, several far-right nationalist groups were already resurfacing in the 1960s. Philosopher Alain de Benoist became its principal voice.

Building on a platform laid out by *Nouvelle Droite*, the National Front opposed liberal democracy and multiculturalism. Instead they promoted ethno-nationalism, and keeping cultures separate. When arguing for this 'right to difference', the ND for example referred to the writings of Johann Gottfried von Herder from the eighteenth century, who, as I discussed in the previous chapter, maintained that nations were naturally constructed, and thus firmly distinct.

One of the main ideological quests of *Nouvelle Droite* was the reinvigoration of European culture and identity. Political scientist Roger Griffin (2002) maintains that the ND combined populist ultra-nationalism with a call for national rebirth. Pierre-André Taguieff (2004) went even further when describing its nationalism as ethnically based xenophobia.

Given the tide of the times, *Nouvelle Droite* gained a surprisingly far-reaching mainstream following. Their ideas were widely reported in the traditional media. Highly respected outlets like *Le Figaro* published their pieces. Their rise to prominence in the public discussion, however, brought criticism of racism, and of upholding at least quasi-fascist views. They were even accused of being in stark contradiction to the liberalist spirit and legacy of the French Revolution: of freedom, democracy and egalitarianism.

IDENTITY POLITICS

Francophone nationalist intellectuals were also among those that initiated the *Identitarian* movement in Europe. Among their leaders was French historian Dominique Venner who promoted a return to European identity, and an active struggle for reconquering what was lost to multiculturalism.

In this quest for some sort of a renewed European Renaissance, the Identitarians simultaneously promoted purging of Middle Eastern influences that had accompanied migrants to Europe. They also advocated the cleansing of American influences flowing across the Atlantic alongside popular cultural imports. According to the Identitarians, Europe's spiritual demise and cultural destruction had already gone so far that it would only return via radical methods. In a sense, this combines opposition to both capitalism and modernity as such. José Pedro Zúquete (2018) argues that identity is here applied as a ethno-centric 'tool for exclusion, legitimizing ignorance, and keeping others apart'.

The European Identitarians offered a dualist nationalism of both country and continent. As well as protecting French culture they also emphasized shielding shared European values. This plays into another dualism of French nationalism, a contradiction that cuts between internal closeness of protecting French-ness, and external openness, which serves the purpose of France being able to assert its influence wider in Europe (Magali 2013).

In their argumentation, the Identitarians blame mainstream liberal democratic leaders for facilitating the dilution of European culture by the opening of gates to migrants and foreign cultural influences. In his dystopian novel *Le Camp des Saints* (The Camp of the Saints), French writer, Jean Raspail (1973) depicts the cultural demise of Western civilization through mass migration of sex-crazed Indians. This fear was also upheld by a founding member of the National Front, writer Francois Duprat, who in May 1976 warned that immigration was causing the disappearance of the true French people, and with them, their identity.

These writings echoed the UK Conservative Party politician and former Classics professor, Enoch Powell, who in an infamous speech in Birmingham in 1968 coined the Rivers of Blood phrase, which later was to be picked up by many nativist populists. Powell criticized mass immigration to the UK of people from the Commonwealth. Quoting a line from Virgil's *Aeneid* he said: 'like the Roman, I seem to see the River Tiber foaming with much blood'.[2]

This conspiracy theory of a White Genocide or Replacement is core to the Identitarian movement. It found wide support in Europe and was entangled into the more general White Genocide conspiracy theory, which nationalist far-right activists have upheld on both sides of the Atlantic. Many of them maintain that immigrants were flocking to predominantly white countries for the precise purpose of rendering the white population a minority within their own land, or even causing their extinction. In the years that followed, identity started to replace issues of class. Gradually, over the second and third wave—as I will discuss further in the following chapters—the fear of replacement focused mainly on Muslims.

In many ways the current evolution of increased polarization and conspiratorialism resembles the Dreyfus affair in the late nineteenth century, when Captain Alfred Dreyfus was supposedly 'outed' as a German traitor and accused of leaking military information to the enemy. Suspiscions were heightened by the fact that Dreyfus was a Jew, spoke German and was an Alsatian. The affair divided the population and polarized society in high level infighting to the extent that principles of law and order were being tested. The French army concocted all kinds of fake accusations which they would spread via the gutter press as being factual. Although later vindicated of charges, Dreyfus was convicted and sent to solitary confinement on Devils Island. As will become evident in the following two chapters, several aspects similar to the Dreyfus affair were to resurface in and around the contemporary debate on Muslims in France.

ALPINE POPULISM

The Alpine region is among those where populism found most fertile ground in the post-war era. Nationalist xenophobes have indeed enjoyed sustained support in Switzerland and in Austria. With both countries nearing top of most lists measuring prosperity, this can seem somewhat paradoxical to populism being—at least partially—a response to crisis and economic hardship. Another peculiarity is that in both cases, previously mainstream parties were retuned in a populist direction.

Due to its neutrality, Switzerland had remained relatively unaffected by the war. Devastations of Nazism were, thus, not felt there in the same way as elsewhere. Perhaps that situation contributed to the fact that xenophobic views were neither completely uprooted. In the early 1970s, several social movements were openly protesting against what they branded as *Überfremdung*, meaning over-foreignization. *Nationale Aktion* (National Action) was among early far-right xenophobic movements campaigning in the early 1960s against the influx of foreign workers. They were especially critical of Italians flocking over the border.

Some of these parties were openly fascist and a few were fully neo-Nazi, such as the *Volkspartei der Schweiz* (People's Party of Switzerland) led by philosopher Gaston-Armand Amaudruz, who was a staunch Holocaust denier. Neo-fascist thinkers in Switzerland were in fact quite influential in Europe. *Nouvelle Droite* in France was influenced by Swiss-born writer Armin Mohler who called for a conservative revolution in Europe, against the liberal policies around immigration and culture.

Switzerland's most influential contemporary populist party was the far-right Swiss People's Party (*Schweizerische Volkspartei*—SvP). Merged out of a few previous movements, the party was in its current form established in 1971. Until the 1990s, the party could be considered mainstream. However, with Christoph Blocher becoming primus motor, it was transformed and geared against both immigration and the European Union.

Austria's Freedom Party

Under leadership of the vibrant Jörg Haider, Austria's Freedom Party (*Freiheitliche Partei Österreichs—FPÖ*) emerged in the 1990s to become one of Europe's most influential far-right populist parties. Although previously rooted in nationalist politics, the party had become firmly mainstream in the decades prior to Haider coming to the helm. The FPÖ's later voyage to political prominence is thus highly interesting when studying the history of nativist populism in Europe.

The Freedom Party was established in 1956 on the base of the Federation of Independents. Initially, it campaigned for Germanic unity, for keeping Austria within a German overstate. Their nationalism was thus based on a pan-Germanic cultural notion. Its first leader, Anton Reinthaller, had indeed been prominent in the Nazi apparatus during the war.

In the following decades, the party became more mainstream, firmly accepting the European liberal democracy which defined the politics of the time. It was not until 1986, when the young and charismatic Jörg Haider rose to the helm, that vigilant nationalism re-emerged. By that time, the FPÖ served as a junior party in government, but was finding ever diminished support.

Haider was quick to rebrand the party as an aggressive far-right alternative to the mainstream. It turned firmly against former collaborators in governments and was also geared against both immigrants and the European Union. Although Haider himself was never a promoter of past-era biological racism, he still came to the defence of those Austrians who had fought for the Third Reich. And like other far-right populists of the time, he was prone to advocate for cultural separatism. 'Vienna must not become Chicago', he claimed when coining one of the party's most famous slogans: 'Vienna for the Viennese' (qtd in Hainsworth 2008).

After this transformation, the party moved from insignificance to immense electoral success, for instance almost doubling its vote between the 1983 and 1986 parliamentary elections. As I will discuss in the following chapter, Haider went on to dominate Austrian politics for the coming decade.

Nordic Chauvinism

Politics in the Nordic countries were shaken in the 1970s when anti-tax parties rushed to the fore in Denmark and Norway. Both were among those initiating the first wave of populist politics in Europe. The fate of nativist populist parties has varied in the region. While populist anti-tax movements rose early in Denmark and in Norway, they only turned more firmly against immigration during the second wave. It was then in the wake of the Financial Crisis hitting in 2008, that populists found significant success in Finland and in Sweden.

Although the parties here discussed share many qualities of populist politics, their policies, style and impact have varied greatly. The Sweden Democrats (*Sverigedemocraterna*—SD) were rooted in neo-Nazism and remained furthest out on the fringe in national politics. The Norwegian Progress Party (*Fremskrittspartiet*—FrP) was perhaps the mildest version of the populist parties and won almost full acceptance domestically. The True Finns (*Perussuomalaiset*—PS)—later referred to as The Finns Party— was primarily Eurosceptic. The Danish People's Party (*Dansk Folkeparti*— DF) was most influential and managed to pull the domestic discourse on immigration into its own direction. All of these movements offered an alternative voice to the mainstream, tapping into the fears of the ordinary public.

In the post-war era, both Denmark and Sweden gained a reputation for being open, liberal and tolerant. An influx of foreign workers, mainly from northern Africa, the Middle East and the Balkans was on the rise in the 1960s, followed by increased flow of refugees. Their numbers were significantly lower in Finland, Iceland and Norway. In Sweden, the open-door policy and tolerance towards the new arrivals was initially deemed being an integral part of Sweden's social liberalism. Multiculturalism thus fitted neatly into the Swedish national identity.

In Denmark, the discourse on immigration drastically changed in the 1970s and 1980s, from emphasizing equal treatment and protecting human rights towards requirements of adhering to fundamental values of Danish society. Nationalism was reawakening and soon immigrants and refugees went through a culturally based neo-racist rhetoric, discursively being constructed as a threat to Danish values and national identity. Manoeuvrings of this kind developed much later and to a lesser extent in the other Nordic countries.

In what was described as an earthquake election in 1973, controversial tax attorney Mogens Glistrup stormed onto the political scene in Denmark with his thick anti-tax rhetoric, waging an all-out political attack on the mainstream, which he claimed was burdening the ordinary man beyond what the public could tolerate. Glistrup defined his Progress Party (*Fremskridtspartiet*—FrP) as an anti-elitist anarcho-liberal movement. Arguing that taxes were immoral, he promoted tax avoidance and boasted of himself for having shrewdly helped many people outmanoeuvre the taxman, something he claimed should be a civil liberty. Glistrup equated tax-avoiders with the brave Danish resistance fighters during the Nazi occupation in the Second World War, claiming that they did a dangerous but important job for the country.

Until this watershed change, Denmark had been considered liberal and tolerant towards diversity and alternative lifestyles, for example, in regard to sexuality and substance use, to name but two categories. It was also among the world's most open country on immigration and asylum. Newcomers gained easy access to civil rights and generous welfare benefits. Imposing Danish values or cultural restrictions on immigrants, which later became commonplace, was absent from the political discourse of the time, and not even considered legitimate.

By the 1973 election, Denmark was at a political juncture. It was becoming quite multicultural and had after a national referendum in the previous year joined the European Economic Community. Fatigue with established parties was growing. Fuelled by his anti-tax stance and a more widely aimed anti-establishment rhetoric, delivered in a rough and humoristic style, Glistrup snatched almost 16 per cent of the vote, making his brand-new party the second largest in parliament. The sudden success came mostly at the expense of the Social Democratic Party, which was losing ground with the blue-collar working class.

Nationalism was reawakening and cultural racism was on the rise. Karen Wren (2001) maintains that Denmark proved especially fertile for cultural racism, turning fundamentally intolerant in the 1980s. She maintains that paradoxically, the former liberal values in Denmark were used to legitimate negative representation of others, especially Muslims and refugees, who were discursively being constructed as a threat to Danish national identity.

Denmark Turning

Over the coming decade, electoral support for the Progress Party slowly declined, and in 1983 Glistrup's past caught up with him when he was sentenced to three years in prison for tax evasion. Absence of the founder gave way to his successor, the likeable Pia Kjærsgaard, who successfully maneuvered to fill the vacuum, adding thick anti-immigrant rhetoric to the mix of tax deduction. An anti-immigrant stance soon became her main errand in Danish politics.

With its anti-elitist rhetoric and growing xenophobia, the Progress Party operated firmly on the fringe, and Glistrup had no ambitions of being accepted by the establishment—with whom he was squarely in opposition. He saw no need in polishing his rhetoric. For instance, when discussing Muslims in Denmark Glistrup once compared them to a 'drop of arsenic in a glass of clear water'. He referred to them as foreign invaders, aiming to 'colonize' Denmark (qtd in Wren 2001).

Though most mainstream parties opposed this chauvinism, the Progress Party was still tolerated by the political establishment. Contrary to what was the case in Sweden, there was no consensus in Denmark of sequestering the populists. Although at the time never considered an ideal partner, the right-of-centre government periodically found a need to strike ad hoc deals with them.

The Progress Party was instrumental in the process of externalizing immigrants and in portraying Denmark as being overrun by foreigners. In the early 1980s the party was becoming increasingly anti-immigrant, especially in response to an influx of refugees from the Iraq–Iran war. It was coming close to fully adopting Herbert Kitschelt's winning formula, which I discussed in the previous chapter, of combining right-wing politics with a policy of anti-immigration. Thus, by adding thick anti-immigrant rhetoric to its anti-tax policy the party was again increasing its support. Full acceptance though, was still far away.

Internal splits were also tearing the Progress Party apart. Pia Kjærsgaard, who had risen to the helm, was later to exit with many of the most active members in toe, and form her own populist party construction, the Danish Peoples Party. Gradually, she was able to start the long and winding voyage towards respectability—which I will explain further when picking this discussion up in the next chapter.

Norway Tags Along

Over in Norway, one Anders Lange set out to mirror Glistrup's success. Lange was linked to nationalistic movements of the interwar years, but—similar to his Danish counterpart—it was his emphasis on breaking up the tax system and claiming to speak for the ordinary man against the elite, that appealed to the public.

In many respects, Norway was still a very traditional society, for example firmly based on its strong Christian heritage. Throughout the ages, Norway had always been the poor and backward Scandinavian. This reversed after striking vast oil fields in the North Sea in 1969. The following boom brought Norway from the poorest in the region to one among the richest in the world.

The debate over Norway's place in Europe has been one of the country's hottest disputed issues. In the wake of the Second World War, Norway joined NATO and also became a founding member of the European Free Trade Association (EFTA) established in 1960. When the UK and Denmark decided to jump the fence and join the supranational European Economic Community (now the EU), the Norwegian public rejected membership by a slim margin. The bitterly fought campaign was quite disruptive. Families were divided and the issue also ran straight through the middle of most political parties. Ever since, the European question has split the country down the spine and caused serious political constraints.

In the European debate, the notion of 'the people' rushed to the forefront in a renewed contest over who were their true representatives. Anti-EU-accession campaigners tapped directly into the understanding of Norway's exceptional history and, in doing so, indicated that the elite was in effect attempting to bypass 'the people'.

It was in this political atmosphere that Anders Lange was able to confront the mainstream parties, grabbing 5 per cent of the vote in the 1973 parliament elections. Similar to Glistrup in Denmark, Lange was a controversial but charismatic figure. His style was chauvinist and he had a strong and aggressive TV presence. Anders Widfeldt (2015) documents how he would often harshly mock his political establishment rivals with his cruel humour, much to the amusement of his audience.

Lange's emergence onto the political stage sent a shockwave through the mainstream parties. He listed fourteen issues that he said ordinary Norwegians were sick of. One was: 'We are sick of politicians who think they own our money' (qtd in Moen 2006). Largely, the party was Lange's own private political enterprise and he refused to build proper democratic structures, which led many of his followers to defect. Lange had an ambivalent relationship with racist and extreme forces. He was surely an outsider at the time but before the war he had held a position of secretary in the quasi-fascist Fatherlands League. Still, keeping hooligan and racist forces down was vital for the success of his party. After Lange's death in late 1974, the party suffered from internal conflict and was not re-elected to parliament in 1977.

Hagen to the Helm

In 1978, Lange's successor in parliament, Carl I. Hagen, rose to the helm. Influenced by Glistrup's party in Denmark, he rebranded Lange's party as Norway's Progress Party. Hagen held onto power in the party for the next twenty-eight years, evolving to become one of the most influential politicians in contemporary Norway. As I will discuss in the following chapters, it was his successor Siv Jensen who later steered the party into government.

Carl I. Hagen was not only a charismatic and skilled orator, he was also a shrewd operator and soon had a firm grip on the party. Under his leadership they re-entered parliament in 1981. The Progress Party grew to simultaneously become perhaps the mildest and most successful right-wing populist political party in Europe. By the late 1980s the anti-immigrant stance had surpassed that of the anti-tax heritage, tapping into concerns with an increased flow of refugees and asylum seekers. Prior to that, Norway was both very homogeneous and held perhaps the most liberal immigrant policy in the region.

One example of the hardened anti-immigrant rhetoric came in the 1987 election campaign. Carl I. Hagen quoted a letter he claimed he had received from a Muslim called Mustafa, effectively describing a conspiracy of Muslim immigrants planning to take over Norway. This was quite remarkable as Muslims accounted for only a fraction of the population. Still, he did not hesitate to uphold the Eurabia conspiracy theory, which I will address later in the book. Although the letter proved to be his own fabrication, in fact a full-fledged political forgery, that did not prevent them from winning 12.3 per cent of the vote—mainly on the anti-immigrant platform.

In passing the psychological 10 per cent mark in electoral support, the party in effect graduated into being taken seriously in Norwegian politics, a position which was confirmed in the 1989 national elections when they secured an impressive 13 per cent of the vote. By then, as I will discuss further in the following chapter, their anti-immigrant discourse had surpassed that of the anti-tax stance.

Agro Populism in Suomi

After the Second World War, Finland was economically devastated. Still, it had been able to protect its fragile independence while simultaneously manoeuvring through delicate diplomatic relations with Russia and developing a robust democratic Nordic-style welfare nation-state.

Finland was a homogeneous country with low level of immigration. Right-wing nativist populist politics were thus not prominent in the latter half of the twentieth century. Still, agrarian populist versions had existed since the 1960s with a noteworthy support. The Finnish Agrarian Party (*Suomen Maaseudun Puolue*—SMP) was established in 1959. It was founded in opposition to the urban elite and claimed to speak on behalf of the common man, referring to the 'forgotten people' in town and country, against the detached ruling class in the urban south (Arter 2010).

Finland had aligned with Germany in the Second World War, mainly because of the threat it felt from its eastern neighbour. Leading up to the war, tension was growing on its border with the Soviet Union. In the so-called Winter War in autumn 1939, Finland lost 12 per cent of its land in Karelia. When the Germans invaded Russia in 1941, the Finns fought alongside them, in what is referred to as the Continuation War, in an attempt to regain lost territories in Karelia.

Beaten back by the Soviets once again three years later and devastated by repeated conflicts, Finland emerged humbled from the war, surely with a sense of suffering but also one of perseverance. The country was not only in dire straits economically but also firmly within the sphere of strategic influence of the Soviet Union. Finnish diplomacy revolved around appeasing their powerful eastern neighbour, for example, by reaffirming neutrality in the Cold War and keeping a low profile in international affairs.

By tapping into the heritage of the old agrarian fascist Lapua movement from the interwar years, the SMP was able to exploit to its advantage this atmosphere of victimhood. The SMP played on the centre–periphery divide in Finland and appealed mainly to rural workers and the unemployed, who felt alienated in the fast-moving post-war society. In a rapid social structural change, Finland was transformed from being predominantly agricultural to a high-tech communication-based society.

Like most other populist parties, the SMP mainly revolved around its leader, the charismatic Veikko Vennamo, who led the party for the first two decades. Populist politics thus rose early in Finland, although initially mostly on this rural base.

The SMP's enjoyed around a tenth of the vote but saw falling support after joining the governmental coalition in the wake of the 1983 election. It ran into serious financial difficulty and was in 1995 absorbed by another nativist populist party, the True Finns Party. Right-wing populist parties as emerged in Denmark and Norway did, however, not gain much popular support until after the Euro crisis hit in 2009.

American McCarthyism

Despite the multicultural nature of America, and the diversified circulation of people around the country, nationalism was always an undercurrent in the United States both in its settlement and subsequently. Already before the end of the Second World War Hans Kohn (1944) maintained that American nationalism mainly revolved around the idea of legal liberty under the constitution. Furthermore, an idea of exceptionalism has for long been floating in the US. John B. Judis (2018) reports on a surprisingly widespread notion existing in the US, of Americans being God's 'chosen people'.

This notion of exceptionality of the American nation has affected political thinking in the US. Among its ideological offsprings is the idea of America's moral leadership in the world, which has for instance led many to believe in the so-called American century, which would follow. This perception of a moral leadership has sometimes contained the classical simplistic division often applied by populists, the struggle between good and evil.

The anti-communist campaign of Senator Joseph McCarthy in the post-war years is a good example of authoritarian tendencies in the US. McCarthy was a demagogue and the Red Scare that he promoted was used to justify the erosion of civil rights of those accused of sympathizing with communist ideals. Many people were coerced by the authorities, and some were blacklisted, preventing them from getting jobs, and in effect from thriving in society. Quite a few were deemed guilty only by association, or even by more obscure suspicions. Correspondingly, American political sociologist Seymour Martin Lipset (1960), who was among the first academics to use the term *populism*, indeed applied it to describe McCarthyism.

The norm-breaking tactics of McCarthy posed a serious threat to US democracy. In the end, it was the mainstream leadership in the Republican Party that tackled it by deeming his methods as being illicit. The response of Chief Counsel to the Army Joseph Welch to McCarthy's false accusations was telling for the turning of the tide against the demagogic red-bait tactics. Welch asked: 'Have you no sense of decency, sir?' Gradually McCarthy fell from grace and McCarthyism became discredited. In the end, his populist methods were dismissed as mere demagoguery.

Since then, many have campaigned on a populist and nationalist platform in the US. However, until Donald Trump emerged on the scene, these kinds of politicians had not found much success. Prior to Trump's rise, the mainstream in American politics had always been able to unite against them. One example was George Wallace, Governor of Alabama, who ran in several Democratic presidential primaries from 1964. Wallace was known for being racist and a staunch segregationist. In his 1963 inaugural address as Governor he promised to protect Alabama's 'Anglo-Saxon people' from 'communistic amalgamation' with blacks. He ended his address with stating that he stood for 'segregation now, segregation tomorrow, segregation forever' (qtd in Raines 1998). Even further out on the fringe was the American Nazi Party established by George Lincoln Rockwell in 1960.

Prior to the 1968 presidential elections, 40 per cent of Americans approved of Wallace. However, in a unified action, mainstream politicians were able to keep him firmly out on the fringe (Levitsky and Ziblatt 2018). In other words, Wallace enjoyed no less of a public support than Trump did when arriving on the scene half a century later. The difference was that by the time of Trump, politics had become polarized in America to the extent that the mainstream was unable to unite against him.

The American governmental system of checks and balances has not only survived because of constitutional design, but much rather as a result of political actors widely accepting shared political norms. In other words, the system not only relies on the written legal text, but its sustainability is perhaps to a greater extent determined by a commonly shared understanding of what is allowed in politics, and what falls outside of the boundaries of US legality. Of course, these democratic norms have often been tested and challenged, but, until Trump emerged as a political force, the two main parties had always kept at bay those disrespecting the system.

The Neocons

The idea of America's greatness, the aforementioned notion of a new American century, suffered a serious blow from the defeat in the Vietnam War. The energy crisis was also biting at the same time. Manufacturing was in decline. Many felt that America was being left behind. It was at this time when the term *The Rust Belt*, was coined, describing urban decay in the Mid-West.

In addition to this double blow, the times also brought demographic changes. Prior to the 1970s most immigrants had arrived from Canada and Europe. Now they were flocking in from other areas, such as from Latin America, the Caribbean, and from Asia. Most of the new arrivals were unskilled, and they accepted low pay.

This was also a time of internal cultural change, with the hippie movement challenging the rigorously strict way of life of their parent's generation. This countercultural movement against social conservatism brought social liberalism, for instance liberty in sexuality and substance use. Coinciding with a call for increased public spending on social welfare, the movement also promoted feminism, human rights, civil liberties, secularism, anti-racism, and so on.

Collectively, these sweeping societal changes brought Christian protestants, particularly in the South, to fear a moral decline in the US. Many of them were supporters of the Democratic Party, but were becoming disillusioned with its leadership, which by then had largely adopted a policy of social liberalism. This drove many of the white evangelic Democrats to unite with social conservatives in the Republican Party. A new creed came to the helm in the Republican Party, the Neoconservatives, often simply referred to as Neocons. These were hawks on foreign policy who opposed the increasing pacifism in the Democratic Party. Disheartened with the counterculture on the left, they wanted to uphold both conservative values domestically and aggressively protect American interests abroad, while also promoting its values around the globe. It was for instance not least on their ideological wings that George W. Bush rose to power around the turn of the millennium, as I will discuss further in the following chapter.

A seminal moment for American politics occurred in 1973 when the Supreme Court accepted women's right to abortion in the famous legal case of Roe vs Wade. Indeed, the debate over women's reproductive organs came to crystallize the ever-deepening divisions between conservatives and liberals. The issue rallied conservative evangelic forces within the Republican Party. The Democratic Party was however fast turning secular, paving the way for the southern religious Democrats jumping the fence. Since then, the two parties have been polarizing even further.

Among those exploiting this change, eventually and unknowingly paving the way for a figure like Trump, was Newt Gingrich, who became the Republican Speaker of the House in Congress. He saw politics as a form of warfare. In a campaign speech, Gingrich (1978) described politics as 'a war for power'. His signature tactics were to discredit his opponents, rather than laying out his own plan for governance. For instance, he accused the Democrats of being non-patriotic traitors, corrupt, pathetic, and, in a word, simply 'sick'. This was a new kind of polarization tactics by use of populist methods, shrewdly tapping into growing discontent among the public. In a combative no-compromise style, when preaching for their ideological purity, Gingrich and his gang struck a tone that was to ring much louder later in US politics. Levitsky and Ziblatt (2018) argue that this was leading to the US system of checks and balances giving way to deadlock and dysfunction.

When Ronald Reagan arrived in Washington leading up the 1980 presidential election, he found a Republican Party that had been fast changing in line with the Neocon movement. Reagan ran on a similar platform as Margaret Thatcher did in the UK. Furthermore, he promoted a renewed sense of patriotism. A nostalgic resurrection of America's greatness. Indeed, one of his main slogans was: Make America Great Again—later adopted by Donald Trump.

NOTES

1. The two-round electoral system in France insures a majority behind the President. If no candidate passes the 50 per cent mark in the first round, a second vote is held between the two frontrunners.
2. See the *Daily Telegraph*. 2007, 6 November. 'Enoch Powell's Rivers of Blood speech'.

References

Arter, D. (2010). The Breakthrough of Another West European Populist Radical Right Party? The Case of the True Finns. *Government and Opposition, 45*(4), 484–504.
Cuminal, I., Souchard, M., Wahnich, S., & Wathier, V. (1997). *Le Pen, Les Mots. Analyse d'un Discours d'extrême-Droite*. Paris: Le Monde.
Frawley, O. (2011). *Memory Ireland: History and Modernity* (Vol. 1). Syracuse, NY: Syracuse University Press.
Gingrich, N. (1978). *1978 Speech*. Presented at the Atlanta Airport Holiday Inn.
Griffin, R. (2002). *The Nature of Fascism*. New York: Palgrave Macmillan.
Guland, O. (2000). *Le Pen, Mégret et Les Juifs: L'obsession Du'complot Mondialiste'*. La Découverte.
Hainsworth, P. (2008). *The Extreme Right in Western Europe*. London: Routledge.
Hobsbawm, E. (1994). *Age of Extremes, the Twentieth Century*. London: Abacus.
Jamin, J. (2009). *L'imaginaire Du Complot: Discours d'extrême Droite En France et Aux Etats-Unis*. Amsterdam University Press.
Judis, J. B. (2018). *The Nationalist Revival: Trade, Immigration, and the Revolt Against Globalization*. New York, NY: Columbia Global Reports.
Kohn, H. (1944). *The Idea of Nationalism: A Study in Its Origins and Background*. New York: Macmillan Publishing.
Levitsky, S., & Ziblatt, D. (2018). *How Democracies Die*. New York: Crown.
Lipset, S. M. (1960). *Political Man: The Social Bases of Politics*. Doubleday.
Magali, B. (2013). The French National Front from Jean-Marie to Marine Le Pen: Between Change and Continuity. In *Exposing the Demagogues: Right-Wing and National Populist Parties in Europe*. Berlin: Konrad Adenauer Stiftung.
Mazower, M. (2009). *Dark Continent: Europe's Twentieth Century*. Vintage.
Moen, E. S. (2006). *Profet i Egen Land: Historien Om Carl I. Hagen*. Oslo: Gyldendal.
Raines, H. (1998). George Wallace, Segregation Symbol, Dies at 79. *The New York Times*.
Raspail, J. (1973). *Le Camp des Saints*. Paris: Robert Laffont.
Sontag, S. (1975, February 6). Fascinating Fascism. *The New York Review of Books*.
Taguieff, P.-A. (2004). *Le Retour Du Populisme: Un Défi Pour Les Démocraties Européennes*. Encyclopaedia Universalis.
Widfeldt, A. (2015). *Extreme Right Parties in Scandinavia*. New York: Routledge.
Wren, K. (2001). Cultural Racism: Something Rotten in the State of Denmark? *Social & Cultural Geography, 2*(2), 141–162.
Zúquete, J. P. (2018). *The Identitarians: The Movement against Globalism and Islam in Europe*. Notre Dame: University of Notre Dame Press.

The Second Wave: The Collapse of Communism and 9/11

The end of the Cold War entailed liberal democracy becoming an almost uncontested new master framework in the West. As I discussed in the Introduction to this book, many scholars wrote that politics would from then on predominantly be conducted within the parameters of representative democratic governance in an open and free market economy. Francois Fukuyama (1992), for instance, wrote that the opening of the Iron Curtain marked the 'universalization of Western liberal democracy as the final form of human government.'

However, history has proved this not to be entirely the case. Only a year later Samuel Huntington contested this prediction of a rosy future when publishing his article and later book, *Clash of Civilizations*. In his famous writings Huntington (1993, 1996) instead predicted that with the collapse of communism Islam would emerge as the main ideological adversary of the West.

In this chapter I analyse the second wave of nativist populism in the post-war era, rising in 1989 in the wake of the collapse of communism and fall of the Berlin Wall. Some of the populist parties finding success in the second and third waves were previously established, a few even initially as mainstream parties, only later turning populist, as was the case in Austria and Switzerland. Aikin to the Oil Crisis of 1972, that had come as a surprise to most people, the political upheaval in 1989 with the collapse of the Berlin Wall also came unannounced. The political class—academics and politicians alike—failed to predict the downfall of the Eastern bloc.

As will become evident in this chapter, the nature of the nationalism introduced in the second wave was somewhat different to that of the previously discussed agrarian populism or the anti-tax neo-liberal populism in the early 1970s. Rather than primarily referring to the social-economic situation of the *ordinary* people, the emphasis moved over to a socio-cultural notion of *our* people.

It can be argued that the nativist populism in the second wave was gradually replacing or at least augmenting the anti-tax and neo-liberal populism of the first wave. Although xenophobia and ethno-nationalism was surely a significant part of the populist message from the outset—as was established in the previous chapter when for example discussing the French National Front, *Nouvelle Droite* and the *Identitarians*—that sort of rhetoric rose much more clearly to the forefront in the second wave. A culturally based ethno-pluralism was now growing beyond that of the primarily economic aspects of the first wave.

Ever Closer Union

Significantly for the backlash against supranational solutions which occurred later, and which I will analyse further in the following chapter, European leaders at the time responded to the dramatic events around the collapse of the Berlin Wall by gearing up their economic co-operation within the European Community (EC), into becoming a fully-fledged economic and political European Union. The Maastricht Treaty of 1992 tightened and deepened the integration process and set in place mechanisms for anticipated accession of most of the newly liberated states on the Eastern side of the fallen Iron Curtain. The new arrivals seeking a 'return to Europe', as it was branded, would have to meet three main overall criteria. One was stability of institutions guaranteeing democracy, the rule of law, human rights and respect for and protection of minorities. Another was the existence of a functioning market economy. A third criteria was on the administrative capacity of absorbing European laws and regulations.

Leading up to the coming Eastern enlargement, the EU signed partnership agreements with each of the candidate countries. Trade relations were fast increasing and after only few years of transition in the wake of the EU accession in 2004 and 2007, citizens of the former Eastern bloc gained the right to work across the region. For a continent that for half century had been separated into two parts, this was a dramatic and initially highly celebrated change.

Another signpost of renewed unison was built when most EU members states united in a single currency, the Euro. Many believed that the Euro would bring a fresh feeling of shared belonging. However—as I will illustrate in the following chapter—when the Euro Crisis hit in 2008/9, many blamed the European apparatus.

As I mentioned in the Introduction to this book, many people were in this period of internationalized liberal democracy predicting the diminishing significance of the nation-state. Philosopher Jürgen Habermas (1998), for instance, went so far as predicting that Europe was moving in direction of a 'post-national constellation'. However, even though the end of the Cold War surely brought renewed unity in Europe, it also led to conflicts. Most notorious was the outbreak of the war on the Balkan peninsula which lasted between 1991 and 2001 and costed 140,000 people their lives.

Re-drawn Dividing Lines

The collapse of the communist Eastern bloc did not only introduce capitalism and democracy to the newly liberated states, it also reinvigorated long suppressed national sentiments in these lands, often channelled through ethno-nationalist parties that were being established across the region. The Yugoslav War brought nationalism back with a vengeance, resembling only that of the interwar period. It proved to be Europe's deadliest war since World War II. In Serbia, Slobodan Milosevic rose on a renewed nationalist rhetoric which promoted creating a 'Greater Serbia' by annexing swaths of Croatia and Bosnia.

The Socialist Federal Republic of Yugoslavia, established after World War II, tied together the predominantly Christian nations of Serbia, Slovenia, Croatia and Macedonia and the mostly Muslim dominated Bosnia and Herzegovina. Its authoritarian leader, Josip Broz Tito, was successful in suppressing nationalism and keeping the coherence of the state. In the wake of his death in 1980, secessionist forces slowly started to re-emerge. With the collapse of the communist block the federal state disintegrated along national lines. In the conflict, both Serbian and Croatian forces turned to ethnic cleansing, with the aim of forcing unwanted ethnic groups out of their lands. The conflict marked the return of separatism in Europe and the renewed rise of authoritarian populism.

Anti-Muslim sentiments surely played a part in the horrendous actions of Serbian forces in Bosnia Herzegovina. It is generally accepted that their actions escalated into the genocide of Bosniaks. The Yugoslavian War furthermore led to a renewed avalanche of refugees fleeing over to Western Europe, mainly to Germany and also to Scandinavia. Once again, millions of people were on the move, many of them undocumented.

In most countries in Eastern Europe, the post-Cold-War era saw a rise of neo-liberal policies. This was indeed a period of Thatcherite privatization politics on steroids. In most instances the communist welfare system was completely dismantled. This led to an immense drop in industrial output, mass unemployment and wide-scale economic hardship for most people, but mammoth wealth accumulation for the few who were in positions of power. In turn, this evolution led to fast progressing inequality, even far beyond Western levels. At the same time, East Europeans were flocking to the West.

Most of the countries in the East were eager to join the EU. In a way it was like rejoining Europe. This led to increased tension in the receiving countries. Many responded with enhanced restrictions and assimilation requirements were hardened. While the European Union, as such, was promoting co-operation with the former communist East, many of its members states were still looking for ways to tighten their borders even further. This caused increased tension on the continent. Doubts regarding the merits of a unified European labour market were increasing. The second wave of nativist populism in Europe thus rose to a significant degree in response to an anticipated integration with post-communist Eastern Europe in the wake of the collapse of the Berlin Wall.

The dramatic changes around the collapse of communism and the dissolution of the Soviet Union also opened up a new space in the conspiratorial milieu in the West. For a long while, the Soviets had been presented as the main enemy of the West, and many tales of evil deeds by the Eastern bloc had thrived during the Cold War. With the opening of the Iron Curtain the arch-enemy of the West was suddenly gone—had vanished into thin air. As will be examined further, this led to a vacuum which was increasingly filled by new mutual suspicions between East and West.

The Rise of the Second Wave

In this chapter I will examine several cases where nativist populism rose in the second wave. Amongst the most prominent in Western Europe were the Flemish Block in Belgium and the Pim Fortuyn List in the Netherlands. This was also the time of the flamboyant Silvio Berlusconi in Italy and Jörg

Haider in Austria. It was likewise in the second wave when Pia Kjærsgaard was able to turn her Danish Peoples Party into one of the most influential in Denmark. Even in West Germany the far-right Republican Party polled around 11 per cent in 1992.

The ugly ducklings from previous eras were showing their faces again; fascism, racism, xenophobia, nationalism, separatism, and so on. As I will discuss in this chapter, this was also the time of more rogue ultra-nationalist movements, even of neo-Nazi movements.

Years later, doubts about European integration were also growing on the Eastern side. In fact, dominant parties in several of the new EU member states were to turn against Europeanization, often indeed—as I will discuss further in the following chapter—on a highly nationalist ground, such as in Hungary and Poland. As result, Europe was unknowingly entering into an era of renewed polarization with growing mutual animosity.

This wave could be separated into two phases: Before and after the terrorist attacks in the US on 11 September 2001. The horrendous event brought increased validity for mainly anti-Muslim sentiments, which spread more easily into the mainstream than before the heinous event. Still, here I deal with the entire period as a single wave. Although its two parts should also somewhat be considered separately, for the purpose of this book it is more useful to treat 9/11 as a fundamental shift within the second wave.

Sneaking Past the Social Democrats

By the 1990s the once-strong links between social democrats and the working class were rapidly evaporating. After the collapse of the communist bloc many social democratic parties in Europe went looking for new kinds of voters and seeking more lucrative alliances in the political centre—in what was branded the new economy—even in some places toying with neo-liberal economic policies.

Social democratic parties who were founded by workers and their representatives had throughout the twentieth century been in close connection with working people. Gradually, however, leadership of these parties started to become filled instead with well-educated political professionals. Surely, many of them were descendants of those that had founded these parties, but increasingly the newer leaders had themselves little personal experience of manual labour.

Over time, this new leadership began to imagine that there was no longer any working class, that the importance of manual labour had diminished. Indeed, on the surface, society had evolved to the extent that the traditional blue-collar workers could no longer as easily be seen on the streets as before.

This, however, was always a fundamental misunderstanding. Although the tasks of workers had changed, the nature of labour had not. The working class might not fill factories in as large numbers as before, still, they could be seen all around in society; clerks in shops, bus drivers, waiters and barmaids, people manning the tellers in institutions, day-care personnel, and so on. The working class are quite simply all those people who live hand to mouth, those who survive from one pay cheque to the next and run into financial difficulties if missing only couple of payments. In other words, the working class is still most people.

However, instead of focusing primarily on the standard of living, of raising wages and on worker's rights, the new social democratic leadership was becoming increasingly occupied with newer and more sophisticated political tasks; such as of gender equality, administrative practices, democratic innovations, higher education and environment protection. In the UK for instance, the Labour Party under the leadership of Tony Blair geared up in this direction and was rebranded as 'New Labour'. The traditional social democratic strongholds in Scandinavia were also severely hit.

As result, social democratic parties were by the late twentieth century losing the support of the blue-collar working class throughout Europe. Many of the traditional working-class voters on the left felt politically alienated. As will be illustrated in the following pages, this change allowed nationalistic populists to sneak past and fill the vacuum.

Chávismo

Over in Latin America, populists were in this period also surging on both sides of the left/right political spectrum. Alberto Fujimori's main initial task when seizing power in Peru in 1990 was in defeating the socialist revolutionaries in the movement Shining Path. Two years after coming to power Fujimori killed off Congress and ended the fragile Peruvian democracy. In other words, Fujimori pulled a similar stunt of eroding democracy by way of democratic elections in Peru, as later was somewhat mirrored in Eastern Europe during the third wave, which I will discuss further in the following chapter.

After a decade in power, Fujimori fled to Japan under accusations of corruption and human rights violations. On the other side of the political spectrum, Hugo Chávez came to power in Venezuela in 1998 on the canopy of the Bolivarian Revolution.[1]

Chávez was a political outsider who campaigned against a corrupt domestic elite. He promised to build a new authentic democracy, by the people and for the poor people, for instance by tapping into the country's rich oil wealth. Chávez rose to power via democratic means. It was not until 2003 that he started to abandon democratic processes for more authoritarian rule. In 2006, the *Chávismo* regime had grown fundamentally repressive, for example by eliminating term limits, locking up disobedient officials and exiling many opposition voices.

Flanders Field

When walking down the winding path into Ypres near the French boarder in northern Belgium to visit the War Memorial of the Flemish town, I recall finding it hard to imagine its dark history. The restaurants encircling the now peaceful main square paved in medieval stone were filled with lively patrons enjoying their steamed mussels and chilled white wine, and not necessarily even contemplating the horrors that the fields all around had witnessed in two terrible world wars. This is where opposing armies had dug their trenches in World War I, reaching from Dunkirk on the northern coast and all the way down to the Swiss Alps. I could not escape feeling the weight of history when listening to the brass band playing under the town's arch gate in commemoration of the fallen.

Were it not for the linguistical duality—Ypres in French, Ieper in Flemish—it might be difficult noticing former partitions. Here is where Julius Caesar ran into intricacy in conquering Gaul. And here is where Napoleon had to retreat from Waterloo in Wallonia for his final battle. Many of the young men who gave up their lives still lie in some of the 170 cemeteries in the area. On 13 October 1918 Adolf Hitler was injured here in a gas attack by the British army. Years later he brought back his troops of the Third Reich. The devastations all around the now tranquil town of Ypres was one of the triggers behind the European integration process. Instead of sacrificing young men on battlefields, officials would assemble in stuffy rooms in Brussels, merely one hundred kilometres away, forced to suffer bad coffee until settling their disputes. In light of this history, the surge of Dutch nativist populism in Belgium, and in the neighbouring Netherlands, carries a magnified meaning.

Amongst those finding support in the second wave was the Flemish Block in Belgium (*Vlaams Blok*—VB, later renamed *Vlaams Belang*), based on a previous Flemish nationalist movement that had campaigned for an independent Flanders. Belgium is a federal state, consisting of Dutch-speaking Flemish people, French-speaking Wallonians and a very small enclave of German speakers. The capital, Brussels, is in a particular situation. Although most of its inhabitants are French speakers it is a bilingual separate Belgian capital region with its own Parliament. In addition, Brussels is the principal seat of the European Union, and thus in effect a highly internationalized metropolis.

Being among only very few 'white on white' xenophobic political parties in Europe, the Flemish Block argued that Flanders was subsidizing Wallonia too much, and sought to break up the Belgian state. Its electoral breakthrough came in the 1991 general elections, when winning 6.6 per cent of the vote. The party, though, only stood in Flanders, where it won 12 per cent. Although sharing the populist space with couple of smaller and more narrowly focused parties, the VB steadily grew in Flanders. The party found increasing support in subsequent national elections. The Flemish Block rose to new heights in the 2003 election, when landing almost 12 per cent of the overall vote, before—for a while—again seeing diminished support.

The VB simultaneously suffered from two contingent difficulties. One was a prolonged *Cordon Sanitaire* that other parties had encircled around it, steadfastly refusing co-operation despite their increasing share of the vote. Although the unifying boycotting of the mainstream served as a useful narrative for attracting voters in the short term, it turned into an obvious disadvantage in the long run. As result of being so firmly kept away from power, the VB saw diminished electoral support. Generally, people don't want to throw away their vote, and can grow frustrated with supporting a party that can't get any of its policies through.

The VB also faced growing competition. The populist ground was becoming increasingly crowded with many movements of a similar ilk standing in elections. The VB was squarely nationalist in their populism. This is in line with the shift from the neo-liberal emphasis of the first wave to a more nationalist focus within the populist realm in the second wave. In addition to its Flemish nationalism, the VB was highly xenophobic, anti-immigrant, social conservative and authoritarian on issues relating to law and order. Their Catholicism was for instance illustrated in fear of moral decay and an emphasis on protecting traditional family values, as well as in opposition to abortion and homosexuality.

The VB was never very anti-European, presumably due to EU membership widely being accepted in Belgium, even celebrated. On the socio-economic axis they were centrist, perhaps rather welfare chauvinist than neo-liberal. This is similar to related parties in the Nordic countries, who I will examine more closely later in this book.

Although the VB was never a one-man show like many other populist parties have tended to be, it still benefitted from one of its two main leader's oratorical skills, Filip Dewinter.

The VB accused the established parties in Belgium of trapping the public within bad policies based on political correctness, for instance by silencing legitimate concerns people might have over multiculturalism, which was fast emerging in Belgium. Jan Jagers (2006) argues that the VB wanted to break up a 'conspiracy' of the mainstream against the ordinary people, and that it positioned itself as the 'only defenders of the silent majority, the popular will and democracy'.

It can be argued that the VB based its nationalism on an Herderian understanding of the Flemish nation, as being permanently distinct from other groups within the Belgium state. As Pauwels (2013) notes, this ethnic nationalism is emphasized in the VB's pursuit for intra-Flemish homogenization in Flanders. Viewing a Flemish nation as so firmly separated is furthermore in line with what Friedrich Meinecke referred to as *Kultur-nation*. The VB's call for an independent Flemish state is thus based on an ethnopluralist ideology of decisive separation between nations. Initially this call for homogenization was aimed against Walloons contaminating Flanders, but gradually, their aim was refocused and turned against non-European immigrants, mainly in opposition to Muslims.

FORTUYN'S LIBERAL NOVELTY

Liberalism had always been a significant part of the domestic political identity in the Netherlands. Correspondingly, post-war populist actors started out from a position of protecting the Dutch socio-liberal heritage. Its first populist to find significant success was the extravagant Pim Fortuyn. His liberal flair separated him from most others of the field in the second wave.

Although political dividing lines between Catholics and Protestants had been quite sharp in the Netherlands, there was perhaps not much that divided the major parties when it came to principal understandings of the government's place in economy and society. The fundaments around the political consensus of the mainstream were first challenged in 1994 when an ethno-nationalist party won seats in parliament, paradoxically named Centre Democrats. The party soon disintegrated, but only after having left the Dutch with a new appetite for populist politics. In its wake, several such parties stood in municipal elections around the country. After this period of activity a party called Liveable Netherlands (*Leefbaarheid*) was established in 1999.

The flamboyant figure Pim Fortuyn soon emerged as its leader. Fortuyn parted from most other populist leaders in his ostentatious lifestyle. Paul Lucardie and Gerrit Voeman (2013) described him as being theatrical and almost exhibitionist in his homosexuality. In fact, Fortuyn was in his own way prototypical for the open, tolerant and social liberal Netherlands.

Fortuyn was a prolific orator and he was able to articulate his opposition to multiculturalism in an exuberant style, which fitted well within the Dutch political culture. He warned against creeping Islamization, which would for instance be to the detriment of homosexuals and other outgroups that enjoyed freedom in social liberal Netherlands. He insisted that Islam was a hostile religion which posed an extraordinary threat to Europe.

Fortuyn was adamant in placing himself on the side of Dutch liberalism. When criticized for xenophobia regarding North-African immigrants he once famously responded. 'I have nothing against Moroccans; after all, I've been to bed with so many of them' (qtd in Ascherson 2002).

Berlusconismo

Italian politics have for long been a hotbed for all kinds of populism. Their flavour and style have varied greatly, travelling the distance from fully-fledged fascism to, for instance, a leftist anti-elite version. In many ways, as I discussed above, the fascism of the interwar years in Europe was born in Italy. The 1980s then saw a rise of authoritarian separatists in the north, the Northern League (*Lega Nord*—LN).

When swiftly seizing authority in 1994, Silvio Berlusconi sent a shockwave through both Italian and European politics. Rising to power on the second wave of post-war nativist populism, Berlusconi resembled the anti-tax populist leaders of the first wave, such as Le Pen in France and Glistrup in Denmark.

In the third wave, his flamboyant style was then also somewhat mirrored in the rise of several rogue strongman outsiders, most clearly by Trump in America—who, as I will discuss in the following chapter, bears much resemblance to Berlusconi. The two were starkly alike. Both were businessmen and rogue political outsiders. They could be classified as anti-politicians, positioning themselves as strongmen alternatives to the failing political class. Both were widely ridiculed in the media, but both also proved to be quite teflonic to scandal. In fact, they got away with behaviour that would ruin most other politicians. Instead they functioned as a tool for the ordinary public to 'stick it' to the political establishment.

Laying the ground domestically, Berlusconi also paved the way for other and more outright populist parties to take control in Rome in the third wave, as for example when Lega and the Five Star Movement *(M5S)* joined in a coalition in 2018. This particular heritage of Berlusconism travelling from the second to the third wave will be tackled further in the following chapter.

When entering politics in 1994, Berlusconi was a rich and flamboyant businessman, a media tycoon owning many of the country's most popular private TV stations, as well as the AC Milan football club. In other words, his business was in providing what the common people wanted to watch. Rumours were afloat that one of his main incentives for entering politics was to avoid prosecution for tax fraud, which he feared was underway by the authorities.

Like many other populist politicians, Berlusconi had no experience in politics. He was a political novice. Instead of travelling the traditional route, rising through the ranks of an established political party, he founded his own, the *Forza Italia*, meaning Go Italy! In bypassing established norms of political campaigning, Berlusconi exploited his position as media tycoon. For instance, he had his TV stations relentlessly running both his advertisements and promoting his political ideas in their programming. No other candidate came anywhere near to enjoying such privileges.

Berlusconi would furthermore promise anything that he though the people wanted, regardless of prospects of being able to make good on his word. In 1994 he promised to create one million new jobs. After the election, Berlusconi was able to scrape together a coalition and became Prime Minister. However, his government collapsed only three months later. His comeback came in 2001 and he governed until 2006. Prior to the 2001 election, Berlusconi led a campaign coalition and offered what he called a contract with the Italians, among other things promising to cut unemployment by half.

Berlusconi was an authoritarian strongman leader. Still, in his flamboyant and capricious behaviour, he could be quite amusing and charismatic. His unorthodox manner, for a politician of his era, also attracted attention abroad. The international media was branding his politics as Berlusconism (Orsina 2014). Initially the term held positive connotations, linked to optimism and laissez-faire entrepreneurism. However, with increased controversies around him, the term got tainted, and, in the end shifted the meaning to populism, scandal, corruption and demagoguery in governance.

Berlusconi departs from many populists of today. When it came to coalition building, he proved to be a skilful political craftsman. He was for example able to build bridges to both the neo-fascist *Allenza Nazionale* and *Lega Nord*. Both those parties were populist, but they were not really on speaking terms with each other.

The Northern League

As stated above, the populist field in Italy is vast. The heritage of Benito Mussolini's fascism was for instance kept within the Italian Social Movement (*Movimento Sociale Italiano*—MSI). Its leader, Gianfranco Fini, however described the party as post-fascist, rather than neo-fascist (Griffin 2000). The MSI joined Berlusconi's government in 1994. Self-described post-fascist, Fini became Deputy Prime Minister and Foreign Minister and he moved on to preside over the Italian Chamber of Deputies.

Among the most influential nativist populist parties in Italy was the Northern League, a far-right separatist party founded by Umberto Bossi in the early 1990s as a federation of regional movements in the north of Italy. The complete name is indicative of its politics: The Northern League for the Independence of Padania. Initially their primary target was the corrupt political elite, which they referred to as 'thieving Rome'.

It was the NL that brought down Berlusconi's first cabinet in 1994, after abandoning the coalition. Reports say that they resented seeing many of their supporters, and even some parliamentarians as well, defect over to Berlusconi's party. Leading up to the 2018 parliamentary election its name was shortened to only *Lega*. As I will discuss in the following chapter, the party entered a coalition government in 2018 with the leftist populist Five Star Movement.

The LN came to master a communicative technique that was later a trademark of many populist politicians. In delivering their highly controversial messages, Bossi and his fellows bypassed the media and started instead to address the public directly, through rallies, speeches, posters and banners. Lorella Cedroni (2010) branded this style as communication without media. Their language of rupture and threat would spur pushback and, thus, bring them attention. Cedroni explains how Bossi and his associates were able to tap into the language of the ordinary people and apply it in politics.

The highly controversial contributions of the NL generally attracted greater media attention than other politicians usually enjoyed. Their rough and demagogic rhetoric, that often carried insults and other kinds of provocation, would indeed be spread through society via the media criticizing their disruptive language—which might be somewhat ironic for the fact that they were so prone to bypass the media.

As I will discuss further in the following chapter, the NL has since been transformed from emphasizing regionality to a more general Italian nativist populism, perhaps most similar to the National Front in France.

HAIDER'S TABLOID POPULISM

As I discussed in the previous chapter, both the Peoples Party of Switzerland and the Austrian Freedom Party were retuned in a populist direction during the first wave of post-war nativist populism. It was during the second wave in the 1990s that these parties found significant electoral success. In 2004 for instance, the Swiss Peoples Party came into government.

In Austria, Jörg Haider steered the Freedom Party to become perhaps the most influential in the country. Haider was energetic and charismatic. He was especially skilful in tapping into the fears and emotions of the ordinary public, while avoiding the more intellectual debates.

The key to his success was found in coupling with the country's tabloid media, mainly the influential daily, the *Kronen Zeitung*, by far the most widely distributed daily in the country. Both party and paper united in defiance against elite, for example turning against the established serious media elite. This recipe was to become rewarding for populists throughout Europe; charismatic leaders backed by the tabloid media, relating to ordinary publics fears of the foreign rather than participating in intellectual political debate.

Twice Governor of Carinthia in Austria, Jörg Haider rose through the ranks of the FPÖ and was its leader from 1986 to 2000. Through the 1990s, the FPÖ found increasing support in many municipal elections. Its greatest national electoral success came in 1999 when winning almost 27 per cent of the vote and becoming the second largest party in parliament. Subsequently the FPÖ formed a coalition government with the mainstream Austrian Peoples Party (ÖVP). After coming to power, the FPÖ saw fast diminishing support. This is in line with populists often having difficulties maintaining their support after coming into positions of power.

Haider was an exuberant leader. He was surrounded by a group of likeminded young men, often referred to as the *Bubelpartie*, or boy-gang. Amongst them was Heinz-Christian Strache, who became party leader in 2005—as I will discuss further in the following chapter. As I mentioned in the previous chapter, Haider retuned the FPÖ away from its pan-Germanic nationalism and towards a more particular *Österreichpatriotismus*, meaning Austrian patriotism. The party programme of 1997 was titled 'Contract with Austria'. It emphasized unified interests and a preference for a single Austrian nation.

The FPÖ found greatest support in the wake of the Iron Curtain coming down. Austria's geographical proximity to the Balkans led to a flow of refugees and asylum seekers rushing across its borders. The FPÖ led the opposition against this sudden flow of migrants who were competing for jobs with Austrians. In the early 1990s, the foreign-born population in Austria surpassed 10 per cent. The FPÖ problematized migrants as both a threat against the county's culture and as a burden on its economy. Reinhard Heinisch (2013) points out that racist and xenophobic rhetoric was also included when pointing particularly to immigrants as major cause of crime in Austria.

Haider's influence reached far beyond Austria's borders. In many ways he paved the way for the softer and more acceptable versions of right-wing populist parties around Europe. This has been labelled the *Haiderization* of politics, the process of normalizing previously condemned views, such as racism, by way of coded rather than explicit xenophobia (Wodak 2015).

Austria First

In 1992 the FPÖ published its programme 'Austria First', declaring that Austria was not and would not become a country of immigration. They especially opposed Muslim migration, stressed protecting the country's Christian heritage and values, and emphasized upholding law and order. At the time, this was mainly aimed against those coming from the Balkans and Turkey. In the early 1990s, Haider insisted that the 'social order of

Islam is opposed to our Western values'. He said that human rights and democracy were incompatible with the Muslim religious doctrine. 'In Islam, the individual and his free will count for nothing; faith and religious struggle—jihad, the holy war—for everything' (qtd in Merkl and Weinberg 2003).

Perhaps strangely for his anti-Islam rhetoric, Haider was criticized for fostering friendly relationships with notorious Arab dictators, such as with Saddam Hussain in Iraq and Muammar al-Gaddafi in Libya. He was even accused of receiving significant sums of money from Saddam Hussain (Mikbakhsh and Kramar-Schmid 2010).

Haider was shrewd in accommodating the concerns of the blue-collar public and he was able to multiply his party's support among low-skilled labourers. The FPÖ was even finding greater support from lower-income people than the Social Democrats enjoyed.

The most controversial aspect of the party's discourse was its apparent anti-Semitism and tendency to dismiss and defend Austria's Nazi past. Haider was criticized for frequent praise of Austrian Second World War veterans, even for former Nazis that had served in the Waffen-SS. He declared that that they were decent people of good character who remained true to their convictions. He was also accused of Holocaust denialism. In a 1991 debate, an opponent criticized Haider's plan of bringing down unemployment by calling it reminiscent of Nazi policies. Haider replied by saying: 'No, they didn't have that in the Third Reich, because in the Third Reich they had proper employment policy, which not even your government in Vienna can manage to bring about.'[2]

Initially the mainstream parties in Austria had tried to isolate the FPÖ. That strategy was abandoned by the ÖVP in 2000 when accepting them into a coalition government. Haider himself was deemed to be too controversial to assume the office of Chancellor, a position he otherwise should have been able to claim given that his party was the largest in the coalition. The government was thus instead led by ÖVP leader Wolfgang Schussel. Haider also stepped aside and ceded leadership of his party to Susanne Riess-Passer who became Vice-Chancellor. Although formally outside of government, Haider was still seen to have great influence on it.

Allowing far-right populists into government caused outrage to many of Austria's partners in the European Union. The *Cordon Sanitaire* which had been upheld around Western Europe in the post-war era, of keeping right-wing extremists at bay and away from power, had been breached. The EU responded by taking measures against Schussel's government, for instance by ceasing co-operation with the Austrian government. In September 2000 the EU abandoned its diplomatic sanctions. The entire episode is noteworthy as years later similar kinds of populists would rise to power in several other EU countries, such as in Hungary, Poland and for a while in Italy, as I will examine further in the following chapter.

After ceding control in the FPÖ, Haider became increasingly at odds with the new leadership. In 2005 he broke away and formed the Alliance for the Future of Austria. Jörg Haider died in a car crash in 2008.

THE NO-QUEEN OF DENMARK

In Scandinavia, nativist populism was also being remodelled during the second wave. With Mogens Glistrup the founder of the Progressive Party running into increasing trouble, the position of Pia Kjærsgaard was growing stronger. While she had been toning down Glistrup's harshness and was shrewdly reformulating the party's policies in a more socially acceptable manner, the hardliners in the party wanted to stick to their old ways of uncompromising anti-politics. The two sides ultimately clashed during the 1995 party congress when Kjærsgaard's pragmatic faction lost. Subsequently, she left with three of the party's MPs in tow to form the Danish Peoples Party (*Dansk Folkeparti*—DF), which domestically was to become one of the most influential right-wing populist parties in the world. The name chosen was the same as that of an authoritarian semi-fascist party of the 1930s.

In the 1998 general election, the Danish People's Party towered above the Progressive Party, winning 7.4 per cent of the vote. By carefully crafting her message to become more socially acceptable, Kjærsgaard's DF was fast moving into the mainstream, toning down Glistrup's anti-tax rhetoric, but still maintaining hardcore anti-immigrant policies. The DF campaigned against Denmark becoming multi-ethnic and what it called foreign infiltration. Gradually they increased their anti-immigrant discourse while downplaying the libertarian rhetoric. In economic term, the party moved much more into the middle ground, for example emerging as a staunch defender of the Danish welfare state. Anti-immigration was becoming the core to the DF's politics, claiming that migrants were threating the welfare system, which the party vowed to protect.

Similar to the FPÖ in Austria, the DF firmly insisted that Denmark was not, and had never been, an immigrant country, forcefully emphasizing that Denmark should not evolve to become a multi-ethnic society. This set the tone for the party's politics for the coming years.

Despite the move of the DF in a more mainstream direction under Pia Kjærsgaard, wide societal acceptance was still not in sight. In late 1999, then Social Democratic Prime Minister, Poul Nyrup Rasmussen, for example, famously stated that Kjærsgaard and her clan would never be 'house-trained' (*stueren*). This prediction was fast proved to be monumentally wrong, when the turn of several events soon played to the DF's advantage.

The first was the referendum on adopting the Euro in September 2000. The Danish Peoples Party had already laid the groundwork in 1997 when campaigning against the EU's Amsterdam Treaty, mainly in playing on fears of mass migration from Eastern Europe. It ran on the slogan 'Vote Danish, Vote No'. Most of the mainstream parties supported adopting the Euro, but the DF aggressively campaigned against abandoning the Danish currency, the *Krone*. Pia Kjærsgaard's relentlessness on the issue earned her the title of the 'No-Queen of Denmark'. When the public indeed refused the Euro, she and her party won much-needed legitimacy and the result underpinned their claim of speaking on behalf of the people (*for folket*) against the unified elite, which, it maintained, was out of touch with the ordinary Dane.

The second event to play to the DFs advantage came in the wake of the terrorist attacks in the US on 11 September 2001, which many in Denmark took as validation of the DF's harsh anti-Islam stance—which I will return to discussing later in this chapter.

Moving Against Migration

Theorists analysing populist politics have long had difficulties with classifying the Norwegian Progress Party. Although the initiator, Anders Lange, had belonged to the quasi-fascist Fatherland League before the Second World War, and even though he had gone as far as voicing support for *Apartheid* in South Africa, he never campaigned on an anti-immigrant platform—it was simply not a pressing political issue at the time in Norway. In fact, Lange forcefully denounced being linked to racism. The FrP was established as a neo-liberal anti-establishment movement rather than nationalist, protectionist or even fully anti-immigrant. Only later on did it emerge to embrace these qualities while simultaneously phasing out its formerly strong neo-liberal stance.

The Norwegian Progress Party was not even fully Eurosceptical, which has been regarded as a common feature of nativist populist parties in Europe. In fact, both Lange and Hagen in 1972, and Hagen again in 1994, voted for Norway's EU accession. The party was split on the issue and only more recently under the leadership of Siv Jensen did it lean further to the No-side, though officially it still remained undecided. In other words, the party was thus constructed out of quite a few contradictory elements.

In the second wave of nativist populism, Carl I. Hagen was clearly steering the party towards the centre, to become perhaps the softest version of populist right-wing parties in Europe. Still, similarly to Denmark, the focus was shifting away from tax reduction towards concerns over Norway being turned in a multicultural direction.

In the early 1990s, the FrP was festered by rivalries between different internal factions. This was a fiercely fought ideological dispute between a libertarian faction on the one hand, and on the other a nativist populist faction, together with a smaller Christian conservative faction. The libertarians were pro-EU, positive regarding migrant workers but critical of the state-funded Church. They were thus almost the polar opposite of the two other factions—bar them all wishing to lower taxes and in promoting private enterprise.

In a dramatic party congress in 1994, the liberal faction lost influence over to the more nationalist Christian conservatives. The FrP's position was moved to protecting Norwegian culture against foreign influences and preventing the welfare system from being exploited by immigrants and asylum seekers. Furthermore, the party turned hostile to the Sami ethnic minority in Norway, for example in a resolution calling for the Sami Assembly being dissolved.

In a classical welfare chauvinistic way, the new mantra of the party was in putting 'our people first'. The party found a way to square this new nativist welfare emphasis with their low-tax heritage by proposing using oil money to fund it. Another sign of the move away from socio-liberalism towards a more authoritative direction was found in a new emphasis on law and order, for example, in arguing that the system favoured criminals over their victims. Anders Jupskås (2013) documents a change in the party's programme, focusing mainly on immigration, criminality and care for the elderly. The immigrant issue was gradually to take up more space in the party's programme and discourse, until it came to the forefront of its agenda.

The US Ultra-Right

The Norwegian Progress Party is among the mildest versions of Neo-Nationalist parties discussed in this book. Several violent ultra-nationalist movements also existed in many countries. Although they largely fall outside of the scope of this book, mentioning some them briefly is of benefit for understanding the breath of nativist populism.

In America, for instance, many violent survivalist nationalist movements have influenced political debates. Most notorious is the white supremacist group, the Ku Klux Klan. Surely, these kinds of groups are out on the furthest fringes of far-right extremism and their actions resonate in no way with non-violent nativist populists. Their extremism is much rather comparable to violent radical-left terror groups in Europe in the 1970s, and contemporary Islamist terrorists. Still, both the violent and milder versions tended to tap into similar political and philosophical sources. This perhaps corresponds to how the violent left tapped into socialist literature, and Islamist terrorists based their horrific deeds on mainstream religious texts.

The story of Timothy McVeigh who blew up the US federal building in Oklahoma in 1995 is telling for the belief system in some of these movements, as his was just one of many violent acts conducted in the name of a good fight against evil domestic authorities. McVeigh repeatedly quoted and referred to white supremacist literature. He belonged to an anti-government survivalist militia, which, after the fall of communism shifted from warnings of Soviet conspiracies to ones aimed against the US federal government. For example, they insisted that US President Bill Clinton's campaign for gun control was a 'prelude to tyranny' (Russakof and Kovaleski 1995).

Gradually, McVeigh came to believe in a series of anti-government conspiracy theories and he visited Area 51, where he believed the government was hiding evidence of UFOs. In a letter to his childhood friend Steve Hodge prior to his action, he pledged his allegiance to the constitution of the USA and accused the government of having betrayed the founding fathers, and that it should be punished accordingly. He wrote: 'I have come to peace with myself, my God and my cause. Blood will flow in the streets, Steve. Good vs. Evil. Free Men vs. Socialist Wannabe Slaves' (qtd in Serrano 1997).

Timothy McVeigh's attack, commonly referred to as the Oklahoma City Bombing, killed 168 people and injured hundreds more. He committed the domestically-grown terrorist attack in revenge for the federal government's handling of the Waco siege in Texas in 1993 where seventy-six followers of the Christian sect the Branch Davidians died, including their leader David Koresh. In letters to his sister Jennifer, McVeigh seemed convinced that the government was plotting a dictatorial New World Order, and that they had already waged war against his people. McVeigh believed that his survivalist movement was under government attack, insisting that he himself was merely a soldier responding to the hostility and defending his country from the government oppressors (ibid.).

Timothy McVeigh was a frequent listener of the conspiracy theorist Milton William Cooper, an Oklahoma-based radio show host who entangled UFO-ism with anti-government conspiracy theories. McVeigh was also plugged into the same network of Christian patriot movements such as the so-called Hutaree, a Michigan-based militia. Members of the paramilitary group believed that the federal government and various law enforcement agencies were all tangled up in a New World Order conspiracy, which the Hutaree pledged to stop. In preparation for an end-of-time-battle with the authorities, the Hutaree declared themselves 'Christian warriors'. Referring to the coming of an Antichrist they wrote: 'The Hutaree will one day see its enemy and meet him on the battlefield if so God wills it' (qtd in Schaeffer 2011).

In 2001, Timothy McVeigh was sentenced to death for the Oklahoma City bombing. In 2012, several members of the Hutaree were arrested and prosecuted for planned violent attacks against government agents.

9/11

At 8:46 on Tuesday morning 11 September 2001, a Boeing 767 passenger plane *en route* from Boston Logan airport to California flew into the north tower of the World Trade Centre in downtown New York City. Seventeen minutes later another plane hit the south tower. At 9:37, a Boeing 757 aircraft penetrated the Pentagon building in Arlington near Washington DC. The fourth and final plane crashed into a field in Pennsylvania after passengers' revolted against the hijackers. Collectively, this was the deadliest terrorist attack in world history, killing 2996 people and injuring over 6000 others. 9/11 also proved to have the greatest effect of any terrorist act in human history.

The perpetrators were identified as being the Islamist terrorist organization Al Qaeda, under the leadership of Osama Bin Laden, established after the Soviet Union invaded Afghanistan in 1979. Nineteen men, most of them from Saudi Arabia, and also the United Arab Emirates, Egypt and Lebanon, carried out the act.

As I have discussed before in this book, cultural polarization between the Christian West and the Muslim Middle East had been growing with greater mutual animosity. While the previous divide between the liberal democratic West and the communist East was closing after downfall of the Berlin Wall, another polarization was separating the Christian sphere from the Muslim world. The increasingly conflictual relationship between the two religious spheres was for example evident in repeated invasions of US-led militaries in the Middle East, such as in the Gulf War of 1990. In his famous previously mentioned writings titled *The Clash of Civilizations*, Samuel Huntington maintained that after the collapse of communism, Islam would emerge as the main ideological adversary of the West.

Despite this growing acrimony, most Americans were on 11 September 2001 wholly taken by surprise. Many sought explanations of why Muslims, in general, hated them. This is what Tim Aistrope (2016) described as an 'Arab-Muslim paranoia narrative'. A similar rhetoric had existed prior to the attacks, such as in the writings of authors like Bernhard Lewis (1990), who searched for 'the roots of Muslim rage' when explaining anti-American hostility in the Arab world. Lewis maintained that this hatred, at times, went beyond hostility and 'becomes a rejection of Western civilization', which, indeed, is 'seen as innately evil', and those who promote or accept it as the 'enemies of God'.

Similar sentiments were also flourishing on the other side of the divide. In a video released by Osama Bin Laden on 27 December 2001, when justifying the heinous terrorist act, the Al Qaeda leader discussed what he called the West's hatred of Islam. He linked it to the crusades of previous times and said that the West in general, and America in particular, 'have an unspeakable hatred for Islam'.[3]

Freedom Fries

9/11 was of monumental importance not only for the USA but also for the entire world. The response to it was also fast and far-reaching. The US government not only invaded Afghanistan, and later Iraq, in an endeavour that was branded as the War on Terror, but domestically they also moved to uproot many fundamental aspects relating to individual and civil rights. The so-called Patriot Act profoundly changed people's rights to privacy, providing authorities with much greater powers to bypass civil liberties in order to prevent future terrorist actions. The legislation was criticized for eliminating judicial oversight of the security apparatus, and for instance permitting the National Security Agency (NSA) to eavesdrop on private communications (Eggen and Vandehei 2006). The Patriot Act seriously limited people's individual liberties.

The terrorist attack led to a massive spike in nationalist sentiments, and it also fuelled anti-immigrant sentiments. Through its ripple effects, the Alt-Right in the US was finding much more fertile ground than before. It can safely be concluded that without 9/11, the mechanics of the Patriot Act would never have passed through Congress. Interestingly, the erosion of individual freedom that was brought with the Patriot Act was justified by being in the name of freedom. Rhetorically, freedom became the buzzword in DC. Illustrative for this turn, was for example when the canteen in Congress changed the name of French fries to freedom fries— in a snipe against France which had opposed the US-led military quests in the Middle East.

Many within George W. Bush's administration had belonged to the Neoconservative faction of the Republican Party, which I discussed in the previous chapter. The Bush administration had taken a hard turn to the right and abandoned most bipartisan attempts. In line with their hawkish foreign politics, their instinct was in taking immediate tough action. This led for example to the invasion into Iraq on 19 March 2003, even though no reliable evidence indicated that the Iraq government, or even any individual Iraqis, had been involved in the attack.

The aftermath of 9/11 saw a wave of hate crimes rising against Muslims in America. Numerous incidents of harassment and violence were reported around the country, including attacks on mosques and religious leaders. Hateful acts included assaults, arsons, vandalism, threats and also several killings. Surveys showed that people of Middle Eastern origin felt discriminated against and were being targeted (Iyer 2001). Anti-Muslim sentiments were now wide-spread, reaching far beyond the shadow communities where racism had always thrived. Domestic opposition to the War on Terror was often dismissed as being unpatriotic and even treasonous. Influential extreme-right radio host, Ross Limbaugh, for example went so far as to link critical Democrats to Al Qaeda (see in Levitsky and Ziblatt 2018).

Almost instantly all sorts of conspiracy theories cropped up. One was created by Donald Trump. In an TV interview on ABC, Trump insisted that Muslims in New Jersey had been celebrating the downfall of the Twin Towers on the other side of the Hudson River that Tuesday morning (see Kessler 2015). This was, though, never true.

The most common and persistent conspiracy theory around 9/11 insisted that US President George W. Bush and British Prime Minister Tony Blair knew about the attacks in advance and let them happen. This is significant as conspiracy theories were in the aftermath of the event being penetrated further into the mainstream than perhaps ever before in contemporary history (see Bergmann 2018). In fact, there is now a vast and far-reaching literature widely available in mainstream circulation solely devoted to questioning official accounts and offering alternative versions of events on that Tuesday morning. A pseudo-academic *Journal of 9/11 Studies* has for instance proved to be a vehicle for the mainstreaming of views that continue to offer alternative accounts of what really happened.

In line with this trend, one David Ray Griffin (2006) has for example insisted that the event was a false-flag operation, concocted by the Bush administration to provide justification for invading Afghanistan and Iraq. Others, for example Peter Dale Scott (2013), drew similarities between 9/11 and the John F. Kennedy assassination, classifying both as what he called 'deep events'. Those, he said, were events that the mainstream media avoided and were only studied by scholars of what he referred to as 'deep history'.

For a decade, 9/11 and its aftermath dominated the US political agenda. It can be argued that only after Osama Bin Laden was killed in May 2011, could Americans move away from allowing the event to contaminate almost all domestic politics. It is in no way overstating the issue, when arguing that the attacks brought a fundamental shift in the sort of populist politics examined in this book.

9/11 did not only mark a turning point in US politics. The horrible event also had far-reaching effects in Europe, where populist parties were indeed fast claiming legitimacy by pointing to their previous warnings against the evil of Islam. Islamophobic prejudice was spreading around the Western world. In Austria, for instance, Jörg Haider proposed that the EU should from then on only accept asylum seekers from Europe.

THE ANTI-MUSLIM TURN

The 9/11 terrorist attacks brought the White Genocide conspiracy theory, which I discussed in the previous chapter, back to the forefront. This notion of cultural replacement has since echoed loudly within many anti-migrant far-right movements on both sides of the Atlantic. Cas Mudde (2016) illustrates how right-wing populists in Europe have been especially successful in depicting Muslim migrants as external threats to the benign native society. In this depiction, Muslims are generally portrayed as a homogeneous group of violent and authoritative religious fundamentalists, who are pre-modern and primarily anti-Western in their politics.

Chris Allen (2010) defines islamophobia in Western societies as the negative positioning of Islam and Muslims as the 'other', posing a threat to 'us'. The archetypical Muslim is, indeed, not only portrayed as inferior, but also as being alien. Anti-Muslim sentiments of this kind have widely become normalized in the West. Muslims are frequently 'featured as invaders', often viewed as part of a 'coordinated plan to conquer Europe' (Kinnvall and Nesbitt-Larking 2010).

Inhered in the theory is an apocalyptic view of Muslims dominating and destroying a liberal and democratic Europe. This intention is generally attributed to all Muslims, irrespective of whether or not they are religious or at all in support of Islamization in the West. As result, those that advocate for multiculturalism and peaceful coexistence can then be accused of naivety and/or of betrayal.

Several influential publications have warned of an Islamist conspiracy of occupying the West. American writer Bruce Bawer (2007)—who later moved to Norway—describes his feelings when arriving in Amsterdam in 1997 as having found the closest thing to a heaven on Earth, that he was finally able to escape the American Protestant fundamentalism. The book titled *While Europe Slept—How Radical Islam Is Destroying the West from Within* describes how he watched Western Europe gradually fall prey to another and much more alarming fundamentalism, that is, to Islam. In a tale of external replacement, Bawer insists that the ever-so-tolerant Europeans were being invaded by intolerant Muslims. Here, Bawer follows a similar intellectual path as Pim Fortuyn did in the Netherlands, that in order to defend Europe's social liberalism, it is necessary to prevent Muslims from contaminating these societies.

This fear of subversion is only the first part of the full theory. Its completion usually also takes the form of accusing a domestic elite of betraying the good ordinary people into the hands of the external evil. Here intentionality is applied, maintaining that covert malevolent powers are bringing about mass migration. This is a core message in the immensely influential book titled *Eurabia—The Euro-Arab Axis*. Writing under the pen name of Bat Ye'or (2005) (in Hebrew, daughter of the Nile), its author Giséle Littman maintains that a particular group of politicians and media people in France were already well on their way to handing the continent over to Muslims. Littman argued that ever since the 1972 Oil Crisis the European Union had secretly conspired with the Arab League to bring about a *Eurabia* on the continent. She said that Europe was now fast being Islamicized and becoming a political satellite of the Arab and Muslim world.

Writer Oriana Fallaci (2006) picked up on this same argument and claimed that Muslims were, in fact, invading and subjugating Western Europe through a combination of immigration and fertility. She wrote that they 'have orders to breed like rats' and stated that these 'eternal invaders rule us already'. She concluded that this was the 'biggest conspiracy that modern history has created'.

THE TIDES TURN IN EASTERN EUROPE

After the collapse of communism and the downfall of the Iron Curtain most countries in Eastern Europe embarked on a quest of implementing a Western-style liberal democracy. Joining the EU was seen as a vital milestone on that road. In a way, it was seen like rejoining the wider European family of states and drawing a line in the sand behind their communist past. However, only few years later, when the rosy promise of fast growth and wide-reaching prosperity was failing to materialize soon enough, some of the countries in Eastern Europe started to move away from liberal democracy. The second wave of nativist populism was also a time of rising authoritarian nationalism throughout Eastern Europe in the wake of the collapsed communist model. Most notorious was ethnic cleansing in the Balkans, discussed at the beginning of this chapter.

In the eastern part of the continent, nationalism was never deemed being as derogatory as it was in Western Europe in the post-war era. Parties of the populistic and nationalist ilk were rising throughout the former communist bloc, such as the Slovak National Party, which was established already in 1990. In Poland, the Kaczynski brothers rose to power with their party Law and Justice. Lithuania similarly saw rise of their version named Order and Justice. In many countries, the rise of the nation was seen in contrast to foreign dominance, and thus, as a source of pride. The voyage of Fidesz, who came to dominate politics in Hungary, is particularly interesting. The party was founded in 1988 by young democrats opposing communism. In the beginning, Viktor Orbán and his compatriots celebrated liberal democracy. They wanted to join the European Union and promoted both social and economic liberalism. Correspondingly to that, the Fidesz party joined the international political federation of liberal parties in 1992.

With the collapse of communism, civil society was fast forming. Free media were reporting. NGOs were operating. Academia was liberated from state control. And soon the Hungarian economy was growing. In a way, Hungary was a poster-child for Eastern Europe's return to liberal democracy. It was only after electoral losses in 1994 that the Fidesz party started its gradual move towards conservative attitudes. Its travel towards more authoritarian tendencies however caused serious splits within the party, with the liberal faction eventually leaving or being silenced. Still, even in his first term as Prime Minister, from 1998 to 2002, Viktor Orbán kept firmly within traditional democratic boundaries.

At the time, it was rather the much more militant Jobbik movement that was promoting authoritarian nationalism. Their message at the time was always contaminated with many of their members blatant flirtation with full-blown neo-Nazism.

Claiming Victimhood

After losing power in 2002, Orbán blamed the liberal media. When winning authority again in 2010, Fidesz had transformed to become fully nativist populist. As I will discuss further in the following chapter, the party has since been accused of abandoning ideals of liberal democracy, to the point of Hungary approaching becoming an autocracy (Schwarz 2018).

One of the main moves of both Fidesz, and the then more rogue Jobbik-movement, was in elevating Hungarian nationalism, mainly by emphasizing the majestic spirit of Magyar King Saint Stephen who lived around the year 1000. Their view of history emphasizes the continuous victimhood of Hungarians by invading armies of Mongols, Ottomans and lastly the Austrian Habsburgs. They would dwell on Hungary's bad fate at Trianon in 1920, when they lost two-thirds of their land and 60 per cent of the population (Judis 2018).

Bringing back the glory of Magyar times was appealing to many Hungarians, while national sentiments were also nurtured by pointing to ongoing threats of foreign dominance. As analysed throughout this book, nativist populism points simultaneously to external threats and internal traitors. In the case of Orbán's Hungary, the external threat was first seen to be the EU, and later migrants. Interestingly, Hungarian-born billionaire George Soros was placed in a precarious hybrid role of both external threat and internal traitor. Although an American citizen, Soros became an important figure in Hungarian business and society after the collapse of communism. He bought up many assets and sought to influence Hungary through his Open Society Foundation. The foundation was tasked with building up aspects of civil society based on liberal democratic ideals.

George Soros for example established the Central European University in Budapest, which became a bastion of both liberalism and multilateralism in international relations. Although Orbán had started out as a beneficiary of Soros, when accepting a Soros scholarship for his studies in England he later turned against him. Gradually, Soros was turned into one of the main targets of nativist populists in both Europe and in America, with many conspiracy theories floating around of his vast-reaching influence. I will return to discussing some of them in the following chapter.

THE KREMLIN'S OLIGARCHIC REFORM

Over in Russia, Vladimir Putin was also slowly moving away from the path leading towards liberal democracy, which had been marked by Boris Yeltsin after the dissolution of the Soviet Union in 1991. Yeltsin's shock-therapy economic reform, including *en masse* privatization, far reaching deregulation and instant devolution of the currency, led to uncontrollable inflation and wide scale unemployment. Between 1991 and 1998 the Russian economy had contracted by almost half. This led many to equate liberal democracy with hardship accompanying Yeltsin's laissez-faire policies.

While the public at large was suffering, many of Yeltsin's cronies were among those able to exploit the havoc and accumulate state property for rock bottom prices. A band of fantastically wealthy *oligarchs* was emerging out of the *nomenklatura*. When Vladimir Putin came along, many Russians had grown frustrated with the apparent injustices around the so-called reform process, which only seemed to benefit those close to the Kremlin elite.

Putin viewed the collapse of the Soviet Union as having been a geopolitical disaster. He has thus strived to resurrect Russia to its former glory, not on a Marxist-Leninist ground as before, but instead based on nationalist ideals. Putin's path towards almost total dominance in Russia was initially paved when striking a deal with many of the country's wealthiest businessmen. In exchange for their loyalty, he would not interfere in their wealth accumulation. Those that did not comply, however, ran a risk of finding themselves incarcerated—like for instance Mikhail Khodorkovsky, who headed the Yukos oil giant. Instead of Yeltsin's wild and violent oligarchic capitalism of the 1990s, Putin turned onto a path of both managed market economy, and, indeed, towards state managed democracy.

After taking office, Putin sought close co-operation with the West. He spoke fondly of the European Union and attended a NATO summit. Reinstating stability brought him popularity. Putin's initial move away from liberal democracy came in the wake of the Chechen War. After successfully squashing the rebels, Putin moved to drowning out dissident voices around this fantastically vast country, for instance by gradually taking control of much of the media. His hard-line actions eventually brought him to collide with the international community, which was growing increasingly concerned with human rights violations in Putin's Russia.

With the collapse of the Berlin Wall, the pendulum in many Eastern European countries had swung fast from socialism to far-reaching neoliberal policies. This was a period of great instability, and in the early new century many of these same countries were rapidly returning to authoritarian patriotism. As I will discuss further in the following chapter, both in Hungary under Orbán and in Russia under Putin, liberal democracy was being eroded via the incremental implementation of slowly evolving authoritarian rule.

GEOPOLITICAL SHIFTS IN FRANCE

By the 1990s, the initial rise of the National Front in France had somewhat receded and the party had also consolidated, enjoying the support of above one-tenth of the population. Several shifts were occurring in the second wave of nativist populism which served to broaden its appeal.

The Cold War saw a move from polarizing tension primarily between socialism and liberal capitalism towards confrontation on another axis. The new axis was contrasting cosmopolitanism with the protection of national values. Similar to changes made by Pia Kjærsgaard in Denmark, in catering to geopolitical shifts accompanying the collapse of communism,

Jean-Marie Le Pen was also starting to downplay the FN's neo-liberal economic position. Instead, he emphasized an anti-immigrant rhetoric. In this period the FN was moving both from neo-liberalism to protectionism, and from promoting European economic integration to campaigning against it.

In line with conventions in French politics, it was expected that the right-of-centre President Jacques Chirac would in the second round of the 2002 presidential elections compete against the Socialist Lionel Jospin for control of the Élysée presidential palace. Surprisingly however, Jean-Marie Le Pen narrowly surpassed Jospin and manoeuvred his way into the run-off. This sent a shockwave down the spine of French politics. And it proved to be a watershed moment. Not only was this significant for French politics, but for populist politics in Europe more generally, which was clearly mounting much more wide-reaching support than before.

Le Pen proved to be especially skilful in riding the wave of post 9/11 anti-Muslim sentiments. In the wake of several violent incidences in France, the 2002 presidential debate largely revolved around law and order. The FN campaigned on a zero-tolerance platform, insisting on much tougher punishment, even of introducing the death penalty. Le Pen successfully linked immigration to increased crime and positioned mainly Muslim migrants as being a 'mortal threat to civil peace' (qtd in Shields 2007).

Jean-Marie Le Pen's rise to significant electoral success coincided with the before-mentioned demise of social democracy. Le Pen had indeed been highly successful in recruiting support from the working class, from the traditional Socialist Party base. After having amended his previously held neo-liberal policies he instead catered to many people's concerns of migrants stealing their jobs, as well as overburdening the welfare system.

Policy changes like these were surely important, but accompanying discursive alterations were also of significance. Although the FN was increasingly focusing on immigration, James Shields (2007) illustrates how its path to success only became clear when simultaneously repackaging the political message into a more refined rhetoric.

Another political change came when Jean-Marie Le Pen turned against Europeanization; for instance, in campaigning against the Euro and what he called the euro-globalism of the Maastricht Treaty which he claimed was ruining ordinary peoples livelihood (Magali 2013). In the 2005 referendum on the EU's Constitutional Treaty the FN campaigned against it. Le Pen described the European Union as being a totalitarian anti-democratic structure.

While Le Pen was turning against the EU, he was—interestingly—simultaneously cultivating a cosy relationship with several authoritarian world leaders. This was similar to Silvio Berlusconi in Italy and Jörg Haider of Austria. Like Haider, Le Pen for example fostered a friendly relationship with Saddam Hussain of Iraq.

NATIONAL (AND EUROPEAN) IDENTITY

This turn against social liberal and a culturally diverse Europe is in line with writings of several intellectuals of the *identitarian* movement, who viewed that identity is the element distinguishing one set of people from another. In his book *Why We Fight: Manifesto of the European Renaissance*, Guillaume Faye (2001) for instance warned that diluting the biocultural identity of the European people would erode European civilization. He thus argued for Europe returning to ethnic consciousness and said that it was necessary to 'defend the biological and cultural identity of one's own people'.

Jean-Marie Le Pen never went as far as Fay did. Still, he identified many enemies of the people. They included immigrants, the domestic elite both in politics and media, and foreign agents. Collectively these actors were painted as posing a threat not only to peoples' prosperity, but also to the very French identity. The FN now also positioned itself as the primary defender of French sovereignty and national identity. They endorsed protectionism and consolidation of state authority. Their programme called for inner expansion by for example promoting pro-birth policies (Magali 2013).

The 2002 presidential election was the first occasion that a far-right populist qualified to the second round in France. The political establishment though, was not willing to fully accept Le Pen's legitimacy. Jacques Chirac refused to face Le Pen in traditional televised election debates, which were cancelled. Socialist Party supporters found themselves forced to back their arch-rival, solely to prevent a far-right populist to be handed the keys to the Élysée palace in Paris. In the run-off, Chirac received an unprecedented 82.2 percent of the vote. In other words, the French voting public staunchly rejected Le Pen's populist stance at the time. He was never able to escape his controversial past. Similar to Jörg Haider in Austria he was accused of being a Nazi sympathizer (Shields 2007).

Fifteen years later however, when his daughter Marine Le Pen repeated her father's success and faced Emmanuel Macron in the presidential run-off in 2017, the mood had altered. As I will discuss further in the following chapter, she received much greater support, and, in effect, won almost full acceptance as a serious candidate standing on an equal footing to her rivals.

Neo-Fascist Movements

The second wave of nativist populism in Europe also saw the rise of a few more rogue and even neo-fascist movements. One of the most influential parties of that kind was the hooligan British National Party (BNP). Founded in 1982, the BNP started out as being firmly far-right neo-fascist and basing its politics on biological racism. They saw the Anglo-Saxon race as being superior to others. Matthew Goodwin (2011) defines it as an extremist far-right party. Initially, the BNP was kept far out on the fringe. However, it drew attention in society around its marches and rallies and through its more militant factions, such as the paramilitary Combat 18, which was created for protecting their events from anti-fascist protesters. The name Combat 18 refers to Adolf Hitler's name.

The BNP rose to renewed prominence in the early 2000s under the leadership of Nick Griffin, who had resumed power by the turn of the century. Griffin set out to broaden the appeal of the party and move it away from its neo-Nazi roots. For instance, by replacing biological racism with ideas of more culturally based ethno-nationalist segregation, stressing the cultural incompatibility of many different racial groups, Griffin was able to significantly increase the BNP's electoral support, especially in municipal elections in north and eastern England. Its greatest win came in 2009 when receiving one million votes in the European Parliamentary elections and sending two MEPs across the English Channel.

On a premise that migration from far-away was undermining British society and culture, the BNP called for an end to non-white immigration. Initially the party advocated compulsory expulsion of all non-whites from the UK, but after Griffin assumed power, they called for voluntary removals. Another change accompanying Griffin's regime was that their previous anti-Semitist stance was exchanged with Islamophobia. In the wake of the 9/11 terrorist attacks, the party launched what it called the 'Campaign Against Islam'. The BNP viewed Islam, as such, as posing a threat to 'our British culture' (Woodbridge 2010). This even related to those that they referred to as 'mainstream Islam'.

The party insisted that every Muslim in Britain was a threat to the country. After the 7 July 2005 London bombing by Islamist terrorists Griffin referred to Islam as an 'evil, wicked faith' (qtd in Copsey 2009). He went on to describe Islam as a 'cancer' that needed to be removed from Europe through 'chemotherapy' (qtd in Trilling 2013).

After coming to reign over the party, Nick Griffin sought to foster relationships with like-minded parties elsewhere in Europe. He was for instance heavily influenced by Le Pen's National Front in France, and he also tapped into the anti-Islam ideology of the French *Nouvelle Droite*, which I discussed in the previous chapter. In 2004, Jean-Marie Le Pen of the National Front was the guest of honour at a BNP-hosted event which they called the Anglo-French Patriotic Dinner. Griffin also sought co-operation with the Hungarian *Jobbik* movement, and with the Italian *Forza Nuova*.

Domestically, the boundaries between the many nationalist movements were somewhat blurred. Many BNP members were for instance involved in the notorious English Defence League led by Tommy Robinson, who formerly had been an BNP activist.

Gradually the BNP saw diminished support, which coincided with the rise of the more benign looking UK Independence Party, which I will discuss further in the following chapter.

Neo-Nazi Movements

Some of these movements were fully neo-Nazi, such as Denmark's National Socialist Movement, which was founded under the leadership of Jonni Hansen in 1991, based on the old Danish Nazi Party of the interwar years.

When I was living in Copenhagen in the latter half of the 1990s, the neo-Nazis were flying high in the national media. They would also hold rallies, marching on the streets in full Nazi insignias, openly celebrating Adolf Hitler and Rudolf Hess. I once interviewed Jonni Hansen for an Icelandic news magazine. Their headquarters were located in a barricaded villa on the Western outskirts of Copenhagen. Hansen received me in their radio studio, where they broadcasted white supremacist heavy metal music in-between enunciating their openly racist political messages. I remember him telling me that their main source of income was in selling Nazi memorabilia to like-minded compatriots in Germany, as merchandise of that kind was forbidden south of the border.

Nativist populist parties were much later to find significant success in Sweden than in most of the neighbouring countries. However, several nationalist—and also a few far-right and extremist movements—had thrived on the margins of Swedish politics throughout the post-war era. The Sweden Democrats—which I will discuss more closely in the following chapter—was founded in 1988 out of the remains of movements closely associated with neo-Nazi forces (Bergmann 2017). Its first proper leader, Anders Klarström, had for example been involved in the Hitler-admiring Nordic National Party formed in 1956.

The Sweden Democrat's international secretary and perhaps main ideologist was Mattias Karlsson. He described the party's quest in quite combative terms, saying that Christian nations in the West were in an 'existential battle for our culture's and our nation's survival (qtd in Becker 2019). The SD, thus, was in the beginning much closer to the skinhead scene and had a much more extreme and xenophobic legacy than nativist populist parties in the other Nordic countries.

Defending Dutch Liberalism by Opposing Islam

Prior to the rise of the Pim Fortuyn List, criticism of the emergence of a multicultural society was almost a taboo in the Netherlands, a critiquing that was not considered as being politically correct. As a homosexual, Fortuyn was able to criticize Islam from a position of protecting the Dutch social liberal order. He accused Islam of being culturally backward and medieval, and, thus, a threat to the open and tolerant lifestyle of the Dutch nation. For the time and place, however, Fortuyn's sharp criticism of Islam caused him to be expelled from his party the *Leefbaarheid* in 2002.

Fortuyn responded with establishing his own party, and in his name, the Pim Fortuyn List. He insisted that his new party's primary errand was to bring power back to the people from corrupt politicians. His main rhetorical contribution to the wider field of nativist populism, was, however, his discursive novelty of shifting away from the traditional authoritarian tendencies of most populists, to positioning himself as the defender of Dutch liberalism, fighting against a threat that was emanating from culturally and socially intolerant Islam.

Aikin to others of a similar ilk, Fortuyn's relatively moderate populism had a clear nationalistic side to it. But his emphasis on social liberalism placed him apart from most other populist leaders at the time. However, as I will come back to in the following chapter, this repositioning of the populist message, the protection of the West's liberalism against authoritarian Islamism, was to be mirrored by several nativist populists in the third wave, for instance in the Nordic countries.

In May 2002, less than two weeks prior to general elections, Fortuyn was killed in Amsterdam by a left-wing animal rights activist. The Pim Fortuyn List surged in the wake of his death, winning 17 per cent of the vote, and becoming the second largest in the country. The party entered government but soon lost credibility.

Out of its ruins, Geert Wilders was able construct his Dutch Freedom Party (*Partij voor de Vrijheid*—VVD) and, as I will document in the following chapter, emerged as one of the most vigilant and successful populist leaders in Europe. Wilders broke with traditional democratic structures. The party remained his own enterprise, and he did not even invite its parliamentary candidates to join it. In 2006, Wilders entered parliament with nine seats. Later his party came to support the government in return for implementing some of its policies. Wilders was a pioneer in adopting a new populist winning formula, in combining socio-economic left-wing views with hard-core right-wing conservative socio-cultural ideas (Lucardie and Voerman 2013). Wilders based some of his politics on Fortuyn's socio-liberalist heritage, but he was soon to steer his party in a much more traditionally authoritarian direction in its opposition to multiculturalism, readmitting to the mix a more generic anti-Muslim rhetoric.

BERLUSCONI'S SCANDALS

In Italy, Silvio Berlusconi was quick to jump on the wagon of the post-9/11 anti-Muslim rhetoric. He insisted that Western civilization was 'superior to Islamic culture'.[4] In its wake, Berlusconi was able to push through stricter immigration policies, including for instance the Bossi-Fini law in 2002, named after his two populist coalition partners. The new legislation provided for the expulsion of illegal immigrants. It was criticized in the European Parliament for being too restrictive and severe.[5] In the 2008 general election, he described jobless foreigners as an 'army of evil' (qtd in Fekete 2018).

Berlusconi staunchly supported US-led military endeavours in response to the 9/11 attack, such as the Iraq invasion. The Italian Prime Minister became cosy with many of the more rogue strongman leaders of his time. For instance, he had good relationships with Muammar al-Gaddafi in Libya and with Recep Erdoğan in Turkey. Although both were Muslims,

Berlusconi was still slowly abandoning Italy's long-lasting political partnership with the Arab world. Instead, he turned to backing Israel and enjoyed his close relationship with Israel's Prime Minister, Benjamin Netanyahu, who he declared was a great leader. In response, Netanyahu called Berlusconi one of Israel's greatest friends.[6] Berlusconi was adamant in maintaining an especially good working relationship with US President George W Bush, and he also fostered a particularly close friendship with Vladimir Putin of Russia. He even reached out to Alexander Lukashenko, the authoritarian leader of Belarus.

Berlusconi's political career was raked with a series of scandals and blunders. He was accused of bribery, abuse of office and of links to the Mafia. There were also several sex scandals around him, including accusations of sleeping with under-age prostitutes. For years the Italian taxman was on his heels, in investigations which Berlusconi dismissed as being an anti-democratic communist witch-hunt against him. In his defence, he once called on supporters to form a freedom army, some kind of civil militia, to come to his aid in defiance against his prosecutors.

As I discussed before, post-war nativist populists have usually refrained from celebrating fascist leaders of the interwar era. Still, Berlusconi repeatedly revealed his ill veiled admiration of Benito Mussolini, describing him as a good leader who only by mistaken loyalty to Adolf Hitler had signed up to exterminating the Jews. Berlusconi insisted that Mussolini 'had been a benign dictator who did not murder opponents but sent them "on holiday"' (qtd in Owen 2008).

In total, Berlusconi served nine years as Prime Minister, making him the longest serving premier in post-war Italy. During his reign, Berlusconi was able to push through several policy changes, undermining the free civil society in Italy. Under his rule, freedom of the press was found to be backsliding. A Freedom House report in 2004 detected increased media concentration in Italy, where 'political pressure led to the downgrading of the country from "free" to "partly free"'.[7] The report said that Prime Minister Silvio Berlusconi had been able to exert undue influence over the public broadcaster RAI. 'This further exacerbates an already worrisome media environment characterized by unbalanced coverage within Berlusconi's enormous media empire.' The *Economist* writer David Lane (2005), found that Berlusconi in effect controlled 90 per cent of all national television broadcasting in the country.

In the field of populist leaders, Berlusconi stands out in many ways. He never completely fitted the profile of the fully-fledged nativist populist.

Still, both his rhetorical style and governance he had a clear populist side. He was prone to offering lofty promises. He would also dismiss the elite and insist that he himself was directly linked to the people. Bobba and Legnante (2016) maintain that Berlusconi was able to turn elections into referendums on himself, rather than allowing them to revolve around the state of governance. However, despite these clearly populist qualities, Berlusconi can also be defined in many other ways. As such, he does not completely qualify as being counted among the contemporary European extreme-right. Rather he should be defined as a centre-right quasi populist.

Finding Legitimacy

When I moved to Copenhagen for my postgraduate studies in 1996, Danes were still flaunting their socio-liberal side. Pia Kjærsgaard was still largely dismissed as a rogue demagogue that would never find influence. This was, though, fast changing. The 9/11 attacks in the US brought new support for the Danish Peoples Party. Most people in the mainstream had consistently and firmly opposed the DF's anti-Muslim politics and the party was harshly criticized for flirting with racism. That was drastically altered after the horrendous 9/11 event. Similar to the significance of the 1973 so-called 'earthquake elections' the 2001 election broke new grounds in Danish politics. First, the DF was gaining legitimacy and was from then on positioned as one of the permanent parties in Danish politics. Secondly, immigration had since become perhaps the country's most salient political issue. After moving away from the anarchist past of the Progress Party, Kjærsgaard was able to present herself and the DF as a credible alternative to the established parties.

For many, the 9/11 terrorist attack served to validate the DF's criticism of Islam. The sudden change boosted confidence among the party's candidates in the coming parliamentary elections held only several weeks later. Mogens Camre, DF representative in the EU Parliament, described Islam as 'ideology of evil' and suggested that Muslims should be 'driven out of Western civilization' (qtd in Klein 2013). He maintained that Muslims could not successfully be integrated into Danish society and that they had indeed come to take over Denmark. Camre said that all Western countries had been 'infiltrated by Muslims', and that even though many of them spoke nicely to us 'they are waiting to become numerous enough to get rid of us' (qtd in Sommer and Aagaard 2003). In reaction to the terrorist attacks the election campaign came to revolve around immigration, and the DF surged.

Many of the mainstream parties soon started to follow the DF's line on immigration. A relatively widespread consensus emerged on the need to stem migration and to impose stricter demands on the integration of foreigners, and of adherence to the Danish way of life. Anti-immigrant politics was becoming mainstream. The debate no longer revolved around the validity of a tougher migration policy, but rather on its means and methods.

A competition thus emerged as to who was the toughest and most credible on migration. Subsequently, immigration was the most covered political topic in media. Roemer and Van der Straeten (2004) found the Danish media to be nationalist and racist in its reporting on immigration, and prone to reproducing a discourse that legitimized ethnic inequalities. In covering migration, the Danish media emphasized crime, social problems and conflict with Danish society (Stainforth 2009).

Danishness

The DF skilfully rode the rise in anti-Muslim sentiments after 9/11, and they were able to set the agenda in the elections. Their anti-immigration rhetoric revolved around three main themes: cultural infiltration, criminality and welfare abuse. One of their election campaign posters asked: 'Your Denmark? A multi-ethnic society with gang rapes, repression of women and gang crimes. Do you want that?'

Anders Jupskås (2015a) found the DF being especially successful in linking other political issues to immigration, such as welfare, the state of the economy and anti-elitism. Immigration was also directly linked to gender issues, maintaining that Islam was incompatible with the level of women's liberation in Denmark. In that regard, the veiling of women in Islam became a central and symbolic issue.

Securing 12 per cent of the vote in the 2001 election and becoming the third largest in the country marked the long and successful journey of the DF from the cold fringe and into the very core of Danish politics. The party's new position of power was cemented when subsequently backing a minority government of *Venstre* and the Conservative Party led by Anders Fogh Rassmussen. Over the coming decade the DF was able to push through restrictions on immigration, tightening demands for integration, implementing tougher measures on crime with stricter sentences, and increased public welfare for the elderly.

In the DF's 2002 principal manifesto, culture was in addition to ethnicity found to be core to Danishness (*Danskhed*). This culture was defined as 'the sum of the Danish People's history, experience, religion, language and common customs'.[8] The manifesto for example stated that Denmark should belong to the Danes. The party argued that immigrants were parasites on the Danish welfare system, which, as result would be severely weakened—to the detriment of ethnic Danes, when in need of services.

The youth movement went further. In a 2003 advertisement, it for example linked Muslims with mass rapes and gang criminality. Gradually, the DF's rhetoric became the dominant political discourse on migration and Muslims. Arguing that cultural racism had found especially fertile territory in Denmark, Karen Wren (2001) maintains that the absence of a significant counter rhetoric has also become institutional and part of the very fabric of Danish society. Even many on the left flank of Danish politics came to accept the anti-immigrant discourse, as I will document in the following chapter.

The Danish Peoples Party grew to become perhaps the most influential in the country, rapidly becoming one of the largest in parliament and prolonging its position of power when repeatedly backing right-of-centre governments. Denmark came to implement one of the toughest legislations on immigration in Western Europe. Criteria around eligible refugees were narrowed, and foreigner's rights tightened. Rights to family reunifications were reduced, to the extent that foreign spouses younger than twenty-four years were no longer allowed residence with their Danish husbands or wives. Asylum seekers faced stricter demands, including passing a tough test on language, society, history, culture and values (for more, see Widfeldt 2015).

While the DF surely pushed the hardest for these tough measures, the other right-wing governmental parties proved to be quite willing participants in the quest. The combined measures had the effect of significantly reducing the influx of non-EU immigrants.

Conflicts and Connections

These troubled immigrant relations only came to international attention in 2005 when the established broadsheet national Danish daily, *Jyllands-Posten*, commissioned several cartoonists to mock prophet Mohammed in drawings published in the paper, causing rage among many Muslims. Karen Wren (2001) argues that cultural racism in Denmark is distinctly anti-Muslim. The DF was successful in demonizing Muslims and in portraying them as invaders.

The provocation with the cartoons was said to be intended to underline freedom of speech as a fundamental value but many saw it as being Islamophobic and racist, even revealing ignorance of the historical impact of Western imperialism.

The Danish People's Party has been connected to many other nationalist movements in Denmark. Similar to France, where the right-wing populist think tank *Nouvelle Droite* was indirectly linked to the National Front, the Danish Association (*Den Danske Forening*—DDF) served as an important intellectual source of ideological inspiration for the DF. Anders Widfeldt (2015) argues that the association had, for example, provided the party with their three-fold argument against immigration; first as a threat to Danish culture and ethnic identity, second, as a cause of crime, and third, as a burden on the welfare state. Pastor Søren Krarup was perhaps their most prominent and articulate spokesman. He said that love of fatherland and the nation-state was one of the loveliest human emotions, closely connected with honesty and decency (qtd in Wren 2001).

The Danish Association viewed Denmark as being a homogeneous Christian nation-state, where migrant workers could only be guests. The continuous presence of foreigners was seen as a threat. In this light, the DDF was instrumental in framing the Danish Peoples Party's argument within an ethno-pluralist narrative, based on the doctrine that even though nations were equal they should be kept separate. Although this discourse derives from fascist traditions, the DF was able to steer it away from the stigma of discredited ideologies such as neo-Nazism.

The DF was adamant in avoiding being linked to the more controversial nationalist movements, for example the before-mentioned Danish neo-Nazi movement, Danish Front or the Danish Forum. DF members have, in fact, been expelled for being associated with these radical movements.

Milder Norwegians

Although populist politics started out on a similar platform in Norway as they had done in Denmark, the Norwegian Progress Party evolved to become a much milder version of their counterparts. Its leader Carl I. Hagen always argued that his party was very different from the DF. He made a firm legitimizing distinction when emphasizing that he was not criticizing the immigrants themselves, but rather the soft and lenient immigration policy of the Norwegian Labour Party.

Still, the development of the two parties was in a similar direction. Anniken Hagelund (2003) explains how the FrP moved from problematizing migration merely on economic grounds to also voicing concerns of its effect on Norway's culture. The party argued that in order to prevent ethnic conflict in Norway, immigration and asylum sought from 'outside the Western culture complex' had to be stemmed.[9] This was a classic nationalist ethno-pluralist doctrine, emphasizing the importance of keeping nations separate, without openly claiming any sort of superiority.

Carl I. Hagen argued that non-Western immigration would bring a culture of violence and gang mentality. Concerns over its effect on the ethnic composition of the nation were increasingly voiced, for example, in a clever way of quoting former Conservative Prime Minister, Kaare Willoch, who once warned against 'too rapid changes in the unified character of our population' (qtd in Hagelund 2003).

Almost from the outset, the FrP found greater acceptance in society than similar parties had enjoyed in most other countries. Already in the 1980s the FrP was within a majority position when supporting state budgets. It thus found legitimacy much earlier than its many counterparts in neighbouring countries. In the period from 1985 to 2001 they held the balance of power between the left-wing and right-wing blocs in Norwegian politics.

By the turn of the millennium, the FrP had become the largest force in some opinion polls. In addition to applying Herbert Kitschelt's winning formula, discussed before, of combining right-wing populism with authoritarianism and a policy of anti-immigration, its success can be attributed to Carl I. Hagen's ability to keep out more extreme forces. By the turn of the century, he set out to purge the party in a series of expulsions of far-right radicals.

By ousting extremists, the party was able to move closer to the power centre of Norwegian politics. In exchange for supporting the right-of-centre government, Hagen was able to secure the influential parliamentary position of chairman of the Committee of Finance for his deputy, Siv Jensen, who was later to succeed him as party leader.

Brave Truth-Tellers

While the FrP firmly refused to be associated with racism their representatives positioned themselves as brave truth-tellers, defying the political correctness of the ruling class. In 2005 the party published a poster depicting a juvenile of foreign descent pointing a gun at the viewer. The text stated that 'the perpetrator is of foreign origin'. When criticized for its xenophobic undertone, the party spokesman said that it was simply necessary to 'call a spade a spade' (qtd in Jupskås 2015b).

The anti-immigrant position of the FrP was based on a new master framework where immigrants were presented as an economic burden and a cultural threat, rather than being biologically inferior (Rydgren 2007). Anders Hellstrom (2016) documents how the immigration issue gained salience in the party's repertoire in the 1990s, when warning against the danger of cultural heterogeneity. He says that immigration was in that way 'transformed from an economic to a cultural issue'.

Anders Jupskås (2015b) identifies five distinctive narratives that defined the FrP's anti-immigration platform. First, that immigrants cost too much. Second, that they exploit 'our' welfare. Third, that they are more prone to crime than the native population. Fourth, that they undermine the Norwegian way of life. And lastly, that they challenge Norway's values, mainly liberal values. Thus, when combined, that they threaten Norway's economy, welfare system, security, culture and liberal values.

Jupskås documents that the first two frames were present from the outset, that the second two narratives emerged in the 1980s but that the last one, regarding the challenge to liberal values, was only presented after 9/11. In any event, it is clear that the cultural emphasis in the anti-immigrant rhetoric, that is, on rules, norms and values, only emerged to prominence in Norway in the 1990s. Simultaneously, the importance of the economic frames gradually decreased.

ETHNO-NATIONALIST NORWAY

Immigrants were not the only population that Progress Party spokesmen portrayed as an out-group in Norway. To a large extent, the same applied to the indigenous Sami population living in northern Norway, as well as in neighbouring Sweden and in Finland. The FrP sought to diminish Sami influence and for example proposed dissolving the Sami Assembly (*Sametinget*) (Iversen 1998).

Despite the FrP's move to distance itself from the Danish People's Party, it still adopted many of their neighbours' policies on immigration; for example in cutting foreign aid and in proposing the mandatory expulsion of foreigners sentenced to jail for more than three months. They furthermore emphasized much stricter rules on family reunifications, including the notorious twenty-four-year-old minimum rule for spouses, and eighteen-year-old maximum rule for children.

Their anti-immigration rhetoric gradually grew more distinctively anti-Muslim. Already in 1979, Carl I. Hagen described Islam as a 'misanthropic and extremely dangerous religion' (qtd in Jupskås 2013). Since then, their anti-Islam rhetoric has grown firmer. Muslim immigration was linked to terrorism, forced marriage and crime (Bergmann 2017). Mulisms were portrayed as a burden on the welfare system and as a threat to Norwegian culture. The FrP furthermore identified a need to fight against Sharia laws filtering through into Norway. In the third wave of nativist populism, discussed in the following chapter, the Norwegian Progress Party was fast moving to become fully accepted in the wider society and landed for the first time in government, in a coalition with the centre-right.

Unquiet Tea Party

The so-called Tea Party faction within the American Republican Party was formed in response to Barack Obama running for president in 2008, becoming the first African American US head of state. Although the Tea Party might be placed in the third wave of nativist populism, I still discuss it here, as the movement was in many ways better aligned with politics operating before the end of the second wave of nativist populism.

The Tea Party advocated for small government and lowering of taxes. The name refers to a pivotal moment in the American Revolution in 1773, when English tea was dumped into the Boston harbour in rebellion against British taxation. Their mantra was: no taxation without representation. The anti-tax emphasis of the Tea Party resembles, perhaps, the neo-liberal populist parties in Europe of the first wave, such as Mogens Glitrup's Progress Party in Denmark, Anders Lange in Norway and the initial rise of Jean-Marie Le Pen's National Front in France.

The Tea Party was not only fiscally conservative, it was also fundamentally socially conservative. Most of its members emphasized Christian traditional family values, tighter security, and they opposed amnesty for illegal immigrants. They rallied in protection of the right to gun ownership, but forcefully campaigned against women's rights to abortion.

The Tea Party was largely funded by the Koch brothers, Charles and David, who in the 1980s had established a political group called Citizens for a Sound Economy. The group's mission was to fight for less government, lower taxes and less regulation. Its first chairman was the libertarian congressman Ron Paul, who three times sought the presidency of the US. Partially, the Tea Party was born out of his failed presidential bid in 2008. The Tea Party would field fringe candidates to challenge those they branded being Republican establishment candidates.

The Tea Party can also be seen a successor of the Neoconservative movement of the 1970s, discussed in the previous chapter. For instance, Neocon leader Newt Gingrich, the former Republican Speaker of the House of Representatives, was among its influential ideologues. Correspondingly, the Tea Party believed in a similar kind of American exceptionalism as the Neocons had done the 1970s. They promoted the aggressive protection of US interests around the world. Both the Neocons and the Tea Party based much of the politics on religious nationalism and indeed on science denialism, which later proved to be a vicious cocktail, as I will discuss in a later chapter when dealing with Donald Trump and, for instance, his response to the Coronavirus Crisis of 2020.

Another forebear of the Tea Party's policies was Pat Buchanan. Interestingly for Donald's Trump's harsh stance on immigration much later, Buchanan's presidential bids in the 1990s were largely based on his claim that if 'we do not build a sea wall against the waves of immigration rolling over our shores' then America will 'become a Third World country' (qtd in Berlet 1999).

American Conspiratorialism

In a norm-breaking manner for what had been customary in American politics up until then, many Tea Party members emerged as leading voices in criticizing Barack Obama and questioning his legitimacy as US President. Several anti-Obama conspiracy theories were spreading at the time. First, a relatively insignificant story was sailing at full mast; that he was not born in the USA and, thus, not legitimate as president. The story, without even any crumb of evidence, soon gained a surprising following.

One of these stories insisted that Obama was an agent for instating a 'one world government' (see Judis 2018). Many conspiracy theories were afloat insisting that Obama was secretly a Muslim. In an email campaign in 2007 it was stated that he had attended a radical Wahhabi school in Indonesia. Another story insisted that he had taken his oath of office for the US Senate by swearing on the Quran (Holan 2007). Never mind the well-established fact that Obama was a Christian and that he visibly took the oath of office on a Bible. Stories of this kind, even though utterly—and indeed provably—bogus, still had their effect. In a 2010 poll, almost one-fifth of responders believed that Obama was, indeed, a Muslim.[10]

In one version, Obama was not only accused of being a Muslim, but also a communist. Iowa Congressman Steve King said that Obama was anti-American and that he would lead the country to becoming a 'totalitarian dictatorship' (qtd in Terkel 2008). Perhaps the most far-fetched story insisted that he was, in fact, the Antichrist (Posner 2008).

These anti-Obama conspiracy theories were not only being spread from the far-right. Suspicions of this sort were also being fed by his mainstream opponents. Even some fellow Democrats, who supported Hillary Clinton, flirted with such tales in hope that it would bring her potential political gain in the primaries before the 2008 US presidential elections. By painting Obama as being the 'Other', his opponents deliberately applied a *Manichean* method of demonizing their adversary. This is a well-known tactic in populist politics.

When seeking the presidency in 2016, Donald Trump successfully positioned himself within the realm of the Tea Party, and he flirted with many of these anti-Obama conspiracy theories. As will become evident in the following chapter, both the politics and the wider cultural social heritage of the Tea Party indeed played a key role in Donald Trump's election as US President. When tracing the rhetoric on immigration in American politics, from the Neocons to the Tea Party and over to Donald Trump, it becomes evident how nationalist policies travel between different populist movements over time—to emerge as distinctly post-war Neo-Nationalism.

Notes

1. A Bolivarian Revolution is named after the President of the Second Republic of Venezuela in the early nineteenth century, Simon Bolívar, who throughout Latin America is largely seen as a liberator in the independence fight against European colonialization.
2. *BBC News*. 2000, 11 February. 'Haider in context: Nazi employment policies'.
3. *BBC News*. 2001, 27 November. 'Transcript: Bin Laden Video excerpts'.
4. *The Independent*. 2001, 27 September. 'Storm over Berlusconi "inferior Muslims" remark'.
5. *Il Fatto Quotidian*. 2013, 23 October. 'Immigrazione, Parlamento Ue chiede la modifica della legge Bossi-Fini'.

6. *The Daily Telegraph.* 2010, 2 February. 'Berlusconi says Israel should be an EU member'.
7. Freedom House. 2004, 3 May. 'Global Press Freedom Deteriorates'.
8. Dansk Folkeparti. 2002, October. 'Party programme of the Danish People's Party'.
9. 'Fremskrittspartiets handlingsprogram 2009–2013', 2009.
10. Pew Research Centre. 2010, 18 August. 'Growing Number of Americans Say Obama is a Muslim'.

REFERENCES

Aistrope, T. (2016). *Conspiracy Theory and American Foreign Policy* (1st ed.). Manchester: Manchester University Press.
Allen, C. (2010). *Islamophobia* (1st ed.). London: Routledge.
Ascherson, N. (2002). Neal Ascherson: The Warning Shot. *The Observer*, London.
Bawer, B. (2007). *While Europe Slept: How Radical Islam Is Destroying the West from Within.* Norwell: Anchor.
Becker, J. (2019). The Global Machine Behind the Rise of Far-Right Nationalism. *The New York Times.*
Bergmann, E. (2017). *Nordic Nationalism and Right-Wing Populist Politics: Imperial Relationships and National Sentiments.* London and New York: Palgrave Macmillan.
Bergmann, E. (2018). *Conspiracy & Populism: The Politics of Misinformation.* London: Palgrave Macmillan.
Berlet, C. (Ed.). (1999). *Eyes Right!: Challenging the Right Wing Backlash.* Boston, MA: South End Press.
Berlusconi Says Israel Should Be an EU Member. (2010). *The Daily Telegraph.*
Bobba, G., & Legnante, G. (2016). Italy: A Breeding Ground for Populist Political Communication. In *Populist Political Communication in Europe.* London: Routledge.
Cedroni, L. (2010). *Il linguaggio politico della transizione: tra populismo e anticultura.* Armando Editore.
Copsey, N. (2009). *Contemporary British Fascism: The British National Party and the Quest for Legitimacy* (2nd ed.). Basingstoke: Palgrave Macmillan.
Eggen, D., & Vandehei, J. (2006). Cheney Cites Justifications For Domestic Eavesdropping. *Washington Post.*
Fallaci, O. (2006). *The Force of Reason* (1st ed.). New York, NY: Rizzoli International Publications.
Faye, G. (2001). *Why We Fight: Manifesto of the European Resistance.* London: Arktos Media Ltd.
Fekete, E. (2018). *Europe's Fault Lines: Racism and the Rise of the Right.* London: Verso Books.

Fremskrittspartiets Handlingsprogram 2009–2013. (2009).
Fukuyama, F. (1992). *The End of History and the Last Man*. New York, NY: Simon and Schuster.
Global Press Freedom Deteriorates. (2004). *Freedom House*.
Goodwin, M. (2011). *New British Fascism: Rise of the British National Party* (1st ed.). New York: Routledge.
Griffin, R. (2000). Interregnum or Endgame? The Radical Right in the 'Post-Fascist' Era. *Journal of Political Ideologies*, 5(2), 163–178.
Griffin, D. R. (Ed.). (2006). *9/11 and American Empire: Intellectuals Speak Out* (Vol. 1). Northampton, MA: Olive Branch Press.
Growing Number of Americans Say Obama Is a Muslim. (2010). *Pew Research Center*.
Habermas, J. (1998). *The Postnational Constellation*. Boston: MIT Press.
Hagelund, A. (2003). A Matter of Decency? The Progress Party in Norwegian Immigration Politics. *Journal of Ethnic and Migration Studies*, 29(1), 47–65.
Haider in Context: Nazi Employment Policies. (2000). *BBC News*.
Heinisch, R. (2013). Austrian Right-Wing Populism: A Surprising Comeback Under a New Leader. In *Exposing the Demagouges*. Berlin: Konrad Adenauer Stiftung.
Hellstrom, A. (2016). *Trust Us: Reproducing the Nation and the Scandinavian Nationalist Populist Parties*. Berghahn Books.
Holan, A. D. (2007). Obama Used a Koran? No, He Didn't. *PolitiFact*.
Huntington, S. P. (1993). The Clash of Civilizations? *Foreign Affairs*, 22–49.
Huntington, S. P. (1996). *The Clash of Civilizations*. London: Simon & Schuster.
Immigrazione, Parlamento Ue chiede la modifica della legge Bossi-Fini. (2013). *Il Fatto Quotidiano*.
Iversen, J. M. (1998). *Fra Anders Lange Til Carl I. Hagen: 25 Ar Med Fremskrittspartiet*. Oslo: Millennium.
Iyer, D. (2001). *American Backlash: Terrorists Bring Home War in More Ways than One*. South Asian American Leaders of Tomorrow.
Jagers, J. (2006). *De Stem van Het Volk! Populisme Als Concept Getest Bij Vlaamse Politieke Partijen*. University of Antwerpen.
Judis, J. B. (2018). *The Nationalist Revival: Trade, Immigration, and the Revolt Against Globalization*. New York, NY: Columbia Global Reports.
Jupskås, A. R. (2013). The Progress Party: A Fairly Integrated Part of the Norwegian Party System. In *Exposing the Demagogues: Right-Wing and National Populist Parties in Europe*. Berlin: Konrad Adenauer Stiftung.
Jupskås, A. R. (2015a). Institutionalized Right-Wing Populism in Times of Economic Crisis: A Comparative Study of the Norwegian Progress Party and the Danish People's Party. In *European Populism in the Shadow of the Great Recession*. Colchester: ECPR Press.

Jupskås, A. R. (2015b). *The Persistence of Populism. The Norwegian Progress Party 1973–2009.* University of Oslo.
Kessler, G. (2015). Trump's Outrageous Claim that 'Thousands' of New Jersey Muslims Celebrated the 9/11 Attacks. *Washington Post.*
Kinnvall, C., & Nesbitt-Larking, P. (2010). The Political Psychology of (de)Securitization: Place-Making Strategies in Denmark, Sweden, and Canada. *Environment and Planning D: Society and Space, 28*(6), 1051–1070.
Klein, A. (2013). The End of Solidarity? On the Development of Right-Wing Populist Parties in Denmark and Sweden. In *Exposing the Demagogues: Right-Wing and National Populist Parties in Europe.* Berlin: Konrad Adenauer Stiftung.
Lane, D. (2005). *Berlusconi's Shadow.* Eastbourne: Gardners Books.
Levitsky, S., & Ziblatt, D. (2018). *How Democracies Die.* New York: Crown.
Lewis, B. (1990). The Roots of Muslim Rage. *The Atlantic.*
Lucardie, P., & Voerman, G. (2013). Geert Wilders and the Party for Freedom in the Netherlands: A Political Entrepreneur in the Polder. In *Exposing the Demagogues: Right-Wing and National Populist Parties in Europe.* Berlin: Konrad Adenauer Stiftung.
Magali, B. (2013). The French National Front from Jean-Marie to Marine Le Pen: Between Change and Continuity. In *Exposing the Demagogues: Right-Wing and National Populist Parties in Europe.* Berlin: Konrad Adenauer Stiftung.
Merkl, P. H., & Weinberg, L. (2003). *Right-Wing Extremism in the Twenty-First Century.* London: Psychology Press.
Mikbakhsh, M., & Kramar-Schmid, U. (2010). Jörg Haiders Geheime Geldgeschäfte Mit Dem Irakischen Diktator Saddam Hussein. *Profil.at.*
Mudde, C. (2016). *34 On Extremism and Democracy in Europe.* Routledge.
Orsina, G. (2014). *Berlusconism and Italy - A Historical Interpretation.* Basingstoke: Palgrave Macmillan.
Owen, R. (2008). Profile: The Irrepressible Silvio Berlusconi - Times Online. *The Times.*
Party Programme of the Danish People's Party. (2002). Retrieved from danskfolkeparti.dk.
Pauwels, T. (2013). Belgium: Decline of National Populism? In *Exposing the Demagogues: Right-Wing and National Populist Parties in Europe.* Berlin: Konrad Adenauer Stiftung.
Posner, S. (2008). Sarah Posner: For Many on the Religious Right, the Prospect of an Obama Presidency Represents the End of Life as We Know It. *The Guardian.*
Roemer, J. E., & Van der Straeten, K. (2004). *The Political Economy of Xenophobia and Distribution: The Case of Denmark.* Laboratoire d'Econométrie de l'Ecole Polytechnique. Working Paper 2004-03.
Russakof, D., & Kovaleski, S. (1995). *An Ordinary Boy's Extraordinary Rage.*

Rydgren, J. (2007). The Sociology of the Radical Right. *Annual Review of Sociology, 33*, 241–262.
Schaeffer, F. (2011). *Sex, Mom, and God: How the Bible's Strange Take on Sex Led to Crazy Politics—and How I Learned to Love Women (and Jesus) Anyway.* ReadHowYouWant.com.
Schwarz, R. (2018). *Democracy under Pressure: Polarization and Repression Are Increasing Worldwide.* Brussels: Bertelsmann Stiftung.
Scott, P. D. (2013). *The War Conspiracy: JFK, 9/11, and the Deep Politics of War* (1st ed.). Skyhorse Publishing.
Serrano, R. (1997). Witnesses Say McVeigh Didn't Refer to Nichols. *Los Angeles Times.*
Shields, J. (2007). *The Extreme Right in France: From Pétain to Le Pen.* London: Routledge.
Sommer, N., & Aagaard, S. (2003). *Succes: Historien Om Pia Kjærsgaard.* Copenhagen: Lindhardt og Ringhof.
Stainforth, T. (2009). The Danish Paradox: Intolerance in the Land of Perpetual Compromise. *Review of European and Russian Affairs, 5*(1), 83–106.
Storm over Berlusconi 'Inferior Muslims' Remarks. (2001). *The Independent.*
Terkel, A. (2008). Rep. Steve King: Obama Will Make America A 'Totalitarian Dictatorship'. *Think Progress.*
Transcript: Bin Laden Video Excerpts. (2001). *BBC News.*
Trilling, D. (2013). *Bloody Nasty People: The Rise of Britain's Far Right* (1st ed.). London: Verso.
Widfeldt, A. (2015). *Extreme Right Parties in Scandinavia.* New York: Routledge.
Wodak, R. (2015). *The Politics of Fear: What Right-Wing Populist Discourses Mean.* New York: Sage.
Woodbridge, S. (2010). Christian Credentials?: The Role of Religion in British National Party Ideology. *Journal for the Study of Radicalism, 4*(1), 25–54.
Wren, K. (2001). Cultural Racism: Something Rotten in the State of Denmark? *Social & Cultural Geography, 2*(2), 141–162.
Ye'or, B. (2005). *Eurabia. The Euro-Arab Axis.* Cranbury: Fairleigh Dickinson University Press/Associated University Presses.

The Third Wave: The International Financial Crisis and Refugees

When the International Financial Crisis of 2008 was chewing into people's livelihoods, distaste for the political establishment had already been building for decades. In its wake, nativist populism rose to new heights, now also spreading far into the mainstream. This was illustrated in wide calls for leadership renewal. In fact, political experience was generally being dismissed, with increased appetite instead for inexperienced newcomers.

This was the time of the political novice. In other words, it was the amateurization of political life in the West. Even in firmly rooted democracies, traditional politics were giving way to populists. The third wave of nativist populism also brought a transformation in their appearance. These were no longer rogue demagogues revelling in Nazi symbolism, as in previous eras. Instead, populist leaders now looked like normal politicians.

As I will illustrate in this chapter, the third wave saw the spread of populist nationalism further into the mainstream in European and American politics than ever before. The new wave brought Brexit to the UK, Donald Trump to power in America and Marine Le Pen qualifying to the second round in the presidential elections in France, where she bagged a third of the vote. Indeed, this was a brand-new world. It is telling for their reach that the four largest democracies in the world—Brazil, Indonesia and India in addition to the US—were all governed by politicians often labelled as being populist.

In Europe, populists came into government in Austria, Greece, Finland, Hungary, Norway, Poland and Switzerland. In Italy, two populist parties,

© The Author(s) 2020
E. Bergmann, *Neo-Nationalism*,
https://doi.org/10.1007/978-3-030-41773-4_5

the Five Star movement and the quasi-fascist Lega, united in government. Even in Germany, far-right populists were also surging.

The president of the *Generation Identitaire*, Arnaud Delrieux, described this change as the 'age of identities, for it is the very essence of the European people that is threatened by the steamroller of globalism, the immigration invasion and multiculturalism' (qtd in Zúquete 2018).

In the third wave, nativist populism had grown far beyond Cas Mudde's (2004) coining of the phrase *populist zeitgeist*. Populist discourse was moved out from the fringe and into the mainstream—even fully adopted by government parties in some instances. Whichever way we dissect this trend, the third wave brought a fundamental shift in the evolution of nativist populism and came to constitute a clear trend of Neo-Nationalism spreading across Europe, America and elsewhere.

The third wave was fuelled by two main consecutive events hitting the Western world, first the International Financial Crisis culminating in 2008, followed by the Refugee Crisis heightening in 2015. Nationalist sentiments were again heightening with the Coronavirus Crisis of 2020.

The Credit Crunch

The International Financial Crisis brought the extraordinary economic boom of the early noughties to a stark halt. Indeed, this was the most serious economic calamity since the inter-war Great Depression. The troubles arose around sub-market housing mortgages in the US in 2007, turning into a full-blown Credit Crunch in the following year. The crisis shook the foundations of Western capitalism, bringing economic uncertainty, severe public austerity and increased hardship on the ordinary public, which largely felt victimized by both business and political elites.

The fall of Lehman Brothers on 15 September 2008 was a watershed moment, turning troubles into a serious banking crisis. In October Iceland, the small island country in the northwest Atlantic, became the poster-child of the global Credit Crunch when all of its oversized international banks came tumbling down within a single week, amounting to one of the world's greatest national financial crises (Bergmann 2014b). This was a financial tsunami without precedent in contemporary times. The crunch also illustrated a vulnerability in the internationalized economy of the West.

In 2009 the crisis was contesting the very fabric of the European economic system and was posing an existential threat to the Euro, the shared currency of many EU member states. Leaders on the continent responded to the crisis with imposing severe austerity measures onto vulnerable countries that were most seriously affected by the malaise. In effect, leaders in Berlin and Paris and other powerful players within the EU were able to coerce authorities in Athens, Rome, Lisbon, Madrid and in other economically weaker EU capitals to accept grave financial burdens in exchange for direly needed bailout, in order to save their countries from defaults—which in turn was threatening to turn into a domino-effect of bankruptcies around the continent.

The austerity measures spurred mass protests among the affected public. With it, the political establishment was largely losing credibility in the eyes of the burdened people, leading to nationalist and populist actors gaining ground in many European countries. On the left flank, populists were gaining ground in Greece and Spain. However, populists were surging more on the right, leading to a paradigm shift in increased support for rogue challengers to the mainstream liberal democratic order.

The Rise of the Third Wave

As I will document in this chapter, the third wave saw nativist populism firmly moving from the fringes to become normalized. Most of these parties had abandoned open xenophobia, rather dressing their messages within more acceptable rhetoric. In the UK for instance, the more toned down populist UK Independence Party was replacing the openly racist BNP, which I discussed in the previous chapter. Later, the Brexit Party took over the rollers for a while. In France, the National Rally (previously named the National Front) found renewed support under the leadership of the more composed-looking Marine Le Pen, who had replaced her more aggressive father Jean-Marie Le Pen.

One of the greatest successes of populist parties in the third wave came in the 2014 European Parliament elections. In Denmark, France and the UK populists surged to the very front. Five years later, populists entered the EP in even greater numbers. Prior to the 2019 elections, European far-right populists had attempted to forge a continental alliance under the leadership of Italy's Matteo Salvini and Marine Le Pen in France. The US far-right strategist Steve Bannon was also trying to unite European populists in his Brussels-based group called The Movement. Bannon described Brussels as the beating heart of the globalist project, and said he wanted to 'drive the stake through the vampire' until the whole system started to disintegrate (qtd in Lewis 2018).

However, as I discussed in the Introduction to this book, it has proven difficult to unite nationalists across borders in a meaningful way, as each is primarily focused on domestic aspects. These parties have thus found difficulties in co-operating in the European Parliament and have, more or less, been split into at least three separate parliamentary groups. One of their dividing issues was that of Russia. While Salvini, Le Pen and Orbán aligned with Vladimir Putin, especially due to his opposition to both the US and the EU, others were more wary of Russia, for instance the Scandinavians and those in the Baltics, as well as also Kaczynski of Law and Justice in Poland.

Euroscepticism was also finding its way to Germany with the rise of Alternative for Germany, which secured significant support in the 2017 parliamentary elections. In the third wave, such sentiments were indeed spreading much further even in many of the more traditionally pro-EU countries than they had done in the two previous waves.

Populism was also on the rise in South America. The Chávismo regime in Venezuela had consolidated power, incarcerated leading opposition figures, and firmly forced much of media and civil society under their will. In 2017, Chávez's successor, Nicolás Maduro, dissolved parliament and shifted authority over to the newly established Constituent Assembly, which adhered to the will of the Chávismo regime.

Over in Greece, different kinds of populists were competing for power. Landing more than a fourth of the vote in 2012, the left-wing populist Syriza was sweeping across the country. When coming into government three years later they for example had to rely on ANEL, a small xenophobic right-wing party. That was necessary for keeping the neo-Nazi, Golden Dawn, from power. Over the course of the Euro Crisis Syriza became more and more domesticated, gradually adhering to demands from EU creditors of implementing austerity.

Left-wing populists also rose up in Spain, where anti-austerity Podemos was contesting traditional politics, taking more than one-fifth of the vote in the 2015 election. The mainstream Popular Party, which had been formed in the wake of Franco's death, was already highly nationalist. Nationalism in Spain also had a secessionist side, most notably in Catalonia and in the Basque country. Rough far-right movements had long found difficulty in breaking through, perhaps because of Spain's relatively recent fascist history. However, in the second general election of 2019, far-right populist Vox party came in third place, winning 15 per cent of the vote, and landing fifty-two out of 350 seats in parliament.

This was also a period of many contradictions. While most of the nativist populist parties were in this period getting rid of their openly xenophobic symbolism, this era also saw several more militant and openly racist parties gaining support in many other European countries. In Bulgaria the Attack Party was growing and the Jobbik movement in Hungary was at the time still outright neo-Nazi.

With many of these parties finding increased acceptability in society, even discredited authoritarian leaders of the past were again being rhetorically resurrected. Jörg Haider of Austria, for instance, dismissed much of the discussion around Austria's Nazi past, and leader of the Italian Lega, Matteo Salvini, openly voiced his admiration of Mussolini. In Russia, Vladimir Putin repeatedly moved to resurrect Stalin's reputation. Notorious policies that for a long while were collectively dismissed—such as of religious and racial segregation—were also emerging to the surface again.

Most horrendous in this third wave were several violent acts committed by far-right extremists. Amongst these were the attacks by Norwegian terrorist Anders Behring Breivik in 2011, and Tomas Mair who murdered MP Jo Cox in the UK in 2016. In 2019, Muslims were targeted by a shooter in Christchurch in New Zealand, and another shooter turned on Latinos in the US border town of El Paso. All of these perpetrators were believers in the extremist-right conspiracy theory called *The Great Replacement*. This is the belief that Muslims or other groups of migrants are actively plotting in secret to conquer the West in a hostile, albeit incremental, takeover.

Instrumental for the rise of nativist populism in the third wave was also the simultaneous growth of social media, which provided for much faster distribution of both fake news and controversial populist views.

SOCIAL MEDIA AND FAKE NEWS

The proliferation of fake news and conspiracy theories coincided with the emergence of digital media. Spreading lies and fabricated news stories to demonize political opponent is of course nothing new. In fact, it is right out of Machiavelli's (1550) playbook. Rumours, urban legends, folklore and other kinds of oral transmissions have always existed in human societies. And fabricated news was also spread by mainstream media outlets in the twentieth century. Distribution of bogus tales is thus not in itself a novel act. However, the emergence of the 24-hour rolling news broadcasts proved to be especially fertile for conspiratorial populists in transmitting distorted information. The take-off for these tales then became exponentially faster with the rapid growth of first online and then the social media outlets that followed. Since 2016, conspiracy theories, disguised as news, were blazing like a snowstorm across the political scene on both sides of the Atlantic.

British journalist and broadcaster Francis Wheen (2005), argued that reason was on the retreat in contemporary political discourse. Instead, he wrote that 'cults, quacks, gurus, irrational panics, moral confusion and an epidemic of mumbo-jumbo' characterizes our era. He warned that the values of the Enlightenment—the insistence on intellectual autonomy, commitment to free inquiry and dismissal of bigotry and persecution—were fast being abandoned.

The research by communications scholars in both Europe and in the US reveal that social media is the primary source of news for most people of the younger generations (Krasodomski-Jones 2019). This is a fundamental shift in the way we learn about the world and how we come to foster opinions. The revolutionary change in the media mechanism which the world rushed through in less than two decades has served to enable conspiratorial populists to bypass the previously powerful gatekeepers of the mainstream media, and instead bring their combative and polarizing political messages directly to the public. As a result, people have become exposed to much more unscrutinized information than ever before.

This overflow of information can render the public incapable of properly interpreting the avalanche of data that they are being exposed to. In effect, too much information can result in preventing us from being able to absorb knowledge in a meaningful way. In this flood of indiscriminate information people can find difficulty in navigating between facts and fabrications. When everything is true, nothing is true. This has opened up a space for misinformation to thrive, leaving the democratic space highly vulnerable to manipulation. Indeed, this has led to the emergence of a new political culture emerging, which has been branded Post-Truth politics.

Distorted information has impacted political discussion to the extent that debates in democratic elections have increasingly come to revolve round false stories. This has also facilitated the increased use of all kinds of informal rhetorical fallacies, which were discussed in a previous chapter. In this change, which has brought contradictions being openly embraced, a discourse appealing to emotions has grown stronger, with diminished emphasis on factual reasoning. This has resulted in public debates becoming more easily disconnected from testable facts. In this climate, discredited knowledge can smoothly rise to an equal prominence with established knowledge.

In both the Brexit referendum debate, and leading up to the US 2016 presidential election, data analysis company Cambridge Analytica was accused of manipulating social media by mining people's online data in order to produce individually targeted messages addressing different fears people were identified as bearing. Voters were bombarded with separate and sometimes contradictory content which was only loosely connected to reality, if at all. Here, we have entered into an era of information warfare, where people's private data has been weaponized and, indeed, often turned against the owner.

As I will discuss throughout in this chapter, conspiratorial populists have within this relatively new climate proved to be especially successful in spreading suspicion of the mainstream media, and against established knowledge which they claimed was produced by the elite, and eschewed in favour of the powerful. Alongside diminished gatekeeping capabilities of the mainstream media it becomes ever more difficult for people to distinguish between factual stories and fictitious news often spread via unscrupulous websites, as both can be presented in the same guise. And as Karen Douglas and her collaborators documented (2017), once a false story of a conspiracy takes hold, it can prove difficult to uproot.

This glut of fabricated information has also infiltrated more traditional media, which often picks up fabricated news and reports it as facts. Jovan Byford (2011) documents how CNN in the US broadcasted the agenda of the so-called Birther movement—the claim that former President Barack Obama was born in Kenya and therefore never eligible to be US President. Some insisted that he secretly was, in fact, a Muslim. Conspiracy theories were blazing during the Coronavirus Crisis of 2020.

The contagions of fake news, which initially were only spread from unscrupulous outlets is completed when it infects the mainstream media which duly distributes the fabricated stories, citing the bogus tales as a credible source. Here the mainstream media is turned on its head to become a far more powerful vehicle for fake news than social media outlets were ever able to do on their own. Only when picked up by the mainstream media does the distorted data find full credibility.

The Spread of Conspiracy Theories

In this new media environment, conspiracy theories have spread more easily than before.

Among the most persistent far-right conspiracy theories are suspicions of a New World Order dominating the world. Tales of the phenomenon have been prevalent over the last two centuries. Most often they revolve around global elites manipulating national governments. Commonly these bands of concealed evildoers are also accused of controlling international organizations behind the scenes, such as the International Monetary Fund, the United Nations and the World Bank.

The European Union is perhaps the international actor most often suspected of being this kind of a New World Order. Hungarian writer Janos Drabik (2017) for instance claimed that the EU 'is the institute of the plutocratic world-elite'. He insisted that the EU was not constructed for the benefit of the European people, but by the world-ruling elite. 'It is the transnational monetary cartel holding power over states that wants to get rid of national states by all means.' Drabik wrote that the global system was 'controlled from one single centre' and moved on to insist that the 'world-ruling elite has gradually annihilated the achievements of the Enlightenment'.

The EU has indeed for long been a target of many conspiracy theorists. Well-paid EU functionaries are popular culprits in many tales of a malignant order of this sort. Some say that the EU is the Roman Empire resurrected, others have claimed that it is a super-state led by the Antichrist. There are even those insisting that the institution itself is the Antichrist. In one version, it took the formation of a computer hiding deep within the Brussels apparatus, keeping track of everyone in the world (Boyer 1995).

A younger and perhaps also a more modest relative of New World Order theories are those of a Deep State controlling countries behind the scenes. In these, a domestic band of clandestine elites is suspected of ruling nations or regions. In these stories, society is seen not to be ruled by its official authorities, but instead by a secret band of hidden actors, a covert bureaucratic class. In Turkey, the term *derin devlet* refers to a cartel of politicians and bureaucrats in different governmental branches together with high-ranking military officials, as well as organized crime, covertly controlling the country.

Clearly, these kinds of suspicions might have some merits. Power can easily lie with people we do not know of. But when relentlessly upheld by populist politicians without evidence, they come to erode trust in society. And when these once peripheral politicians gain support and acceptance, and indeed power, then conspiracy theories become competitive knowledge.

Deep State theories rose to renewed prominence around the Tea Party in America. They were then elevated to new heights in the presidential campaign in 2016, which brought Donald Trump to power. In this latest version, a clandestine elite within the state apparatus is accused of manipulating American politics and government in a co-ordinated and systematic manner. Most proponents of this theory point to bureaucracies of the military complex and to spy agencies. Among them was the president himself. Donald Trump for instance described the Deep State as 'real, illegal and a threat to national security' (qtd in Porter 2017). In a 2017 poll, *ABC News* and *The Washington Post* found that almost half of Americans believed in a conspiratorial Deep State in the US.

During the Coronavirus Crisis of 2020 a range of conspiracy theories were spreading around the world. One, which was, for example, promoted by Republican Party Senator Tom Cotton, insisted that the virus had been created in a weapons lab in China to undermine Donald Trump. Trump's campaign advisor, Roger Stone, was amongst those that suspected that Bill Gates might have been involved in creating the virus in order to plant microchips in people (Fredricks 2020). A Pew Research Centre study in April 2020 found that 29% of Americans believed that Covid-19 was made in a lab (Schaeffer 2020).

The Great Replacement Theory

Another category focuses on external threats that can either be posed from aggressive foreign actors or infiltrators. As I have already mentioned, the most prominent theory around dangerous outsiders in contemporary time is that of Muslims occupying Europe and America—the fear of Muslims replacing the Christian population with Islamists. These have included notions of a White Genocide and the Eurabia theory.

In 2011 a deeply controversial French philosopher, Renaud Camus, titled his book as *The Great Replacement*. He argued that European civilization and identity was at risk of being subsumed by mass migration, especially from Muslim-dominated countries, and because of low birth rates among the native French people. Camus became one the most influential thinkers of the French *Identitarian* movement, which I discussed previously. This movement has grown fast among nativist populists, rooting in countries like Austria, Denmark, Germany, Italy and the UK.

Numerous nativist populist leaders in Europe have since promoted this theory, for example by nurturing the myth that migrants—especially Muslims—were taking over our national soil and heritage. This fear was nurtured by Geert Wilders of the Freedom Party in the Netherlands, who said that immigration was the greatest threat facing European culture. Wilders said that if Europe failed to defend itself against these malignant forces, it would be because Europe no longer believes in the superiority of its own civilization. On Twitter Wilders (2017) wrote: 'Our population is being replaced. No more.' Wilders linked his words to a video clip showing Muslims dominating the streets in Amsterdam. The video was titled 'Is this Iran or Pakistan? No, this is Amsterdam, the Netherlands.'

After pointing to this external threat to the nation, Wilders—in a classic Neo-Nationalist move—turned to accusing the domestic elite: 'In the Netherlands we are dealing with a social elite who are undertaking what I call an attack on the nation state, who undermine the Netherlands, who are hostile to the Dutch identity—hence multiculturalism, open borders, the European Union' (qtd in Duyvendak and Kesic 2018).

This is but one example of many similar moves made by several Neo-Nationalist leaders in Europe indicating that Europe was facing a hostile Muslim takeover. In Austria, H. C. Strache wrote that the Great Replacement had already taken place under mainstream governments. In Belgium, Dries Van Langenhove of the Flemish Block (VB) said 'we are being replaced' (qtd in Davey and Ebner 2019). In the 2019 federal elections, the VB had regained its former strength and again landed almost 12 per cent of the overall vote, becoming the second largest party nation-wide.

As will become evident in this chapter, the Great Replacement theory rose to new heights in the third wave of nativist populism. Sometimes proponents of the story have alluded to the full conspiracy theory, of malignant domestic forces orchestrating a population change in a campaign of ethnic cleansing aimed against the Christian white population.

An extensive quantitative study measuring the spread of the theory found that between April 2012 and April 2019 one and a half million tweets referred to the Great Replacement theory (Davey and Ebner 2019). The volume steadily grew over the period. The theory has also been fast moving into the mainstream. Both the mainstream media and traditional political parties started to follow suit.

Before the 2017 general election in the Netherlands, the centre-right Prime Minister Mark Rutte took out advertisements in several national newspapers where he criticized immigrants who refused to align with Dutch society. One of them read: 'Act normal or go away.' The aim was obviously not solely to convince Muslims in the Netherlands to change their ways. Rather the purpose was to reassure voters that they could trust Rutte to stand firm on migration, and that there was, thus, no need of supporting Wilders in order to take a tough stand on immigrants (Fekete 2018).

SHARIA PANIC

The Great Replacement theory was also alive and well in America. Senior editor at the *Atlantic* magazine, Adam Serwer (2011), identified a conspiracy theory he called the Sharia panic. This is the fear of American Muslims trying to undermine the US constitution and planning to overthrow the government. This was evident in the chants of neo-racist protestors in Charlottesville in Virginia in 2017, as I will discuss later in this chapter. Another and more specific version insisted that Muslim terrorists were hiding in about twenty-two to thirty-five secret training camps around America (see in Potok and Terry 2015). As I will also discuss later in this chapter, Latin American immigrants have also increasingly been portrayed as foreign invaders and as posing a threat to the demographic composition of the US.

Among those buying into this Great Replacement theory were several violent actors, such as the Australian terrorist in New Zealand who on 15 March 2019 killed fifty-one people in Mosque shootings in Christchurch. A seventy-four page so-called manifesto published by the shooter was simply titled *The Great Replacement*. It followed all the tropes of the White Genocide conspiracy theory and pointed to classical antagonism between the Christian and the Muslim world, and indeed alluded to a global war between the two.

The twenty-eight-year old attacker referred heavily to the French *Identitarian* movement, and he had donated significant amount of money to them (Davey and Ebner 2019). He also hailed Donald Trump as 'a symbol of renewed white identity and common purpose'. The shooter furthermore revealed that prior to the attack he had gotten the blessing of the notorious Norwegian terrorist Anders Bhering Breivik. Writing in the *Guardian*, Jason Wilson (2019) notes that the Christchurch shooter was brought up in Australia in a period when racism, xenophobia and anti-Muslim hostility had been normalized.

Tellingly for the times, the notorious act was livestreamed on Facebook and shared with millions of people. Australian senator for Queensland, Fraser Anning, wrote in the aftermath of the attack that the violence was the fault of migration and Muslims. 'The truth is', he wrote, 'that Islam is not like any other faith. It is the religious equivalent of fascism.'[1]

As previously mentioned, these same notions were also upheld by the murderer of Jo Cox in the UK, and the Norwegian terrorist Anders Behring Breivik, who believed that the Labour Party in Norway was in on the plot with the Islamists. I will return to discussing these violent responses to the Great Replacement theory where appropriate later in the text.

Conspiracy theories around Muslims have indeed been abundant in the milieu of the Neo-Nationalists. One insisted that a Muslim caliphate created the horrendous 2014 Ebola epidemic in Western Africa, and planned to weaponize the virus, for example by blowing up an Ebola victim on the busy Times Square in New York City. Perhaps the most far-fetched claim is that Islamic fascists inhabit the centre of the moon.

The progression of these tales in society is indicative of the snowballing effect of populism. Given the right conditions and texture they can trundle like an uncontrollable avalanche down a hill.

The Syrian War and the Refugee Crisis

The Great Replacement theory was elevated to new heights with the Refugee Crisis peaking in 2015 and 2016. In the wake of the conflicts in Syria and other countries in the Middle East and North Africa, Europe met with a sudden increased influx of refugees from Muslim-dominated countries. This brought renewed tensions over migration and counts as a significant shift within the third wave of nativist populism.

In fusing the frustrations of the Financial Crisis which was burdening the ordinary man, with fear of mass Muslim migration from war-ridden countries in the Middle East, nativist populism was growing to new levels. Underlying these fears was also the ongoing threat of Muslim terrorism—in less than a decade more than dozen major terrorist attacks had been committed by Muslim actors in Europe.

With the increased flow of migrants from Muslim-dominated countries, right-wing populists in Europe have firmly moved away from their anti-Semitic stance of former times. Instead they have come to focus on a covert Islamist plot of taking over control in Europe. This is one of the distinctions between the fascist version of nationalism in the interwar years and the nativist populist Neo-Nationalism of the post-war years.

Although we have surely seen a significant evolution in the demographic composition of Europe since the Second World War, with increasing numbers of people coming from the Middle East and North Africa, the sudden flood of refugees out of Syria in 2015 did not alter the demographic construction on the European continent in any drastic way. Still, that is exactly what many nativist populists have maintained. In wake of the crisis, which receded in 2017 and 2018, Muslims accounted for only roughly 5 per cent of the population in the European Union. An estimation by the Pew Research Centre indicates that by the year 2050 the Muslim population will rise to between 7.4 and 14 per cent.[2] Many of these people are, however, expected to move away from their traditional Muslim heritage and integrate into the contemporary European lifestyle.

Studies have found that people tended to overestimate the Muslim population. In France, respondents in the before-mentioned study thought that Muslims stood at 31 per cent, when in reality they were 8 per cent. In America, respondents on average thought that Muslims amounted to 17 per cent of the population, when in reality they were only around 1 per cent (ibid.).

Despite the relatively low percentages of immigrants in the West—compared to the intensity of the public debate about them—fears of immigration were still dominating much of politics in Europe. A poll in 2016 found that around two-thirds of respondents in countries like Denmark, Hungary and Germany said that immigration was the most pressing political issue at the time (Mounk 2018). Correspondingly, a UK study found that immigration was the most common concern directing a Leave vote in the Brexit referendum (Judis 2018).

Given this distortion between perception and reality it is perhaps not surprising that immigration was often found to be the most pressing political issue, only surpassed by fear of terrorism.

ALTERNATIVE FOR GERMANY

Germany is an especially interesting case for analysing the third wave of nativist populism. Mainly due to the desolations of the Nazi past, nationalism had in the post-war era been discredited and indeed firmly suppressed in Western Germany. However, during the Euro Crisis, and the following Refugee Crisis, nationalism was also re-emerging in Germany. Over the past two decades Germany had in a way sublimated its nationalism into the European Union. In other words, its pro-EU position can be seen as a kind of cloak for national ambitions on the world stage.

Similar to the True Finns in Finland, the party Alternative for Germany (*Alternative für Deutschland*—AfD) was established in 2013 in opposition to bailing out mainly southern European countries during the Euro Crisis. Due to several academics present in its leadership they were initially and ever so cosily branded as the Professors' party. Soon though, they broadened their appeal. The influential tabloid *Bild* also threw its weight behind that same message. One of its many headlines on the subject read: 'Stop! No More Billions for the Greedy Greeks' (qtd in Barfield 2015).

With the Refugee Crisis rising to new heights, another movement was also gaining more ground: Patriotic Europeans against the Islamization of the Occident (PEDIGA) took to organizing many protest rallies against Muslims and migrants around the country, mainly in the former eastern part. Among their slogans was 'Wir sind das Volk', meaning 'we are the people'.

The Refugee Crisis of 2015 marked a turnaround for populist politics in Germany. At its height, Chancellor Angela Merkel reversed her policy of stemming the tight of refugees and decided to allow Syrian mass migration into Germany. 'We can manage this', she famously declared. Within a year more than one million refugees were allowed entry into Germany.

This was a reversal of her previous opposition to immigration. Previously she had catered to the concerns that many nationalist conservatives had over immigration. At a conference of the party's youth movement in Potsdam in 2010 she declared that multicultural society had 'utterly failed', maintaining that the idea of different cultures living happily side by side 'did not work' (qtd in Fekete 2018).

With her decision in 2015, Angela Merkel then became the (unlikely) spearhead of the multilateralist and liberal democratic Europe. The leader of the conservative Christian Democrats—an east-German daughter of a protestant pastor, and a staunch believer in transatlantic relations—was now being celebrated by the social liberal left in Europe. For the brave decision, *Time* magazine in America crowned her Person of the Year.

Not all were happy though. She instantly came under massive criticism from conservatives and nationalists. After several criminal incidents committed by migrants in Germany, nationalist and anti-Muslim voices grew louder. After the 2015/16 New Year's Eve festivities in Cologne, news stories were breaking of mass mobs of migrants sexually harassing and even raping native German women. This spurred an outrage across the country and seriously undermined Merkel's open-door policy. Nicole Hörchst, AfD Member of Parliament, used the opportunity to place her nativist populist party as the only protector of women's rights in Germany, pointing to the 'danger of losing the freedoms and rights of women for which we've fought for centuries' (qtd in Chrisafis et al. 2019).

When the stories of harassment were later rolled back as blown out of all proportion, and indeed for being mostly false, many within the nativist populist milieu dismissed the correction as coming from the lying press, *Lügenpresse* in German (Fekete 2018.).

THE NEW NATIONALISTS

To understand the sudden rise of nativist populists in Germany, like elsewhere in the third wave, it is necessary to examine the conjunction of these two otherwise separate crises, the Refugee Crisis following the Euro Crisis. These two trends gradually found a unified platform within the AfD. For the first time since the Second World War, prominent forces in Germany were defying the defamation of nationalism in Germany. Underground far-right nationalist movements had of course, always existed in the post-war era. In 2011, a neo-Nazi terror cell called the Nationalist Socialist Underground was revealed as having over previous decades committed several murders and other violent acts, against mainly Muslim migrants (Fekete 2018). By 2017, however, nationalism was no longer only underground in Germany.

With the Refugee Crisis, AfD representatives were no longer primarily focused on rolling back European integration and stopping financial aid to crisis-ridden countries. Under Frauke Perry, the party firmly set its sights against migration, rejected the ideals of multiculturalism and declared that 'Islam does not belong in Germany' (qtd in Judis 2018). Party leaders have said that people of non-German ethnic origin cannot be considered as belonging to the German nation. Perry also wanted to widen the appeal. Similar to attempts made by the Sweden Democrats—discussed later in this chapter—she wanted the AfD to fill the vacuum left by the German Social Democratic Party.

AfD representatives have also questioned taboos around the country's Nazi past, suggesting that Germans should be allowed to be proud of their military actions in the past. Björn Höcke for example questioned the relevance of the Holocaust monument in Berlin, saying that Germans 'were the only people in the world to plant a monument of shame in the heart of their capital' (qtd in Judis 2018).

In the 2017 election, Alternative for Germany won 12.6 per cent of the vote and became the third largest party. This was the first time a far-right nationalist party got elected to the German parliament since the Nazi party in 1933. The rise of the AfD is perhaps one of the most significant indicators of how far into the mainstream Neo-Nationalism has travelled in the third wave. Echoing the rhetoric of Trump in America, and that of the Brexit campaign in Britain, AfD leader Alexander Gauland set out 'to take our country back' (qtd in Snyder 2018). The two main parties responded with again forming a grand coalition across the political spectrum, leading the AfD to become the country's primary opposition party.

Since the Refugee Crisis of 2015 the AfD has been promoting the Great Replacement conspiracy theory, discussed above. Migrants were placed as the external threat to Germany, while mainly the Western German political elite were cast as the domestic traitors. Before the 2019 European Parliament election, the party ran posters depicting a naked white woman surrounded by Muslim men, having a brown-skinned finger placed in her mouth. The caption said: Vote for us so that Europe won't become Eurabia.'

Support for the AfD has been greatest in eastern Germany, in the former DDR regions, such as Brandenburg, Saxony, Thuringia and Mecklenburg. Many felt left out during the economic boom, which was mainly enjoyed in Western Germany. Jobs were still low-pay and insecure. Interestingly the support of PEDIGA and AfD was much greater in these eastern areas where there were fewer immigrants. AfD representatives have squared that by saying that they wanted to reserve eastern Germany for white Christians (see Fekete 2018).

Although the AfD was more popular in eastern Germany, its support was never limited to only the usual suspects of far-right voters, that is, the lower-educated blue-collar and backward-looking losers of globalization. The party also enjoyed significant support from people of other creeds, young and old, prosperous and poor, educated and illiterate (Klages 2019). The only factor apart from geography separating AfD supporters from others were their attitudes to refugees and migrants. In other words, xenophobes from all levels and swaths of society supported Alternative for Germany.

Germanic Differences

When it comes to the prominence of nativist populist parties, Austria differs from Germany in fundamental ways. As I discussed in previous chapters, such parties had for decades held a strong position in Austria. In the third wave, they still grew stronger.

Similar to trends elsewhere, in countries where nativist populists have found prolonged and significant support, the mainstream in Austrian politics was suffering. This became especially evident in the 2016 presidential election. Leading up to the vote both the Social Democrats and the conservative Christian Democratic People's Party, the ÖVP—the two had effectively alternated in occupying the largely ceremonial presidency—found diminished support.

In the run-off, both were surpassed by challenger parties, the Green Party and, indeed, the far-right populist Freedom Party. This forced even mainstream conservatives to support their polar opposite in Austrian politics, the Green Party candidate, Van der Bellen. In unifying against the nativist populist candidate, the mainstream was only narrowly able to prevent Freedom Party's Norbert Hofer from being handed the keys to the Hofburg Imperial Palace in Vienna. Similar to other populists, Hofer claimed to have the people with him. You have high society behind you, he said, but I have the people.

The Freedom Party also did well in the 2017 parliamentary election. And although the ÖVP won the election, its leader Sebastian Kurz felt forced to in invite the Freedom Party into his government. Not so surprisingly it proved to be a struggle for Kurz to keep his populist partners in check, leaving the government tainted by their offensive and often racist comments. Leader of the Freedom Party, Vice Chancellor Heinz-Christian Strache, played into the Great Replacement conspiracy theory when stating that it was necessary to fend off a 'population exchange' (qtd in Shields 2019). Illustrative for his politics, the Freedom Party released a photo of Strache taken when he was attending a campaign against building a mosque in Vienna in 2009. Dressed in black, the photo showed him holding a large white cross, appearing as a warrior and saviour of the pure people (see Wodak 2015).

As I mentioned above, there are fundamental differences between the two German-speaking countries. While nativist populism has been prominent and sometimes dominant in Austria, their rise was much more recent in Germany.

Up North

The range and variations of nativist populism in the Nordic countries makes the region an interesting case for understanding the phenomena more broadly. Prior to the rise of the third wave these brands of parties had only found success in two out of the five Nordic states. As was established in previous chapters, Denmark had in the wake of the Second World War started out being open, tolerant and social-liberal. However, from the 1970s two populist parties were able to turn the small Nordic state to implement perhaps the toughest legislation on immigration in Western Europe. Since the turn of the millennium, migration has become the most discussed topic in Denmark, mainly revolving around concerns over Muslims in this predominantly Christian society.

The cultural nationalism in the Danish Peoples Party's discourse was, for example, found in its emphasis on Christian values and the link between the state and the Evangelic-Lutheran Church. On that ground the party positioned itself as a protector of Danish culture, in a word, of Danishness (*Danskhed*). In doing so, DF representatives often referred to specific Danish values, which primarily consist of Christian values and family values in addition to the Danish cultural heritage, all framed within the parameters of the Danish national identity (Gad 2010).

The party clearly defined nationality by ethnicity. Still, although they were highly instrumental in the 'othering' process of foreigners, it should, however, be stressed that no evidence of outright racism was found in the party's material. While avoiding being openly racist the DF was especially skilful in separating immigrants from ethnic Danes, that is, in distinguishing between 'others' and 'us'. Its nationalism thus combined both cultural and ethnic elements.

This identity-based rhetoric was also moralist. In firmly relying on a moral frame of 'us', 'others' were negatively represented as culturally inferior (e.g. Boréus 2010). Swedish political scientist Jens Rydgren (2010) defines this as a 'neo-racist rhetoric', where national values were portrayed as being under threat from immigration.

The DF's 2009 manifesto concluded that a multicultural society was destined to be 'without inner context and cohesion' and 'burdened by lack of solidarity' and, therefore, 'prone to conflict' (qtd in Widfeldt 2015). To prevent such a travesty, party members argued that Danish society should be shielded from foreign impact. As a result, the presence of ethnic minorities was discursively problematized and presented as a threat to a fragile homogeneous Danish culture. Karen Wren (2001) described this depiction in Denmark as 'a historically rooted set of traditions now under threat from globalization, the EU, and from "alien" cultures'.

On law and order, the DF started out from a quite authoritarian standpoint. The party emphasized traditional Christian family values. However, when criticizing Islam for intolerance, they would move to place themselves on the side of social liberalism. In their 2009 manifesto, Islam was identified as an enemy of the LGBTQ community, saying that 'in recent decades, homosexuals have come under pressure from intolerant Islamic groups'. The DF vowed to work determinedly against oppression and discrimination against homosexuals. Similar to the German AfD, discussed above, the Danish Peoples Party had turned around to become the protector both of women and gay rights.

From the Fringe

The Danish People's Party gradually grew to become perhaps most influential political party in the country, a positioned it held for almost two decades. It also influenced most other political parties, who one after another—across the left/right dividing lines—gradually became much more anti-immigrant than before, to the extent that even the previously condemned policies of the DF were now largely upheld by the mainstream.

Supporting right-of-centre governments without accepting ministerial posts worked to the DF's advantage. The party found significant influence while also being able to distance itself from the government's more unpopular decisions. From that position, the DF was able to push through perhaps the strictest immigration laws in the entire Western world. Their polarizing division between 'us' and 'them' evolved to become a commonly shared understanding in the immigrant debate across the political spectrum.

After landing in opposition, the DF only went from strength to strength. In the 2014 European Parliament elections, they came out on the very top. In the following year, the DF won one-fifth of the vote in the general election and became the largest party on the right flank in Denmark. Under leadership of Kristian Thulessen Dahl, who had replaced Pia Kjærsgaard at the helm—she became Chair of Parliament—the DF went back to supporting *Venstre*'s right-wing minority government.

The DF did not meet many hindrances on its road to hardening the already punitive Danish immigration policy even further. Their first demand was to stop accepting quota refugees, and then to tighten border control, for example by reinstating checks on the German border. This occurred again after an increased flow of Syrian refugees. Other European countries followed suit, for example Sweden, which even introduced temporary border control on the Øresund Bridge.

Throughout the process of acquiring mainstream acceptance, the DF firmly kept up its anti-immigrant rhetoric, as illustrated in the following two examples.

In a TV debate in November 2010 Pia Kjærsgaard suggested banning satellite dishes in immigrants' 'ghettos', because, she said, they were ugly and because they brought Muslims in Denmark access to Arabic TV channels such as *Al-Jazeera* and *Al Arabiya* (Klein 2013).

In the wake of the Paris terrorist attack in late 2015, where Muslim jihadists mainly from Belgium and France killed 129 people, the DF's Foreign Policy spokesman Søren Espersen (2015) said in a TV interview that Western military forces should now start bombing civil targets in Syria, specifically also in areas where there were women and children.

Nativist Welfare

The DF was especially skilful in catering to its voter base. Their supporters were of a relatively low level of education, more in manual labour than specialist, more rural or suburban than urban, and either young or old rather than middle-aged. DF supporters were equally split across left and right. They had a relatively low level of trust in other citizens but believed more in their own leader than members of other parties tended to do.

When analysing the success of the Danish Peoples Party a specific winning formula can be detected. Rather than adhering to Herbert's Kitschelt's formula of combining an anti-immigrant stance with neoliberal economic policies, the DF instead combined social welfare policy and nationalist-chauvinist ideas. Here, the party struck a chord with less educated voters who in the past had voted for the Social Democrats. As I mentioned above, many right-wing populist parties in Europe have indeed tapped into the traditional voter base of social democratic parties. The DF success similarly came at the expense of the Danish Social Democrats.

As I have already discussed, the DF was successfully transformed from being a fringe party with marginal impact to become one of the most influential parties in Danish politics. Interestingly, it did this by changing the political discourse in Denmark on immigration and Islam rather than by altering its own message. Their once-condemned policies not only became fully normalized, but also much more widely supported in society. Generally, the debate had shifted away from accommodating migrants, which it had centred on in the 1960s, to measures of expelling them from the country. In 2018 a law was introduced that set longer sentences for crimes committed in immigrant ghettos. A DF member of parliament, Martin Henriksen, also proposed that children living in these ghettos should be subject to evening curfews, which would be enforced by wearing ankle bracelets (Graham-Harrison and Rasmussen 2018).

Frustrated by seeing their support bleed over to the Danish Peoples Party, the Social Democrats—the once hegemonic power in Danish politics—began to follow in the direction of the DF. During the 2015 general election debate, the then leader Helle Thorning Scmidt embarked on a campaign advocating imposing stricter rules on asylum seekers, and of demanding tighter demands on immigrants to adhere to Danish values. The Social Democrats voted in favour of a law allowing the state to strip refugees of their jewellery and other valuables.

A much more significant shift occurred after Mette Fredriksen assumed stewardship in 2015. With Fredriksen at the helm the Social Democrats took several further steps to abandon their former socio-liberal stance against the DF's callous immigration policy. Instead, they more or less made it their own, for instance in proposing a cap on non-Western immigrants, and of shipping asylum seekers to reception centres in North Africa.

Paradigm Shift

The story of the DF's impact on the Social Democratic Party in Denmark is interesting for understanding the dynamics between populist and mainstream parties. In the so-called Paradigm Shift legislation of 2019, the Social Democrats even came to support the right-wing government's increased restrictions on immigrants. The measures included a ban on wearing the burqa, and increased the automatic repatriation of refugees out of Denmark—although by then Denmark had already been all but closed to refugees.

By the 2019 general election the DF had fallen victim to its own success and saw its support cut by more than half. The downfall was mainly caused by other parties closing in on their space, largely by copying DF policies. First, *Venstre* had regained some of its lost support by adopting the strict anti-immigrant stance of the DF, followed by the Social Democrats who leading up to the 2019 elections were vigorously targeting the more authoritarian working-class voters.

Simultaneously, the DF also felt squeezed from the other side, from the even further out and more extreme right. In addition to others stealing their anti-immigration policies, two new parties, positioned further out on the fringe, ran with far more extremist views than had ever been heard before in prominent Danish politics—including a call for expelling all Muslims out of the country.

The two new parties, New Right and Hard Line, emerged to challenge the DF from the fringe. New Right was much more firmly nativist, anti-EU and economic right-wing than the DF, and Hard Line was outright racist. In other words, the DF was outflanked—perhaps similar to what both Glistrup and Kjærsgaard had done before.

After themselves becoming an established party in a position of power, the DF was no longer seen as a challenger. Instead it had become the new mainstream, now contested from the outer periphery. The difference was that after they had over decades gradually been able to turn the discourse on immigration to become much tougher than before, the new challenger parties had to go much further in their defiance than their predecessors had. Leader of Hard Line, Rasmus Paludan stated that mass migration had turned Danish streets into rivers of blood—here, the previously mentioned rivers-of-blood notion of Enoch Powell is reproduced. In a video to his followers posted on YouTube, Paludan said: 'The best thing would be if there were not a single Muslim left on this earth. I hope that will happen someday. Then we would have reached our goal' (see Elabdi 2019).

Although the style of the new parties and their position in Danish politics was perhaps comparable to the Progress Party and the Danish Peoples Party when they had emerged onto the scene in Danish politics, the stance of the new parties was much tougher. As result, the anti-immigrant field had become much more fragmented in Danish politics. Only the milder version of the two, New Right, won seats in parliament. Hard Line fell just short of the threshold.

What stands out from the 2019 election is that even though the DF massively lost support, their politics was still the greater winner. In fact, political positions that previously had been kept out on the fringe were now the new normal. After the election, Mette Fredriksen came to lead a Social Democratic minority government, which continued to uphold much of the immigration policy pushed through by the Danish Peoples Party.

Not everyone was happy with this move. When accepting the Nordic Council 2019 Literary Prize, young Danish writer Jonas Eika confronted his Prime Minister, who was sitting in the front row, for continuing the former government's racist language and policies. Not only had racism become widely accepted, but he insisted that it had been institutionalized in Denmark. Eika went on to criticize other Nordic leaders in the audience, saying that many of them were contributing to the militarizing of the EU borders in a process that risked the lives of thousands of migrants.

SNEAK ISLAMIZATION

Further north, immigration had also evolved to become the issue most discussed by the Progress Party of Norway, being mentioned twice as often in the 2009 election campaign than health care, the next most frequent topic of party members. Party leader Siv Jensen, who had succeeded Carl I. Hagen in 2006, warned against what she referred to as 'sneak Islamisation' (qtd in Jupskås 2015). The notion alludes to a hidden process already in place, which eventually would alter Norway and turn it away from its liberal Christian roots towards becoming a Muslim-based society. In flirting with the Great Replacement conspiracy theory, Siv Jensen maintained that demands of the Muslim community, such as on halal meat being served in schools, the right to wear hijab and of public celebration of Muslim holidays, were all examples of such sneak Islamization.

Despite the tough anti-Islam rhetoric, the FrP succeeded in portraying itself as a much milder right-wing nativist populist party than those on the continent. They refused being compared to the Danish People's Party or the French National Front (now the National Rally). Siv Jensen was also successful in broadening the FrP's political platform, moving away from the initial anti-tax campaign, and later immigration, to emerging as a more normal multi-issue party, which eventually brought it closer to the mainstream. Their principal manifesto for the period between 2013 and 2017 stated that it was a liberal party based on 'the Norwegian constitution, Norwegian and Western tradition and cultural heritage, founded on the Christian outlook of life and humanistic values'. Their success in this regard is evident in the fact that they never faced similar boycotting attempts and isolation by the political establishment as did several other populist parties.

In the 2009 general election, the FrP won almost one-quarter of the vote, by then the best result of any populist party in the region, and among the very best Europe-wide. Despite striving to distance itself from extremist parties elsewhere, the FrP always had a clear populist verve. They firmly positioned themselves as defenders of the ordinary people, of '*folk flest*' as the phrase goes in Norwegian. Similar to the Danish Peoples Party they successfully tapped into the voter base of the Labour Party and repositioned themselves as Norway's workers' party. Their voter base was also similar to populist parties elsewhere, mainly the under-educated working class or unemployed of the youngest and oldest voter groups. Surveys showed that the most important issue for their supporters was indeed immigration, law and order, care for the elderly and reduced taxes (Jupskås et al. 2016).

Similarly to the influence of the Danish Peoples Party in Denmark, it has also been documented how both the Labour Party and the Conservative Party of Norway gradually came to adopt much of the FrP's rhetoric on immigration (Simonnes 2011).

The Breivik Effect

Although the FrP was of a relatively milder kind within the realm of nativist populism, Norway has still seen its fair share or violent far-right extremism. The most horrible and traumatic incident was the terrorist attack of Anders Behring Breivik on 22 July 2011, killing seventy-seven people in a bomb blast in the administration quarter in Oslo, and in a gun massacre at the Labour Party Youth movement camp in Utøya, 38 kilometres west of Oslo. Eight were killed in Oslo and sixty-nine slaughtered in Tyrilfjorden, most of them were teenagers and very young members of the Labour Party Youth Movement. Although a lone wolf attacker, Breivik claimed to belong to the international Christian organization of Knight Templars fighting a holy war against Marxism and multiculturalism.

Breivik previously belonged to the FrP but had not found success meeting his ambition. He never got beyond Vice-Chairman of the party's youth movement for Western Oslo. He had also grown frustrated with the party being too soft on immigration.

The effect of the domestic-grown terrorist attack in Norway was one of unification, perhaps best captured in the pledge of Prime Minister Jens Stoltenberg, of more openness, more humanity and more democracy. An influential critic of welfare-oriented and social-liberal Norway, American expat Bruce Bawer (2012) wrote a book describing how the social-liberal left had used the terrorist act as a tool to silence the debate about Islam. He went so far as to accuse Labour Party supporters of being the new Quislings of Norway.[3]

The Breivik attack caused the Progress Party grave difficulty and threatened its hard-earned legitimacy. The party leadership campaigned vigorously to disown him and instantly toned down its anti-Muslim rhetoric. For that, Pia Kjærsgaard of the Danish People's Party was critical and said that Siv Jensen 'lacked spine' (qtd in Skarvoy and Svendsen 2011). Siv Jensen was only happy to use the opportunity to distance herself and her party from Kjærsgaard and her crew in Denmark. Still, the FrP was severely punished in the 2011 local elections.

The setback proved only to be temporary. Two years later they had won back much of their lost support and landed in government, as a junior partner in a minority coalition with the Conservative Party.

The Breivik attack revealed a hidden sub-culture in Norway, simmering underneath the surface on the Internet—a network of racist and Islamophobic groups operating around the country. One of the main forums for this politics was the online platform *document.no*, where Norwegian racists exchanged their views.

Breivik's main hero on the platform called himself *Fjordman*. This 'dark prophet of Norway', as he was referred to, warned that ethnic Norwegians would soon be in a minority if the political elite continued to destroy European culture and turn the continent into a 'Eurabia'. Fjordman also contributed to the web portal, *Gates of Vienna*. The name refers to the siege of Vienna in 1683, where Europeans defeated an invading Ottoman army. The overall narrative was of unravelling a socio-liberal cabal conspiring with Islamic forces of turning the continent into Eurabia. Breivik responded with a call to all cultural conservatives of defying the demographic infiltration of Muslims and proposed taking actions to expel all Muslims from Norway (Seierstad 2015).

Numerous other far-right movements have existed in Norway. Norwegian racism usually does not accept being racist at all. Public versions had indeed surely and squarely moved away from being biologically based, towards being culturally based. However, such former versions did still exist, as evident at the time of the Breivik trial when Roma people set up camp in Oslo. The camp suffered numerous attacks and they were described as 'rats' and 'inhuman' (see Booth 2014).

DOG WHISTLING

As discussed, the initial response to Breivik's attack was severe and almost universal. But it did not lead to the demise of nativist populist tactics. An interesting example of the FrP's dog-whistle racism came before the September 2017 parliamentary elections. For several days Norway's integration minister, FrP's Sylvi Listhaug, let almost the entire political debate revolve around her planned visit to the Stockholm immigrant-dominated suburb of Rinkeby, in neighbouring Sweden. Seeing falling support ahead of the election, Listhaug played out the one card that was most likely to turn the tide for her party—the anti-Muslim card.

In front of the media cameras she warned against lenient immigration policies, like those in Sweden. Calling them 'no-go zones', Listhaug told tales of 'parallel societies having developed in more than sixty places in Sweden'. In these no-go zones, she said, were 'a large quantity of people with immigrant backgrounds'. She went on to insist that they were festered with 'conditions of lawlessness and criminals in control'.[4]

The Norwegian minister for integration repeatedly warned against a foreign policy she referred to as the 'Swedish condition'. The *Financial Times* wrote that the term was a code for 'gang warfare, shootings, car burnings and other integration problems' in the neighbouring country (Milne 2017).

Although Listhaug's statements were widely debunked and dismissed as unfounded, that did not cause her or her party any suffering at the polls. On the contrary, the FrP only saw increased support in the wake of the controversy. After rewinning her seat in parliament, she continued to uphold similar rhetoric, and in March 2018 she posted on Facebook an accusation that the Labour Party put the rights of terrorists above national security.

True Finns and the Crisis

Although Finland had surely seen its fair share of wide-ranging nationalist movements, right-wing populist parties similar to those in neighbouring countries only rose to prominence when the True Finns Party surged in the wake of the Euro Crisis hitting in 2009. Their charismatic leader, Timo Soini, was quick to position his party against EU bailout for crisis-ridden countries in southern Europe. Soini saw his party as a forceful channel for the underclass and asked, 'why should Finland bail anyone out?' He called for Greece to be expelled from the Eurozone and said: 'We won't allow Finnish cows to be milked by other hands' (qtd in Judis 2018).

In the European Parliament election of 2009, the True Finns won almost one-tenth of the vote. Two years later they surged in the general election, landing almost one-fifth of the vote. Their success came by hijacking almost the entire political agenda when debating the Euro Crisis.

With the EU and the European Central Bank seemingly powerless, the True Finns said that the system favoured elites over ordinary citizens. One of its most vocal members, Jussi Halla-aho, wrote on Facebook that Greece's debt problems would not be resolved without a military junta.

The True Finns were able to break up a stagnant party system where three mainstream parties had for decades alternated in ruling the country. From 2009, however, Finnish politics came to a significant degree to revolve around the Finns Party and its populist politics. Prior to finding success, they had widely been dismissed as a joke, a harmless protest movement, a nuisance on the fringe of Finnish politics (Raunio 2013). Their discourse was deemed to be aggressive and crude, and the media mostly only saw entertainment value in them. After the 2011 election, however, they had surely become a force to be reckoned with. They clashed with the mainstream parties and called for the end of the one-truth cosy consensus politics of the three established parties. Soon, some of mainstream parties began to follow suit and came to adopt much of their anti-EU rhetoric.

In the 2015 election Timo Soini led his party to land in government for the first time. Since then, it has seen diminished support. Interestingly, unlike many other parties of a similar ilk, the True Finns accepted the populist label. Timo Soini, who had actually written a master thesis on populism, even celebrated the label, saying that their aim was indeed to please the ordinary man. Soini however refused the extreme-right label. Accordingly, the English version of the party's name was changed to the Finns Party.

Contrary to the Progress Parties of Denmark and Norway, the Finnish populists never flirted with neo-liberalism. Rather, they inherited the centrist economic policy of the SMP, which I discussed in a previous chapter. Its right-wing populism was thus never socio-economic, but rather only socio-cultural.

Three main themes emerged as the political platform of the Finns Party. First, resurrecting the 'forgotten people', the ordinary man, to prominence and speaking in their name against the elite. Second, fighting against immigration and multiculturalism. Third, stemming Europeanization of Finland.

The Forgotten People

Despite Finland being a classic Nordic welfare state based on a long-standing tradition of consensus politics, its heritage was also one of deeply rooted polarization. The dividing lines ran between East and West, Socialism and Nationalism, Urban-rich versus Rural-poor and between the Cosmopolitan and the Local.

Like the SMP the Finns Party was highly successful in exploiting the centre/periphery divide, effectively exchanging the agrarian-focused populism for a more general cultural division based on a more ethno-nationalist programme. The phrase the 'forgotten people', referred to the underprivileged ordinary man neglected by the political elite.

In this formulation, the political elite was presented as corrupt and arrogant and it was continuously accused of having suppressed the ordinary blue-collar man. Positioning themselves against the urban Helsinki-based cosmopolitan political elite, the Finns Party claimed to speak in the name of the 'forgotten people', mainly in rural areas.

Drawing on traditional Christian values, the Finns Party discursively depicted the 'forgotten people' as pure and morally superior to the privileged elite. This sort of moralist stance was widely found in their 2011 election manifesto, including claims of basing their politics on 'honesty', 'fairness', 'humaneness', 'equality', 'respect for work and entrepreneurship' and 'spiritual growth' (see Raunio 2013).

CHRISTIAN VALUES

The Finns Party proved to be staunchly conservative on issues like religion, morality, crime, corruption and law and order. They campaigned for Christian values, for families and family size firms, increased military and police spending, while simultaneously arguing against gender equality, openness, social diversity, same-sex marriage and sexual liberties (Norocel 2017). It was thus rather authoritarian than libertarian, tough on crime, and took a tough moralist line on drugs and alcohol abuse, cemented in Christian society and family values.

The Finns Party was surely anti-elite, but they were in no way anti-system. Indeed, the party firmly supported the Finnish state, its institutions and democratic processes, including keeping the relatively strong powers of the President. The political programme emphasized ethno-nationalism, strongly focusing on Finnish national cultural heritage. They were suspicious of Swedish influence, dismissive of the Sami's heritage in Suomi, and outright suppressive in regard to the small Gypsy population.

In a classical populist 'us' versus 'them' style, a running theme was on Finnishness, of distinguishing Finns from others. Rather than a mixing of cultures within the naturally drawn nation-state, the Finns Party instead emphasized a mosaic of co-existing nations in Europe (Pyykkönen 2011).

The Finns Party promoted patriotism, strength and unselfishness and suggested that the Finnish miracle should be taught in schools, emphasizing how this poor and peripheral country suppressed by expansionist and powerful neighbours was by internal strength and endurance able to fight their way from under their oppressors to become a globally recognized nation of progress and wealth.

Like both the Danish Peoples Party and the Progress Party in Norway, the Finns Party was welfare-chauvinist. On ethno-nationalist grounds they emphasized first protecting native Finns but excluding others. On this platform, a more radical and outright xenophobic faction thrived within the party. Jussi Halla-aho, who became perhaps Finland's most forceful critic of immigration and multiculturalism, led the anti-immigrant faction. After an internal split which saw the back of Timo Soini and many of the more moderate faction out of the party, Halla-aho became party leader in 2017.

AGAINST (NON-EXISTENT) ISLAM

Jussi Hallo-aho has frequently been accused of racial hatred. In 2012 he was convicted for disturbing religious worship and of ethnic agitation (see Dunne 2014). When discussing immigration on his blog, he wrote that 'since rapes will increase in any case, the appropriate people should be raped: in other words, green-leftist do-gooders and their supporters'.[5] Hallo-aho described Islam as a 'totalitarian fascist ideology' and wrote that the prophet Muhammad was a paedophile. He insisted that Islam indeed sanctified paedophilia.[6]

Many other examples of defiance against immigration exist among members of the Finns Party. A well-known party representative, Olli Immonen, posted on Facebook in 2015 a photo of himself with members of the borderline neo-Nazi extreme-right group, the Finnish Resistance Movement. He wrote that he would give his life for the battle against multiculturalism. In another Facebook post, he said that he was 'dreaming of a strong, brave nation that will defeat this nightmare called multiculturalism. This ugly bubble that our enemies live in, will soon enough burst into a million little pieces (qtd in Winneker 2015).

Jussi Hallo-aho contributed extensively to the anti-immigration online forum, *Homma*. He said that our era would forever leave a mark on the future of the Finnish nation. 'I have strong belief in my fellow fighters. We will fight until the end for our homeland and one true Finnish nation. The victory will be ours' (ibid.).

The shift in the rhetoric from placing the EU and its bailout programme for crisis-ridden countries in southern Europe as the main external threat, to Muslim migrants replacing Brussels as the arch enemy of the Finnish people, simply follows the progression in time, as is discussed above, from the Euro Crisis to the Migration Crisis.

Many other prominent populist and extreme-right associations existed in Finland. In the wake of the 2015 Refugee Crisis, a group calling themselves Soldiers of Odin took to patrolling the street of several Finnish towns. Dressed in black jackets, decorated with Viking symbolism and the Finnish flag, they claimed to be protecting native Finns from any potential violent acts of foreigners. Perhaps it is significant that this they did despite Finland never having belonged to the Viking heritage.

In the 2019 parliamentary elections the Finns Party became the second largest, following closely on the heels of the Social Democrats. The liberal democratic mainstream in Finland responded by forming a five-party coalition, which mainly served to keep the Finns Party out of government.

The Swedish Exception

In an attempt to explain why right-wing populists had not found similar success in Sweden as elsewhere in Europe—that is, until they did—political scientist Jens Rydgren (2002), wrote about what he called the Swedish exception. However, in 2010 the Sweden Democrats entered parliament, finally passing the threshold of relevance. Until then they had been kept firmly out on the fringe in Swedish politics.

Sweden had accepted more refugees and asylum seekers per capita than any other country in Europe. The Sweden Democrats forcefully criticized both the open-door policy and what they called a lenient immigration policy of the mainstream parties. They insisted that it had caused segregation, rootlessness, criminality, conflict and increased tension in society (Hellstrom 2016). They described the Rosengård block complex in Malmö and other immigrant communities as ghettos that had become no-go areas for Swedes. Although not true, they still claimed that the police even hesitated to patrol these areas. They implied that the Social Democrats had effectively turned these places into foreign-held territories, occupied by Muslims who were the country's greatest foreign threat, and had even partially introduced Sharia laws on Swedish soil (Åkesson 2009).

Leader of the Sweden Democrats, Jimmie Åkesson, said that Muslim refugees posed the 'biggest foreign threat to Sweden since the Second World War' (qtd in Becker 2019). He argued that Sweden should be kept as 'an ethnically and culturally homogeneous nation' and warned against the emergence of a multicultural society. The party emphasized national separatism based on biological and cultural differences.[7]

Loosening the Cordon Sanitaire

Prior to the 2010 electoral breakthrough, the SD had been widely dismissed as an evil outsider. In 1998, their share of the vote was not even a half per cent. In 2006 they gained some attention when almost 3 per cent of the electorate voted for them, though falling short of the 4 per cent parliament threshold. By 2018, their share of the vote had risen to 17.6 per cent.

The establishment in Swedish politics, other political parties and the mainstream media alike, first responded by ignoring the SD, and then by boycotting them all together, thus effectively applying on it a firm *Cordon Sanitaire*. Their legitimacy was also compromised by repeated incidences of aggressive xenophobic expression by party loyalists. They surely mobilized 'angry young men' into protest against immigrants, but also unwillingly attracted a following from more radical and violent neo-Nazi forces. In a demonstration in Stockholm in 1991, skinhead members of the party were heard yelling *Sig Heil*! The same Nazi salute was again frequently heard in 1993 at an SD-organized celebration of the late King of Sweden, Karl VII (Hellstrom 2016).

Although the SD's move from the far-right fringe of xenophobic and neo-Nazi extremism was initiated earlier, its full transformation was first achieved after young Per Jimmie Åkesson and his clan took over the helm in 2005, just prior to his twenty-sixth birthday. They rerouted away from the party's previous neo-Nazi past and instead turned towards the model of the Danish People's Party, the National Front in France and the Austrian Freedom Party.

The new leadership set out to systematically abandon extreme and banal views such as open biological racism, for instance by stepping back its policy of deportations of all post-1970 non-European immigrants, and of reinstating the death penalty (Widfeldt 2015). They also completely redressed. The rogue demagogic neo-Nazi skinhead look, the black army boots and tattoos with Norse and Nazi imagery were closeted and exchanged for suit and tie, close shave and neat haircuts. Furthermore, members expressing extremist views risked expulsion. In November 2011, Jimmie Åkesson announced a policy of zero-tolerance for racism. Several expulsions followed.

With the rascals out, the most severe hindrance towards electoral success had been moved from their path. Slowly, and even though falling short of winning full legitimacy, the party was eventually able to reach the ears of the electorate. The *Cordon Sanitaire* was loosening. In fact, the SD was able to play on their stigmatization and boycott, and present themselves as victims of bullying tactics of the establishment. In the end, playing the underdog, bravely standing against an overwhelming force of the entire establishment, worked to their advantage.

Since cleaning up its image, the SD was able to travel far from its neo-Nazi origins, claiming to be an alternative but legitimate voice. They positioned themselves as social conservative protectors of the Swedish national identity and traditional family values as well as advocators of law and order. Put more simply, they maintained to be speaking on behalf of the ordinary man, who the establishment had left behind. They accused the ruling elite of being preoccupied with the interests of the privileged few. Despite this effort the SD was not fully able to fend off accusations of extremism, such as of its ongoing and not so well-hidden xenophobia, and of still-visible links to neo-Nazi forces. In fact, the SD still lacked what Elisabeth Ivarsflaten (2006) referred to as a reputational shield.

Equal But Separate

In an ethno-pluralist 'equal but separate' doctrine, the SD avoided openly describing Swedish culture as superior. Instead Swedish culture and identity was portrayed as being unique and firmly separate from others. Each nation was here understood to possess one ethnically determined culture. The Swedish culture thus became a dividing line separating the native population from others in society, who were presented as a threat to internal social cohesion. Arguing that each nation embodied a singular culture based on ethnicity, they said it was the responsibility of Swedes to protect their own culture and identity from external contamination. On this ground, their 2011 manifesto emphasized turning Sweden back into a culturally homogeneous society, where the interest of the native population always came first.

In manoeuvring their way into a position of at least limited legitimacy, the real tactical breakthrough came by shrewdly adopting the social democratic notion of the People's Home (*Folkehemmed*). This was similar to moves made by both the Danish Peoples Party and the Norwegian Progress Party. Jimmie Åkesson claimed that the Social Democrats had abandoned their long-asserted promise of the People's Home, the all-embracing welfare society. Instead, he insisted that the SD was now the true representative of the Peoples Home. The SD skilfully played on a nostalgic wish of reverting back to a simpler and happier time. This was a classical discursive creation of a Golden Age when the close connection between the ethnic people, democracy and welfare are emphasized in an exclusionary understanding of the nation (see Elgenius and Rydgren 2019).

Vitally for achieving this discursive move, they were able to attach their own nationalist agenda of protecting the native population to the unifying metaphor of the People's Home, which in its essence contained the Swedish national identity (Hellstrom 2016). They furthermore accused the Social Democrats and other mainstream parties of abandoning the people, and only working on behalf of its own interests or for external forces. Former party leader and long-standing Prime Minister in the late twentieth century, the late Olof Palme, was placed as the main domestic culprit, accused of rapid internationalization and for promoting multicultural views.

The SD was firmly socio-culturally conservative, but unlike many right-wing nativist populist parties in neighbouring countries, it was not at all neo-liberal. In fact, the SD attacked the Social Democrats for having weakened the welfare state and for having lowered benefits resulting in the suffering of native Swedes who relied on the system. In this regard, they adopted the winning formula of the Danish Peoples Party and of Geert Wilder's Freedom Party in the Netherlands. Nordic populists indeed generally unite in embracing the newer winning formula of linking people and culture to the nation-state, that is, in protecting the redistributive welfare state for only the ethnic population, and, thus, placing migrants as a threat to it.

New Master Framework

The new master framework consisted of combining ethno-nationalism and anti-elite populism with welfare chauvinism. Jimmie Åkesson maintained that the unique Swedish welfare system could not handle too much immigration. He thus presented welfare and immigration as mutually exclusive and asked the electorate to choose. This was illustrated in an SD advert in 2010. A native woman pensioner slowly moving with her wheeled walker is overtaken by a group of fast-moving Muslim women in burqas, who cash out the social security coffers before the Swedish woman finally arrives. Their slogan read: 'Pensions or immigration—the choice is yours' (cited in Klein 2013). In a traditional welfare chauvinistic way, Åkesson and his team thus positioned themselves as the guardians of the welfare state, claiming that voting for immigrant friendly mainstream parties was a vote against the traditional heritage of Swedish welfare, while a vote for his party protected the universal welfare system.

By discursively stealing back the metaphor of the People's Home, the SD set out to achieve several goals at once. The first was simply to capitalize on the myth of the Swedish heritage. Secondly, they positioned themselves as the true representatives of the welfare society, the defining factor of Swedish national identity. Thirdly, this was simultaneously a way to criticize the current leadership of the Social Democrats for having let down the native population for a naive celebration of multiculturalism. A final positive side effect was the portrayal of the contemporary Social Democrats as alienated elitists—out of touch both with its past and present society.

This is the classical before-mentioned three-phase discourse of nativist populists: first, Muslim migrants are placed as the threat to the ethnic and cultural nation, then the Social Democratic leadership is accused of betraying the people, while, lastly, the SD position themselves as their protectors.

PERSISTANCE

After their breakthrough in 2010 the Sweden Democrats were able to persist in Swedish politics, thus disproving the thesis of a Swedish exceptionalism. The SD was primarily a nationalistic anti-immigrant party, but after 2005 the new leadership started to broaden its scope and attempted to mobilize voters on several other issues as well. It was no longer solely a single-issue party. In line with its socio-conservative stance, the SD was initially sceptical on gay rights. Over time, however, the party repositioned itself as protectors of homosexuals against a threat to sexual liberalism accompanying mass Muslim migration. In 2010 the party published a report titled 'Time to Speak Out About Rape'. The focus was not on the crime in general, but rather on Muslim immigrants raping native Swedish women, claiming that Sweden was experiencing a rape wave, which was directly caused by immigration (see in Moffitt 2017).

The newfound social liberalism was always quite selective, and seemed mostly to be aimed against Muslim socio-conservativism. For example, when the small town of Sölvesborg, a SD stronghold, banned flying the rainbow flag often used by the gay and queer rights movements at official buildings in 2019. Council member, Louise Erixon, wife of Jimmie Åkesson, said this was because of respect for conventions.

Gradually, the *Cordon Sanitaire* loosened. The SD gained access to the media and was allowed to find its place on the map of Swedish politics, tolerated though perhaps not fully accepted. While surely moving to the mainstream, they still firmly flagged their anti-immigrant colour. This was well-illustrated in an open letter to the Finns Party in 2015, written by the leadership of the SD's youth movement, warning their neighbour of repeating the same mistakes as in Sweden. In the letter titled 'Finland, you do not want the Swedish nightmare', they wrote that over the decades Sweden had been 'destroyed' by immigration after 'undergoing an extreme transformation from a harmonious society to a shattered one'. They said that many Swedes totally opposed this system of 'mass immigration, extreme feminism, liberalism, political correctness and national self-denial' (Kallestrand et al. 2015).

This mirrored Åkesson's previous positions. In a newspaper article in 2009 he framed Muslims as the greatest foreign threat to Sweden, and, indeed, to Europe. In line with the Great Replacement conspiracy theory he claimed that Western societies were becoming Islamized and were under threat from Sharia law (qtd in Nordensvard and Ketola 2015).

In the 2018 general election the Sweden Democrats surged again to another record high of 17.5 per cent. Although the result caused a prolonged political crisis, the Social Democrats in the end held onto power in a minority government backed by other mainstream parties. After grave difficulties, the *Cordon Sanitaire* on the SD held, for the time being.

ICELANDIC NATIONALISTS

Until the 2017 parliamentary election, when at least two quasi-populist parties passed over the threshold and took up seats in parliament, such parties had not found significant electoral success in Iceland. In previous publications (see Bergmann 2017) I have identified three main reasons halting their rise. First of all, nationalism was never a discredited ideology in Iceland, like it was in most other Western European countries after the Second World War. The small island country gained its independence from Denmark in 1944 and its postcolonial national identity was firmly based on nationalistic sentiments (Bergmann 2014a). There was thus no need to challenge the political establishment with nationalistic views from the fringe, as nationalism had never been marginalized.

Secondly, nativist populist parties in Europe had found most success when opposing mainly Muslim migrants. Muslims are scarce in Iceland and there are no areas where the semantics of an Arab culture dominate the scene. And thirdly, populist parties have usually found success when under leadership of charismatic leaders. Until recently, far-right populists in Iceland were rather unlucky in that regard.

However, the Financial Crisis which hit Iceland especially hard in 2008 brought political upheaval and unleashed quite a few populist actors (Bergmann 2014a). Through the so-called Pots-and-Pans Revolution several protest movements emerged. In 2009, the Citizens Movement entered parliament; later it was succeeded by the rather left-leaning quasi-populist Pirate Party.

On the wave of the crisis, a completely renewed leadership also took over the country's old agrarian party, the Progressive Party (PP), which was rapidly retuned in a more populist direction: geared against foreign creditors, international institutions and eventually partly towards anti-Muslim rhetoric—even in the absence of a significant Muslim population.

In 2013, the young and new PP leader, Sigmundur Davíð Gunnlaugsson, came to head a government in a coalition with the mainstream previously hegemonic right-wing conservative Independence Party—which had been ousted in the Pots-and-Pans Revolution. Gunnlaugsson had risen to prominence on the canopy of public protests against foreign governments and creditors who were pressuring Icelanders to shoulder the debts of the fallen Icelandic banks abroad (Bergmann 2016).

After being exposed by Wikileaks in the so-called Panama Papers for his family holding a small fortune in unregistered offshore accounts, Gunnlaugsson lost leadership in the party. He responded with constructing his own, the Centre Party, which was a more clearly nativist populist forum. Gunnlaugsson was also prone to upholding a wide range of conspiracy theories. He insisted that George Soros had orchestrated his demise by leaking the Panama Papers. In the 2017 general election, the Centre Party won more than one-tenth of the vote. It was then elevated further in 2019 when manufacturing controversy around the EU energy legislation, which Iceland adopted through the EEA agreement.

Another quasi-populist party also found support in the 2017 election. The Peoples Party was prone to uphold welfare chauvinism. Its leader, Inga Sæland (2016), counted the cost of admitting asylum seekers versus helping poor Icelanders. She insisted that while skint Icelanders suffered hardship, asylum seekers, funded by the state, were living in comfort. Rhetorically she asked whether that money might instead be better used by helping poor Icelanders. This is a classic case of creating false oppositions.

Despite the lack of a significant Muslim community in Iceland, there were still a few movements that made campaigning against Muslim influences their primary purpose. In 2017 I for example attended an event where Robert Spencer, founder of Jihad Watch in America, was a keynote speaker. When I arrived I felt a tense ambience in the packed conference room. Herds of stern looking security guards were roaming around, ready to silence anyone who might protest against the message on offer. I was at the time collecting data for the research published in this book. After the meeting concluded I asked to pose a couple of questions to Mr Spencer. I was not only refused but fast turned away by the heavily built guards, and in no uncertain terms made to exit the premises. The foreign guests left via a side door and were immediately whisked away in a waiting car. The heavy handling was highly unconventional for other public gatherings in Reykjavik.

An Illiberal East

With the fall of the Berlin wall, many of the countries in Eastern Europe who were escaping from communism entered onto a path of far-reaching economic restructuring. They would even apply neo-liberalism policies more vigorously than had been done in the free market states in Western Europe. As I discussed in the previous chapter, this transformation brought serious hardship to the public. When the promise of liberal democracy failed to deliver the anticipated prosperity, many people grew frustrated and authoritative nationalists were shrewd in exploiting the situation. This was the case in the *Visegrád* countries. Populists came to power in all of them, the Czech Republic, Hungary, Poland and Slovakia.

As I discussed in the previous chapter, Hungary was in the 1990s firmly *en route* to liberal democracy within the international architecture of cross-border institutions. On that long winding road, the public was however growing frustrated with the lack of improvement in their living standards. Inequality was growing and the grotesque coteries of the *nouveau riche* were showing off their wealth. Large swaths of the general public felt left out. And when the ruling class was increasingly seen as being in bed with the new breed of capitalists, the common man was not only getting fed up, many were also getting ready to consider other routes than only those leading to liberal democracy—which had, up until then, not provided the Hungarian people with much economic progress.

After winning a full majority in the 2010 general election, in the wake of the Financial Crisis biting hard, Fidesz party leader, Viktor Orbán, started to consolidate state power into his own hands, for example by controlling and oppressing free media, ousting liberal academia, reducing judicial independence and tightening control of the entire state apparatus. He filled the constitutional court with his own trusties and rewrote the constitution as well as gerrymandering electoral districts for his own advantage (Levitsky and Ziblatt 2018). Orbán controlled the state media by placing it under a Fidesz-led council. Private media outlets and journalists were also made to register with the government. If the authorities found their reporting not being balanced enough they could be fined. Next, Orbán prevented the opposition from getting their messages across, for example by banning campaign material in private media.

Gradually, Fidesz was able to turn Hungary towards a governmental system that Orbán himself described as a Christian illiberal democracy. Hungary in effect became a one-party state. Orbán stated that democracy should be hierarchical rather than liberal. His vision was for Hungary to become an 'illiberal new state based on national foundations' (qtd in Mahony 2014). Orbán celebrated Donald Trump's victory in the US, saying that his election marked the transition from liberal non-democracy to real democracy. In essence, his vision was for an authoritative democracy without individual civil rights. In a hierarchical illiberal democracy the leader is trusted to interpret the will of the people.

The Ethno-Centric View

Victor Orbán's understanding of the Hungarian nation was also highly ethno-centric. Speaking at an ethnic Hungarian summer camp in Romania in 2014, he said that the Hungarian nation was not just the sum of individuals in the country. Rather, it was an community that 'must be organized, reinforced and in fact constructed' (qtd in Judis 2018).

In wake of the Syrian Refugee Crisis, Orbán took an even firmer stance against migrants, refusing to adhere to collective EU response and instead hired thousands of border hunters while fencing of the Hungarian border with a gigantic defence wall. He said this was his duty, otherwise the Hungarian nation would die out. Orbán placed refugees seeking asylum in Hungary as a threat to the ethnic Christian Hungarian nation, insisting that Hungary should be kept for Hungarians alone. In an address in 2018, he stated that 'we do not want to be diverse and do not want to be mixed: we do not want our own colour, traditions and national culture to be mixed with those of others.'[8]

In his fight against asylum seekers, Orbán launched a renewed attack on George Soros, also discussed in previous chapters, who had in the 2015

Refugee Crisis advocated that Europe should accept migrants from the Middle East. Orbán insisted that Soros was, aided by the EU, seeking to ruin the Hungarian nation by way of migration. The government splattered posters of Soros around the country, for instance reading: 'Soros wants to transplant millions from Africa and the Middle East. Stop Soros.' Another simply said: 'Let's not let Soros have the last laugh' (Judis 2018). Some of the posters suggested that Orbán was indeed controlling the European Union behind the scenes.

During the Coronavirus Crisis of 2020 Orbán used the opportunity to rush through emergency legislation which in effect gave him powers to rule by decree. Parliament was sent home and anyone found disseminating information which authorities deemed being false or disturbing could be incarcerated. Hungary had travelled far from core criteria of EU membership, those of respecting human rights and the rule of law.

Two of a Kind

Over in Poland, authorities under Jaroslav Kaczynski and his largely hegemonic party in the post-communist era, Law and Order, have more or less followed suit in the direction of Fidesz in Hungary, for example by increasing government control over state media and packing the Supreme Court with cronies. Poland was turned away from the path laid by *Solidarnosc* towards market economy and liberal democracy, to become one of the most polarized in Europe.

Nationalist sentiments in Poland, like in Hungary, often rest on ideas of victimhood and foreign oppression. Kaczynski also defined the Polish national identity on ethnicity and pointed to refugees as contaminating the Polish people. He insisted that Syrian refugees brought new and dangerous diseases to Poland and argued that Europe was facing a serious crisis of consciousness, saying that accepting refugees showed the willingness of EU leaders to sacrifice European cultural and ethnic identity.

Finding increasing support at home and seeing similar-minded parties flourishing in many other Eastern European countries has galvanized both Hungary and Poland in defying the European Union's immigration plans. Orbán rejected the EU refugee quotas, saying that the EU's migration policy had failed: 'It is clear that the European people don't want immigration, while several European leaders are still forcing the failed immigration policy.'[9]

Interestingly, given the history of race-related victimhood in the Second World war, anti-Semitism was also on the rise. The right-wing newspaper, *Tylko Plolska* (Only Poland) for example ran a frontpage story explaining to its readers how to spot a Jew, listing anthropological features and character traits. A headline read: 'How to defeat them? This cannot go on' (qtd in Osborne 2019).

Both Hungary and Poland have been in violation of the Copenhagen criterions of the European Union, which lays out the bloc's fundamental accession requirement rules, such as respecting democracy, human rights and the rule of law. In autumn 2018, the European Parliament triggered against Hungary its Article 7 procedure for countries found being in breach of democratic governance and for human rights violations.

Domestically, Orbán was then able to use this external interference to play up fears of renewed foreign oppression. Catering to national myths as discussed in the previous chapter, the EU was positioned as yet another foreign power seeking to dominate Hungary and erode its sovereignty.

Conspiratorial Russia

Russia is the country in Eastern Europe where this trend away from the promise of liberal democracy has perhaps gone the furthest, turning this Eurasian superpower into an at least quasi-authoritarian regime. After coming to power, Vladimir Putin gradually started to abandon Boris Yeltsin's policy of bringing Russia into the international family of liberal democracies. Instead, Russia has travelled far on the path of post-Cold-War illiberalism. On the way the West was, after having for a short while been considered a partner in a shared quest for a liberal future, redefined to again become the arch-enemy of Russia. One of the most powerful tools in this turn was the use of conspiracy theories, which always have been a prevalent feature in Russian culture.

Anxiety and feelings of powerlessness in post-Soviet Russia led to a growing nostalgia for past Soviet times and a simultaneous rise in anti-Western attitudes. Ilya Yablokov (2018) illustrates how tales of anti-Western attitudes framed the nation-building discourse in Putin's Russia and that by doing so, the strong leader was able to suppress dissident voices. The European Union was especially targeted and portrayed as decadent and hostile. The West was in general treated as the ultimate Other, seeking to prevent Russia from flourishing. This narrative helped to reinforce two vital notions. One was of Russia being different from the West, and that it should not imitate its liberal democracy. The second notion underlined Russia's greatness, which, vitally for the story, was that the West was aiming to destroy Russia.

I can take an example from my own experience. In 2015, I was invited to give a presentation at the Moscow State Institute of International Relations, run by the Russian Foreign Ministry. In discussions with governmental officials, faculty members and students alike they all insisted that the West—mainly Germany, France, the United Kingdom and the United States—was actively undermining the Russian state a by variety of means. Not least because of that, they insisted that Russia had to develop its own kind of democracy instead of adopting the liberal style of the West—which, they said, was just ongoing Western colonialization. In our conversations they argued for an alternative model, what they called an illiberal and authoritative variety of democracy, which would fit much better for Russia and its political heritage. When challenging them on how it would work, I came to understand that meaningful democratic-decision making was not a core ingredient of the governmental system they described to me. In fact, calling it a democracy was just another oxymoron.

For this turn, the Russian state media played a pivotal role. The Moscow-based state-controlled English language 24-hour television news station *Russia Today* (RT), was made available to a global creed of conspiracy theorists. They would welcome onto their airwaves almost anyone with a story undermining the credibility of the West, including the notorious far-right commentator Alex Jones. RT presenters seriously discussed covert actions of, for example, the Bilderberg group, 9/11 Truther Movement theories and stories of climate change conspiracies, treating them as credible news (Byford 2011).

Far-fetched and unfounded conspiracy theories of aggressive outsiders were actively promoted by the Kremlin for their domestic political gain. As *Guardian* columnist Natalie Nougayrede (2015) writes, this rhetoric centres on the notion that Western powers were engaged in covert manipulations with the intent of ultimately 'dismantling the very statehood of Russia'. Collectively, this turn constituted a systemic campaign of misinformation upheld by the authorities themselves. In an attempt to capture this kind of politics, Peter Pomerantsev's (2015) unauthorized biography of Vladimir Putin was titled *Nothing Is True and Everything Is Possible*.

External Aggressors

This discursive creation of external plots served to rally support behind the Kremlin in fighting against their internal political opponents. By depicting domestic dissidents as covert aggressors from abroad, Putin and his clan not only claimed the right to crush nonconformist voices domestically, but also insisted that the Russian state was obliged to do so. Taking them on at home was thus part of the good fight against foreign enemies.

This political construction furthermore provided the authorities with means to blame almost anything that went wrong on the external enemy and its internal covert collaborators. In this vein Vladimir Putin was prone to point a finger against what he perceived to be continuous US-led aggression against Russia.

This is a classic case of how a nativist populist places himself as a protector of the nation against a foreign threat which he himself had discursively created. In applying this simplistic dualist worldview, the nativist populist can also turn against any disobedient domestic voices, as they are simply branded as traitors of the people in the good fight.

In these cases, the leader equates himself with the people against both external threats and domestic traitors. Discursively, the people and their leader become a single entity. This is similar to that which Donald Trump attempted in the United States, by branding the media as the enemy of the people.

As has been discussed, fears of Western subversion became a key instrument for the social cohesion of the Russian nation. Gradually there was a shift from fears of Western forces as the primary threat to the country, towards also including fears of migrants. This turned into an evolving belief in the Great Replacement conspiracy theory, that external forces were now also plotting to ruin Russian society by migrant infiltration.

Traitors Within

This leads us to the importance of the notion of traitors within for understanding contemporary Russian politics. The young women of the protest punk band Pussy Riot, for example became in handy as perceived perpetrators. In February 2012, five young women attempted to perform what they called punk-prayer in the Cathedral of Christ the Saviour in Moscow. The title of their song was telling for their aim: *Mother of God, Drive Putin Away*. Ahead of the presidential elections, the all-girl punk band became a leading voice of much larger ongoing protests against Vladimir Putin's regime. At first, the young women were dismissed as some sorts of hooligans. But soon after the stunt in the Moscow cathedral they were treated as enemies of the Russian nation. Three of them were arrested and sentenced to two years in prison. Since then, several members of the band have faced repeated arrests and incarcerations.

To deal with the domestic protestors, Russian authorities launched an aggressive media campaign, in which the young Russian women were depicted as being agents of a Western-led plot to undermine the very Russian statehood, and, indeed, to prevent Russia from fulfilling its full potential at home and in the world. In these invented stories the domestic dissidents were directly linked to foreign intelligence agencies and branded traitors of the people, posing an existential threat to the Russian nation and its cohesion.

Within the Kremlin many argued that Pussy Riot was a Western revenge plot, sent to demoralize the Russian nation, and to demonize the Russian government for standing up to Washington's intention to destroy Syria. In this vein, the regime was able to assert that they were faced with disruptive forces that threatened the very unity of Russian society.

In this discursive creation, domestic criticism of the Russian regime was dismissed as mere undermining tactics of Western forces, with the aim of weakening Russia for the West's own geopolitical gain. By this rhetorical internal division of 'us' and 'them' authorities could treat the domestic protestors as foreign infiltrators who were undermining an otherwise united Russian nation. By depicting them as foreign conspirators, the Kremlin was able to portray dissenting actors as posing a major threat to Russian statehood. Members of the domestic punk band were via this method treated as invaders who aimed to destabilize, and, indeed, to emasculate Russia.

The Kremlin went further and dismissed the young girls of Pussy Riot as immoral deviants, sexual perverts, witches, blasphemers and provocateurs who were supported by the West and utterly alien to the ordinary Russian people (Yablokov 2014). Via media reporting, the young women of Pussy Riot were discursively turned into 'others', and thus made distinct from the Russian nation.

The case of Pussy Riot was only one of many leading to a highly conspiratorial discourse following in the Russian media. Another case in point was the treatment of opposition leader Alexei Navalny, who on dubious grounds has repeatedly been incarcerated and barred from standing in elections. Almost all domestic dissenting voices were subsequently portrayed as part of the overall Western conspiracy of ruining Russia. In the media campaign, the protesters were depicted as being a conspiring minority within the nation, perhaps much like a cancer that needed to be uprooted. Furthermore, all criticism from abroad of the harsh treatment of the young women could be scorned as part of the external plot. Indeed, critical reporting from abroad was taken as proof of the Western-led conspiracy.

Misinformation Tactics

In its dispute with the West, Russia has been accused of deliberately applying misinformation tactics in order to discredit Western authorities. The Kremlin was for instance found to have interfered in both the Brexit referendum debate in the UK in 2016 and the US presidential elections later that year. They have also been caught funding actors in Eastern Europe who cast doubts on the European Union, for instance in the Czech Republic, Slovakia, Hungary and Poland (Snyder 2018). Russia has also supported anti-EU far-rights populist parties in Europe, including Le Pen's National Rally in France. The aim of these actions was to disrupt the unity of liberal democracies of the West. It is estimated that before the European Parliament election in 2019 more than half of the voters had been exposed to disinformation campaigns emanating from Russia (Scott 2019).

During the Coronavirus Crisis of 2020 many similar conspiracy theories were detected coming out of Russia. One insisted that the virus was a biological weapon made in America by the CIA. Another which was widely discussed by pro-Kremlin actors on Russian state TV maintained that the UK was sitting on a vaccine and would only roll it out at the height of the crisis, for their monetary gain.

The Kremlin forcefully supported Donald Trump for US President, openly and behind the scenes. One of the most influential ideologues of the Kremlin's quest for a spiritual rise of Russia as a Eurasian superpower was Alexander Dugin. Prior to the US elections he urged American voters to support Donald Trump and posted a video titled: 'In Trump We Trust'. Although the extent of the operation is not known, it is uncontested that the Kremlin actively sought to get Trump elected. Sources close to the Kremlin leaked large amounts of emails that had been harvested from Hillary Clinton's server. The timing of their release in July 2016 clearly hurt her in the elections (Snyder 2018).

The office of the United States Special Prosecutor, Robert Mueller, indicted thirteen Russian nationals and three Russian companies—including a notorious Troll Factory in St Petersburg called the Russian Internet Research Agency. The indictment issued in 2018 stated that the Petersburg-based agency had conspired to 'defraud the United States by impairing, obstructing, and defeating the lawful functions of the government through fraud and deceit for the purpose of interfering with the US political and electoral processes, including the presidential election of 2016'.

Troll Factories

Robert Muller's investigation found that the Russian computer Bot Farm had invested large amounts of money interfering in the US election debate. The investigation found that these Troll Factories had continuously spread pro-Donald Trump propaganda and fake news on social media platforms such as Facebook and Twitter. In 2017 alone a task force set up by the EU mapping fake news coming out of Russia—the East StratCom group—detected 1310 such fake news stories of various kinds.[10]

One insisted that Angela Merkel was the secret daughter of Adolf Hitler. Another said that Sweden was on the verge of a civil war. Many of these stories ridiculed the political correctness of the West. One cited a fabricated directive of the European Union regulating children's formations of snowmen. The story said that anyone building a white human from snow would also have to include a yellow and a black version, otherwise the EU would fine them €5000 for racism.

Several of these stories also spoke to the perversion and demoralization of the West. Denmark was said to have legalized animal prostitution. Another story said that the mainstream media was silencing the grim fact that due to immigration rapes in Sweden had increased by a 1000 per cent between 2015 and 2017. According to these stories, the Swedish authorities were no longer investigating rapes committed by refugees (Palma 2017).

Sweden was a popular source for such stories. One claimed to unravel a secret plan of Sweden's Foreign Minister Margot Wallström, to sterilize all white men in Sweden to prevent them from breeding further. Incidentally, that was never true, and reported rapes in Sweden in 2017 were up by only 1.4 percent from 2015.

Among the main themes identified in these stories was of a US plot to occupy Europe. One of these stories reported that the US Air Force had in 2017 bombed Lithuania. Another indicated that French President Emmanuel Macron was a secret agent of the US Department of the

Treasury. The report said that Macron was backed by homosexual lobbyists and also by the wealthy Rothschild family. In another version authorities in Berlin were also accused of a plot to turn Europe into a German colony.[11]

In these stories the West was systematically treated as the ultimate Other, as hostile and seeking to prevent Russia from flourishing. The Kremlin flirted with many conspiracy theories catering to this notion. One was upheld by Putin's crony Vladimir Yakunin, former head of the Russian railways state company, who maintained that the West was deliberately spreading homosexual propaganda around the world in order to reduce birth rates in Russia, and therefore weakening the Russian state (Snyder 2018).

In these stories, Russia, however, was usually seen as the innocent and moral actor under siege from an iniquitous and violent Western aggressor. Putin was prone to elevate Russia from not only being a nation-state on planet earth but also into some kind of divinity. Once he even described Russia as a spiritual condition (ibid.).

Many of the stories vilifying the West were centred on Germany, the epicentre of post-war liberal democracy. One insisted that Germany was a deteriorating but aggressive state in support of Nazis in Ukraine. According to the story, Germany was, via a large scale Nato build-up in the Baltics, planning to invade St Petersburg.

Via this depiction, Russia was able to present its own invasion into Ukraine, when annexing Crimea in 2014, as a defensive act against Western aggressors. The Kremlin ran a series of fabricated stories claiming that pro-Western authorities in Kiev were crucifying children. As result, the fight of Russian soldiers across the border was merely in protection of the innocent against an external evil.

Gayropa

A common theme of these stories of the West harming Russians revolved around Europe having fallen into the hands of immoral homosexual authorities. This was the notion of Gayropa. One story revolved around a Russian mother in Norway who after divorce had lost custody of their children to her Norwegian husband. Irina Bergseth became a media sensation in Russia, with her story of mischievous Norwegian authorities stealing Russian children and giving them to homosexual domestic nationals.

More broadly she described Scandinavia as having been gayofied and maintained that Russia was now the last bastion of traditional values, the only one opposing 'a sodomite dictatorship' which Europe had become. Her message fitted well into the dominant Russian narrative, which represented non-heterosexuals as sex-radicals. Often the story implied that the imperialist West was imposing gay-ism to undermine Russia (Persson 2015).

Many of these stories revolved around the tarnished morals of the West. One insisted that in Sweden schools were forcing all pupils to pray to Allah. Another said that Christmas was being renamed the 'Winter celebration' to avoid offending Muslims in Sweden. The root to that story was a single headline in the Swedish daily *Sydsvenskan*, which referred to Christmas as a 'winter celebration'. Several Russian web outlets followed up on the story by publishing a video from a Western-style shopping mall where a mob of people was ruining a Christmas tree, apparently in an attack on a Christian symbol (Lacarpia 2016). Several Coronavirus Crisis conspiracy theories depicted the West as inept and dysfunctional, for instance, indicating the dissolution of the European Union as a result of mismanaging the crisis.

Brexit, Brexit, Brexit

The debate leading up to the vote in the United Kingdom of leaving the European Union—Brexit—in June 2016 proved to be highly nationalistic, populist and conspiratorial. Of course, wanting to the leave the EU is not in itself populist. Not at all. It is a perfectly legitimate political position to hold, also keeping in mind that the UK had for long been somewhat hesitant in regards to the increased supranational nature of the EU. However, in the referendum campaign the aforementioned three-level rhetorical tactics defining nativist populists were all clearly present: Discursively creating an external threat, blaming the elite of betraying the people and positioning oneself as the true defender of the nation. Through the progression of the debate, the external threat pointed to would interchangeably be the European Union and/or migrants. The Labour Party leadership and the Remain elite of the Conservative Party were cast as traitors to the people. Vote Leave campaigners, as well as the more rogue UKIP leadership, then positioned themselves as the liberators of the British people.

There was also an interesting shift in the positioning of the external threat, depending on whether it was seen stemming from the EU or from immigrants. In arguing against migration, the EU would be placed in the role of the elite that was betraying the people. However, oftentimes the

EU would itself also be targeted as being the outgroup threatening British identity. As I will illustrate on the coming pages these rhetorical manoeuvrings were tailored to meet each argument when it fitted the debate.

As would also be the case in the US presidential elections later that year—discussed ahead in this chapter—sophisticated misinformation tactics were used to influence voters. The data analysis company Cambridge Analytica was accused of manipulating people's personal data on social media to target individual fears directly, irrespective of reality. Here are some examples of the misinformation tactics openly applied in the Brexit debate.

'Let's give the NHS the £350 million the EU takes every week.' This was the message on the first billboard of the Vote Leave campaign— unequivocally insisting not only that EU membership costed UK taxpayers this vast sum of money every week, but also that the enormous amount would be available to fund the UK National Health Service after leaving. The same message was printed widely in Brexit campaign materials, famously, for example, on the side of their campaign bus. At best, this was very misleading. Not only was this a gross figure blown out of all proportion and did not take into account returns through EU programmes, but also did it not even deduct the so-called UK rebate, adding to the calculation amounts that never even left Britain.

This kind of depiction fits with classic populist positioning. EU membership was here linked to the NHS being underfunded. In other words, this is a classic case of false polarizing, where funding the NHS properly was directly linked with leaving the European Union. Furthermore, this served to oppose 'Us' with 'Them', protecting *our* NHS against paying into the foreign EU. By this positioning, the EU was placed as an external threat to proper healthcare in Britain. Unelected EU administrators were here placed as an external authority, burdening the British with their corrupt ways. Vote Leave chief strategist Dominic Cummings said that everyone knew that 'Brussels is a very corrupt place full of bureaucrats who have done no good to this country' (qtd in Harrison 2019). In this vein, the Vote Leave slogan of 'take back control' speaks directly to the notion of fighting an external power which had sucked authority from the country. This was simultaneously a call for bringing power back to the people and of resurrecting Britain to its former glory. In many ways this was a nostalgic turn back to previous times when free and independent Britain was a world-leading empire. Boris Johnson, who came to lead Britain through in the Brexit conundrum, indeed played on these nationalist notions, both prior to and after becoming UK Prime Minister.

Brexit has also to be examined in relation to the severe austerity which the UK underwent in the post-Financial Crisis era. Before the vote in 2016 the government had implemented several measures to meet costs inhered by the 2008 crisis. This led to monetary fatigue in many deprived places. Correspondingly, the support for Brexit was greatest in areas most severely hit by the crisis (Becker et al. 2017).

Taking Back Control

Another classic tactic applied in the Brexit campaign was in discrediting specialists that called out the false information upheld in the campaign. When criticized by many specialists for his simplistic and antagonistic attitude to the situation, a leading Brexit campaigner of the Conservative Party, Michael Gove, replied: 'I think the people in this country have had enough of experts' (qtd in Bennett 2016). With his words, Gove applied at least two rhetorical fallacies, a *red herring* deviation from the topic, and also an *ad hominem* attack on the accusers.

Instead, he insisted that after the referendum the UK would instantly 'hold all the cards', and that it would be incredibly easy to make a great deal with the EU (see Henley et al. 2018). The opposite turned out to be true. When Boris Johnson rose to power in 2019, he made Gove his de facto deputy Prime Minister in control of no-deal preparations. It can be argued that suspicions of specialists had made the government slow to respond to concerns leading up to the Coronavirus Crisis of 2020, which hit the UK especially hard.

Taking back money was but one of many messages that were only loosely linked to reality during the Brexit debate. Leading up to a visit by US President Barack Obama, who was expected to come out against Brexit and say that in the case of a leave vote, it would take a long time to negotiate a trade deal between the USA and the UK, many of the Brexiters took to undermining the US president's credibility. Ahead of the visit, in the tabloid *The Sun*, the then London Mayor Boris Johnson said that due to Obama's part-Kenyan ancestry, Obama had a dislike of the British Empire. To underpin the claim, Johnson insisted that precisely because of that reason Obama had removed a bust of Winston Churchill from the Oval Office in Washington upon taking office as US President. After Johnson was criticized for covert dog-whistle racism UKIP leader Nigel Farage came to his defence. Farage wrote that Obama indeed 'bears a bit of a grudge against this country because of his grandfather and Kenya and colonialization' (qtd in Bennett 2016).

Boris Johnson proved to be highly conspiratorial during the campaign, for example when stating that the EU had the same goals as Adolf Hitler, that of creating a European superstate: 'Napoleon, Hitler, various people tried this out, and it ended tragically. The EU is an attempt to do this by different methods' (qtd in Ross 2016). After becoming UK Prime Minister in summer 2019, Mr Johnson restated the similarity between the aims of the EU and Nazi Germany.

Mr Johnson was not new to concocting stories about the EU. When he was Brussels correspondent for the *Daily Telegraph* in the 1990s, he became infamous for fabricating funny but false news stories about the EU. One of his frontpage stories insisted that the then President of the European Commission, Jacques Delors, was planning to rule Europe. Johnson however mainly made a name for himself with more quirky stories, ridiculing the EU. One ran under the headline 'Italy fails to measure up on condoms.' Johnson mockingly wrote that 'Brussels bureaucrats have shown their legendary attention to detail by rejecting new specifications for condom dimensions.' He said that this was 'despite demands from the Italian rubber industry for a smaller minimum width'. Johnson concluded that the whole thing had left 'Italian egos smarting' and finished by quoting an official spokesperson, Willy Hélin, who he said insisted that 'this is a very serious business' (qtd in Rankin and Waterson 2019). Johnson was notorious for fabricating quotes, but that did not stop his highly entertaining stories being picked up in papers around the continent, shaping the minds of many that read them. Mr Johnson was indeed a pioneer in the industry of fabricating political stories, and he helped to pave the way for the later avalanche of fake news.

There were also those that went much further in Brussels bashing. UKIP's Gerard Batten seemed to believe that the EU was conceived by Nazi Germany (Stone 2016). He also insisted that the notorious Bilderberg group was secretly plotting to prevent Britain from leaving the EU. It is worth mentioning that after Nigel Farage left UKIP and formed the Brexit Party, UKIP became much more clearly nativist populist, and even joined up with several more authoritarian and racist movements.

The Muslim Card

Another conspiratorial aspect of the Brexit campaign was related to fears of the possible accession of Turkey to the EU and, thus, of increased Muslim migration to the UK. While dismissing the fact that all EU member states hold a veto of new members, Vote Leave still insisted that the UK would, in practice, not be able to stop the Turks from getting their hands on EU passports.

In the third wave of post-war nativist populism, the UK Independence Party had surpassed the British National Party (discussed in the previous chapter) and firmly occupied the populist space in the country. Its leader Nigel Farage had become the primary voice advocating for Brexit. He forcefully maintained that 75 million poor Turks were on the verge of gaining access to the UK, 'to use the Health Service, to use our primary schools, to take jobs in whatever sector it may be' (qtd in Bennett 2016). They insisted that the Brexit vote was indeed a referendum on the massive migration of Muslims into the UK.

This was in the midst of the Refugee Crisis stemming from the war in Syria. Farage went on to argue that even combatants of the terrorist organization Isis would also filter through to the UK with Syrian refugees coming from Turkey. Here, the positioning of the European Union had shifted. It was no longer placed as the external threat, such as when accused of undermining the NHS. When it came to migration, the EU was instead cast as a traitor to the British people, facilitating uncontrolled flow of Muslim migrants to the UK. Nigel Farage referred to them as 'hordes' of foreigners' (qtd in Harrison 2018). The discourse was highly xenophobic. Migrants were linked to loss of identity and the erosion of British culture.

In a speech promoting Farage's message, prominent Conservative Party member Theresa Villiers said: 'If people believe there is an immigration crisis today, how much more concerned will they be after free movement is given to Turkey's 75 million citizens?' Former Conservative Party leader Ian Duncan Smith similarly maintained that the EU had made it very clear that Turks 'are going to get free travel and then enter the EU'. In a statement, Vote Leave went on to state that the high birth rate in Turkey would lead to one million Muslim Turks coming to the UK within eight years (Bennett 2016). A prominent Vote Leave campaigner Penny Mordaunt said that a vote for remain was a 'vote to allow people from Albania, Macedonia, Montenegro, Serbia and Turkey to move here freely when they join the EU soon' (Lister 2016).

Messages playing on these largely unfounded fears were actively built into the campaign material of Vote Leave. Neither country was on any kind of route towards EU membership. Still, with the focus in the campaign shifting to imagined Turkish membership and invented increased

Muslim migration into the UK, the polls started to move in the favour of Leave.

A third poster showed a photograph of a seemingly endless flow of refugees crossing through the Balkans, mostly young males. Its text read: 'Breaking point—the EU has failed us all.' At the bottom, the message continued: 'We must break free from the EU and take back control of our borders.' Collectively, this constitutes a systemic campaign of misinformation.

When accused of racism, Farage used the well-known rhetorical fallacy of attacking the accuser, saying that anyone calling his party racist was, directly because of that, part of the establishment.

Communication studies have shown that coverage of Muslims in UK media is predominantly negative, especially in outlets supportive of the Conservative Party (Waterson 2019). Accordingly, surveys showed that majority of Tory Party members believed Islam was generally a threat to Western civilization, and a threat to the British way of life.

A Violent Turn

As has been seen in many other cases, such as with the Breivik attack in Norway and by the aforementioned shooters in Christchurch and El Paso, this sort of rhetoric can lead to violence. The misinformation discussed above was among the political messages that Thomas Mair proved to be overtly susceptible to. A week before the vote he pulled out a sawn-off rifle and knife and shot and stabbed a forty-one-year-old woman who in the early afternoon was heading for the library entrance on the Market Street in his West Yorkshire town. Jo Cox was a Labour Party MP on her way to a constituency surgery. She died as result of multiple wounds and Mair was sentenced to life in prison without the possibility of pardoning.

Jo Cox was a staunch believer in European integration and a firm supporter of both immigrants and a multicultural British society. Her killer had come to believe that left-wing liberals in politics and in the mainstream media were responsible for much of the world's evil, and, indeed, for his own misfortune (Bennett 2016). Mair was a racist who believed in the Great Replacement conspiracy theory. He was obsessed with notions of white people facing increasing aggression. And he had the utmost contempt for those whom he called white traitors of their own people. In his eyes, Cox was one of these left liberals responsible for ruining the Western world. He saw her as one of 'the collaborators' of these external aggressors and a 'traitor to white people' (Cobain et al. 2016).

Thomas Mair was plugged into many far-right groups, including the notorious English Defence League, where he attended many gatherings. His house was filled with Nazi memorabilia and white supremacy literature. Noticeably, he had kept press cuttings about the case of Anders Breivik.

'My name is death to traitors, freedom for Britain.' This was the reply he gave when asked in the Westminster Magistrates Court to confirm his name (qtd in Booth et al. 2016). Mair had a long history of mental health problems. During the case procedure, it became evident that he had been influenced by much of the rhetoric upheld by the nationalist right in the Brexit campaign. Witnesses before the court testified that during the attack he had cried out 'this is for Britain', 'keep Britain independent', and 'Put Britain first' (qtd in Cobain and Taylor 2016).

The judge on the case said there was no doubt that Mair had murdered Jo Cox 'for the purpose of advancing a political, racial and ideological cause, namely that of violent white supremacism and exclusive nationalism most associated with Nazism and its modern forms'.[12]

Although the politicians and activists campaigning for Brexit at the time cannot, of course, be held directly responsible for this horrendous act of a madman, it is still equally impossible to completely escape the fact that political messages are sometimes received in different ways than they are intended to be interpreted. As Alex Massie (2016) wrote in *The Spectator*: 'When you shout BREAKING POINT over and over again you don't get to be surprised when someone breaks.' Massie argued that when politics are presented as a matter of life and death as in the Brexit campaign—as a question of national survival—'don't be surprised if someone takes your word for it'.

As the debate leading up to the exit progressed some would go even further. One such person was Alan Craig, former leader of the Christian Peoples Party. Speaking at the UKIP annual conference in 2018 he said that Muslim sex gangs had for decades abused and raped white English girls, to the extent that it had become a 'holocaust of our children' (qtd in Bloom 2018).

Political Predicament

Despite Michaels Gove's insistence that Britain would after the vote hold all the cards in the coming negotiations with the EU, it still proved to be difficult to finalize a beneficial exit agreement. Several contradictions in the UK's position did not help, for example keeping frictionless commerce with Europe while breaking out of the Single Market and striking independent trade deals around the world. Britain soon plunged into political predicaments and there were also increased reports of clashes in the streets between native Brits and foreigners (Schindler 2017). It seems that as Brexit was largely seen as a vote against immigration, some of those that had been accused of racism during the campaign felt vindicated by the results.

The spread of conspiratorial fake news about the EU was also increasing alongside prolonged difficulties in finding a viable path for Brexit. On social media many people were falsely quoting the Lisbon Treaty, claiming that by 2020 Britain would lose its veto on fishing and agriculture, and that by 2022 it would be forced to adopt the Euro (Toynbee 2019). Ultimately this was a misinformation campaign saying that if Britain could not get out in time it would be trapped as a subjugated state within a European federation. One story said that Britain would lose control of its borders to the Schengen scheme, and that it would have to hand the military over to Brussels. Another insisted that the London Stock Exchange would be moved to Frankfurt (ibid.)

In the wake of the Brexit vote, the previously stable UK party system was being tested. Political dividing lines in the UK were no longer primarily defined by the Left/Right divide, but rather by a new Remain/Leave division, which was threatening to rip the British socio-political fabric apart. In the 2019 EU Parliament election, the Brexit Party came out on top and became the largest UK party in the EU Parliament.

Under Johnson, the Conservative Party responded to this threat by more or less adopting the approach of the UKIP/Brexit Party on the Brexit process. This is similar to moves made by Mark Rutte in the Netherlands, and that of the Social Democrats in Denmark when adopting the policy of the Danish Peoples Party on immigration.

When the exit negotiations had broken down and Johnson was embarking on his first visit as Prime Minister to EU capitals, he blamed rebels within his Conservative Party for the EU's harsh stance in the negotiations, saying they were undermining his negotiating strategy. Measuring this on the populist rhetorical stencil, discussed before, we see here how the EU was positioned as the external enemy and rebel Conservatives as the internal traitors.

After Johnson finally struck a new exit deal, amending the one that had been negotiated by then Prime Minister Theresa May, he was refused ratification in the House of Commons, and the UK once again headed for a general election in December 2019. By his firm stance on Brexit, Johnson was able to hold the Brexit Party at bay and won with a huge majority, paving the way for the UK to leave the European Union.

In Trump We Trust

Populism was also taking a Neo-Nationalist turn in America in this period, culminating in the election of the flamboyant real-estate tycoon and reality TV star, Donald Trump, to the Oval Office in 2016.

Similar to what had occurred in the Brexit referendum, and in many other recent elections around the Western world and beyond, the US presidential campaign proved to be highly populist and conspiratorial. Many studies have documented the turn of Donald Trump and his supporters to populism and conspiratorialism. Content analysis of his speeches and other communications indicate that Trump was more than any other candidate prone to apply rhetoric that was 'distinctive in its simplicity, anti-elitism and collectivism'. Eric Oliver and Wendy Rahn (2016) found that Trump supporters were 'distinctive in their high level of conspiratorial thinking, nativism and economic insecurity'.

Illustrative for the more general move of the US Republican Party towards right-wing populism was for example when both Nigel Farage, and Marion Maréchal-Le Pen of the French National Rally, were in 2018 invited to address a high-level conservative and Republican gathering near Washington DC, where both US President Donald Trump and Vice-President Mike Pence were also among the speakers.

In line with the turn to nationalism and populist operations, Trump's then senior political advisor, Steve Bannon, set out three main priorities in the early days of the administration in 2017. The first marked the turn to nationalism, with primary emphasis on enhancing security and sovereignty, and the second on rebuilding America to greatness on the platform of economic nationalism. The third priority was of a populist nature, bringing about the deconstruction of the administrative state (Goldberg 2018). This last part speaks to the Deep State conspiracy theory upheld by Donald Trump and his crew, insisting that a covert vast complex of bureaucrats was ruling the country behind the scenes and without mandate from voters or elected officials. In his election campaign, Trump famously vowed to 'drain the swamp'.

With his rhetoric, Trump appealed to the white working class that had felt betrayed by the established elite. Many in the so-called Rustbelt, such as in the states of Michigan, Wisconsin, Ohio and Pennsylvania, had felt their dignity being removed by way of the fast-moving global economy. Trump's success was gained by tapping into the frustrations that many traditional Democrat Party voters felt about their out-of-touch political elite. His supporters would not necessarily believe that Trump could reverse the situation or make their lives much better. But as they had become increasingly dissatisfied with their societal situation, many of them proved to be happy to support someone who was prepared to stick a spanner in the works of the Washington machine.

Adam Enders and Joe Uscinski (2019) maintain that the main factor explaining the support for Trump is not necessarily partisanship or even, as such, anti-elitism, sexism, nationalism or xenophobia. But rather, that his supporters were primarily those who felt their status in society being threatened, irrespective of whether their lives were being disturbed by women, minorities or by political correctness. All of the above had to be taken into account. They thus offer a host of factors that have caused grievances for many people of the working-class whites, often over a prolonged period.

Trump ran on two main slogans, both relating to the notion of America's fatigue under the liberal elite: 'Let's Make America Great Again', and 'America First'. Both are in line with long-standing ideas of American exceptionalism. As I mentioned in previous chapters, both also echoed the rhetoric of previous eras. Ronald Reagan had run on the platform of 'Making America Great Again'. And the public face of the 'America First' movement in the 1930s was Charles Lindbergh, aviation hero and Nazi sympathizer.

Trump's nationalism was geared away from multilateral treaties and alliances. In many ways it was aimed against the very international institutional architecture that the United States had led in constructing in the post-war era, discussed in a previous chapter. Instead, Trump held a Hobbesian view of the world, where the international arena was seen as a zero-sum game of competition and survival. In this anarchical world, the President would be able to throw the United States' muscle-power around to strike great bilateral deals, allegedly for the benefit of Americans. In a speech in Washington in 2016, Trump for example stated that 'the nation-state remains the true foundation for happiness and harmony'.[13]

In line with the drive to relegate international institutions, the Trump administration demoded the diplomatic status of the European Union's Delegation in Washington from state equivalent embassy to the mission of an international organization. This attitude downgraded the USA to a diminished diplomatic role, which, for example, became evident during the Coronavirus Crisis of 2020. Trump's vast insults aimed at various world actors, and his unilateral tariffs, sanctions and boycotts, did not help in managing this global crisis.

A Post-Truth President

Compared to his predecessors—and indeed to most other prominent US politicians up until then—Donald Trump had an especially loose relationship with truth. The fact checking site, *PolitiFact*, found more of Mr Trump's statements to have been 'absolutely false' than of any other candidate in the race.[14] For example, he upheld the bogus claims of diverse topics such as Obama's birthplace, vaccination, climate change and immigration.

By fuelling the previously discussed so-called Birther movement, suspecting Barack Obama of being foreign-born in Kenya, and, thus, not legitimate as US President, Trump and other conspiratorialists inserted doubts about his Americanness. Instead, Obama was cast as foreign, and un-American. In other words, this was the process of 'othering' even the sitting US President.

At a fundraising speech in March 2018, Mr Trump boasted that in a meeting with Canadian Prime Minister Justin Trudeau he had, without knowing the facts, made up information, insisting that the US ran a trade deficit with its northern neighbour (Smith 2018). In many communications he also claimed that climate change was a Chinese plot, designed to damage the US economy (Aistrope 2016).

When studying some of these statements, it seems that Mr Trump did not care much whether his words were true or not. These were not necessarily all deliberate lies, told to convince people of specific alternative versions of events or interpretation. Rather, these were just bullshit, uttered to divert and distort what was deemed to be correct and right. Mr Trump's relationship with truth is perhaps rather that of a bullshitter than a deliberate and committed liar. Thus, it can perhaps be concluded that Donald Trump was an archetypical example of a post-truth politician, discussed above.

Trump used similar tactics to demonize his opponents, splattering all kinds of negative labelling around. He would for example systematically brand Hillary Clinton as 'criminal' and 'crooked' and repeatedly declared that she 'has to go to jail' (qtd in Levitsky and Ziblatt 2018). In his crowded rallies he welcomed a frequent chant from his supporters: 'Lock her up.' During these rallies he would sometimes flirt with violent tendencies and often applauded when critics were forcefully removed from the audience. Some of the footages brought memories of militias that fascist parties of past eras often used.

After the 2018 House of Representatives elections, Trump ran into a series of clashes with a group of Democrat Party congress women of colour. He referred to them as 'hate-filled extremists' and, although most of them were US born, suggested that if they didn't like America they should go back to their countries of origin: 'They're always telling us how to run it, how to do this, how to do that. You know what? If they don't love it, tell 'em leave it' (qtd in McCarthy 2019). A familiar sounding chant at Trump campaign rallies was growing louder, 'send them back'.

As I mentioned in the previous chapter, Trump's populism perhaps most resembled that of Silvio Berlusconi in Italy, and perhaps also that of Andrej Babis, the Czech Republic billionaire and media tycoon who came to ride the populist surge.

Enemies of the People

Like so many other nativist populists, Donald Trump was a political novice. Although he did not establish his own party, which is extremely difficult to do in a first-past-the-post electoral system, he was able to win over the Republican Party, initially against the will of its establishment.

In many ways, Trump was an odd representative of the nationalist Christian right in America. With many sex scandals around him, he was never much celebrated for particularly strong morals. Previously he had upheld quite liberal views, such as on abortion and gay rights. Trump had never been particularly religious and even supported restricting gun ownership. By the time of his presidential bid, this had all changed, and he advocated the cohabitation of both Christianity and American nationalism. Quite smoothly, he emerged as the heir to the heritage of Reagan, Gingrich and the Tea Party.

With relative ease, Trump was then able to subdue the party apparatus under his own will and move it away from many fundamental principles relating to professionalism, decency and civil rights. To make up for his lack of political backing, Trump was shrewd in utilizing the media. In the election debates he would drum up controversies that would attract attention to him rather than to his opponents. Many of the mainstream media took the bait, including *CNN* and the *New York Times*, who covered Trump far more than his rival, Hillary Clinton. Although much of the reporting was critical, the exposure he gained was worth millions in free press-coverage.

It is also telling for the post-truth times we are living in, that after being accused of promoting fake news stories Donald Trump turned the allegation on its head and started systematically branding the mainstream media of being fake news outlets. He even labelled established news outlets like *The New York Times* and *CNN* as 'enemies of the American people' (qtd in Mounk 2018). Steve Coll (2017), of the *New Yorker* magazine, finds that Trump's definition of fake news seems simply to be 'credible reporting that he doesn't like'.

Some incidents around Donald Trump were outright bizarre. One occurred when he sought to buy Greenland. The huge and largely glaciered island is an autonomous country within the kingdom of Denmark. Initially, most took it as just a yarn, but later it emerged that Trump was serious about the purchase. When being explained that Greenland was not a property for sale, but a country belonging to the population living there, the US President in protest cancelled a long-planned state visit to Denmark. He got offended by the Danish PM's rebuff, who had stated that the request was 'absurd'—Greenland was not a territory that Denmark could sell. The American President responded by calling the Danish PM a 'nasty woman' and complained that Denmark did not pay enough for NATO's defence.

The whole conundrum stunned most Danes. Former Danish Foreign Minister, Villy Søvndal, said the decision 'confirms that Donald Trump is a narcissistic fool' (qtd in Nielsen 2019). These exchanges are unprecedented between Western allies in contemporary times and indicate that we had indeed entered completely new territory in international affairs.

Interestingly, this was not the only time Trump called a woman nasty. In fact, that was perhaps his most common insult for women he did not like. The list of women he has called nasty is long (see Jones 2019).

Vilifying Migrants

Donald Trump proved to be unilateralist and isolationist in international relations. In many ways he was the archetypical Neo-Nationalist, fusing economic nationalism with cultural nativism. A major theme in his rhetoric, both prior to and after taking up the presidency, was in drumming up fears of migrant invasion across the US southern border. In doing so he would on several occasions flirt with the Great Replacement theory. When kicking off his campaign, he started by vilifying Mexican immigrants, linking them to rapes and the US drug problem. He retweeted a message by a white supremacist who falsely claimed that blacks were responsible for 80 per cent of murders of white people in America, and he also wrongly insisted that inner city crime was at a record high (Potok 2017).

In January 2019, I was transitting through Orlando, Florida, on my way back home from Medellin in Colombia. In Medellin I had encountered some of the many refugees that were fleeing the economic devastation of Maduro's far-left populist Chávismo regime in neighbouring Venezuela. Many of them relied on begging while others performed arts in the street in hope of few pesos. Their future seemed very uncertain. In Orlando I also met newly arrived Venezuelans. One of them was looking forward to starting work as a taxi driver. I asked him whether he expected many of his countrymen that were on the move to attempt entry into the United States. He said that he hoped not. In fact, he turned out to be a staunch Trump supporter, and was enthusiastic about building a border wall against Mexico, so as to prevent others from following him into the US. Our conversation reminded me that political patronage does not always follow the lines that we might expect. And, as is not all that uncommon among immigrants, the newly arrived Venezuelan refugee I met in Orlando feared that his own possibilities of succeeding might be diminished if many more followed. Thus, he now supported a president who had fought against people like himself coming to the country.

Another of my brief acquaintances in Orlando, a white working class American, told me that he had voted for Mr Trump because unlike most politicians, Trump did not speak at him, but to him. This is in line with the before-mentioned findings of Enders and Uscinski, that most Trump supporters were disillusioned with the eloquent and well-spoken elite. My white working-class acquaintance in Orlando then explained to me how refreshing it was to have a candidate who wasn't articulate, but instead sounded like one of the people. Precisely in this feeling is where much of Trump's appeal lies.

In vilifying migrants, Trump would interchangeably refer to Latino refugees and Muslim immigrants. Among promotors of the Great Replacement conspiracy theory was also Steve Bannon, former editor of *Breitbart* news and key advisor to Donald Trump. Bannon repeatedly referred to Raspail's (1973) before-mentioned novel, *The Camp of the Saints*. Like Marine Le Pen in France, Bannon saw the story as a prophecy, that Muslim refugees were now starting an invasion of Europe. Referring to Syrian refugees in October 2015, Bannon said: 'It's been almost a Camp of the Saints-type invasion' (qtd in Blumenthal and Rieger 2017).

Donald Trump often went out of his way to vilify Muslims, even though their communities in the US were relatively quiet, and—quite frankly—insignificant. He even went so far as implying that Barack Obama was the founder of the Muslim terrorist organization Isis. Although admitting that Obama might not himself have physically established the terrorist organization, he still insisted that Obama had been the most valuable actor in their formation: 'I give him the most valuable player award.' Trump moved on to also implicate his rival in the presidential election with the founding of Isis: 'I give her, too, by the way, Hillary Clinton.' When criticized for without merit implicating Obama with the notorious terrorist organization, Trump reiterated his claim: 'I don't care. He was the founder. The way he got out of Iraq was, that was the founding of Isis. Ok?'[15] Indeed, this was Mr Trump's *modus operandi*—irrespective of the circumstances he was prone to always double down on his opponents. In line with his science denialism, his disrespect for the establishment and experts, Trump initially brushed off most warnings around the imminent Coronavirus Crisis in early 2020, calling it a 'hoax' and saying for example that the matter was 'under control' and that the virus would 'miraculously disappear' (Paz 2020). Prior to the outbreak he had undermined, and even in some cases dismantled, several institutions tasked with analysing threats like these, for instance when shutting the National Security Council's pandemic unit. He didn't seem to comprehend the calamity, claiming instead that the crisis was being overblown in media to hurt him in the upcoming elections. The failure to respond left the US unprepared, leading to a far greater crisis than occurred in countries where authorities responded earlier and in accordance to established knowledge and advice of experts.

The Coronavirus Crisis

The crisis even led to the very federal union of the USA coming under question, with increased friction between Trump and many state governors over division of power in dealing with the catastrophe. Later, Trump blamed several outsiders for the crisis, most often China where the virus originated, but also the European Union, and most notoriously the World Health Organization, which had criticised those countries that failed to take the Covid-19 disease seriously enough. When the virus was ripping through the US Trump responded by halting funding to WHO. He had also moved to exploit the crisis to promote some of his most contested policies, such as of building his border wall to Mexico. In contrast to the chaos that reigned in the USA, China attempted to present itself as a responsible world leader, not so subtly seeking to exploit the opportunity to advance its place in the international order, at the expense of the United States.

THE MUSLIM CONNECTION

Relationships between the United States and many Muslim countries have been strained for a long while. The strife is for example evident in repeated invasions of US militaries in the Middle East, and in terrorist actions of Arabs in the USA, as I discussed in the previous chapter.

The controversy around the planned Islamic community centre in lower Manhattan—Park51—is illustrative of the combative attitude. Opposition soon rose, branding the project as the 'Ground-Zero mosque'. The leading campaigner, Pamela Geller (2010), wrote that this was 'Islamic domination and expansionism. The location is no accident. Just as Al-Aqsa was built on top of the Temple in Jerusalem.'

Geller claimed to be at the frontline of a cultural war: 'To allow a mosque at a place a Muslim gang destroyed on 9/11 would amount to formally blessing Islam's 1400-year-old tradition of exclusivity and suppression of all persons of all other faiths. It would be a 100 per cent victory of Islam and Sharia law over the US Constitution and America's time-honored democracy and pluralism.'

This rhetoric gained wide political backing in the USA. Former Vice-Presidential candidate Sarah Palin tweeted that the community centre would be a 'a stab in the heart' of Americans. Previously discussed former speaker of Congress, Newt Gingrich, also echoed Geller, warning that the mosque was a step towards replacing the US Constitution with the totalitarian supremacy of 'Sharia law', and that the project, in effect, amounted to a case of 'cultural, political and legal jihad' (qtd in Wright 2016).

President Donald Trump struck a similar tone. He proposed that authorities would operate a database keeping track of American Muslims. When in 2016 he argued for banning many Muslims from entering the

USA, he said: 'I think Islam hates us' (qtd in Schleifer 2016). After becoming president, he indeed found ways around hindrances to allowing citizens of several Muslim-dominated countries from travelling to the USA.

Like his aid Steve Bannon, the US President also voiced his concern regarding the Islamization of Europe, especially in the UK. In 2015, he tweeted that British authorities were disguising 'their massive Muslim problem' (qtd in Walters 2015). He maintained that more Muslims in the UK joined Isis than enlisted in the British army. He went on to claim that parts of London and Paris were 'so radicalized' that police officers were 'afraid for their very lives'. Once he retweeted three unsubstantiated anti-Muslim videos posted by British far-right activist, Jayda Fransen. One of them showed a Muslim destroying a statue of the Virgin Mary, another showed a group of Muslims pushing a boy off a roof, and a third indicated that a Muslim was hitting a Dutch boy on crutches (see in Weaver and Jacobs 2017).

At a rally in Florida in 2017, Trump turned his sights on Sweden: 'You look at what's happening last night in Sweden. Sweden! Who would believe this? Sweden … They took in large numbers. They're having problems like they never thought possible.' This was quite stunning as nothing really noteworthy had happened in Sweden that night. Possibly, the American President had been watching *Fox News* that had aired a dystopian view of Sweden after accepting large numbers of asylum seekers (Becker 2019).

As already established, Donald Trump has long made false claims about Muslims. For instance, he insisted that Muslims knew in advance about the San Bernardino mass shooting in December 2015 and did not report it. Famously, he accused Muslims in New Jersey of having celebrated the terrorist attacks on 9/11. In a television interview on *ABC News* in November 2015 he told presenter George Stephanopoulos that 'thousands and thousands of people were cheering as that building was coming down' (qtd in Kessler 2015). Like so many others of his statements, his claim was not substantiated with evidence. It has been well documented that some Arabs in the Middle East did celebrate the attack, but no evidence at all existed that Arabs in New Jersey were cheering as the towers fell.

All of these statements were untrue. Perhaps it is telling for Mr Trump's overall relationship with the truth that he announced his plan of banning citizens from several Muslim-dominated countries from entering the USA on conspiratorialist Alex Jones's radio show.

Donald Trump's rhetoric has unavoidably filtered out and impacted his aides and supporters. Illustrative of that was when his National Security Advisor, Michael Flynn, tweeted that to fear Muslims was rational. Flynn went on to describe Islam as a 'malignant cancer' (qtd in Potok 2017).

WHITE SUPREMACISTS

Mr Trump has not only been classified as an American nationalist, but he has also been suspected of sympathizing with white supremacist movements. Although he has often surely refused to condole their actions, he has also on several occasions been hesitant in condemning some of their hateful speech. It is also telling that the racist radical-right in America sincerely celebrated Trump's election. One such person was Andrew Anglin, founder of the neo-Nazi website, *Daily Stormer*—named after the German Nazi propaganda gutter press known as *Der Stürmer*. He wrote: 'We won, brothers. All of our work. It has paid off. Our Glorious Leader has ascended to God Emperor. Make no mistake about it: we did this.' He went on writing: 'All my friends in Europe are texting me "NOW WE'RE GOING TO GET TO KICK OUT THESE MONKEYS!!!!"' In conclusion he wrote that 'the White race is back in the game' (qtd in Ennis 2016).

Internationally recognized white supremacist Richard Spencer insisted that Trump's election marked a victory for identity politics (Potok 2017). This is significant, as promoting identity is indeed the core to Neo-Nationalism, that is, the post-war populist version of nationalism analysed in this book. When Trump was elected, Spencer led a modified Nazi chant: 'hail Trump, hail our people, hail victory' (qtd in Snyder 2018).

Anti-Muslim attitudes in the US have, like in Europe, sometimes taken a violent turn. One such example occurred in Charlottesville, Virginia, in 2017. White supremacists clashed with counter demonstrators over the removal of a statue of confederate legend, General Robert E. Lee. In the early afternoon on Saturday 12 August the twenty-year-old James Alex Fields Jr of Ohio ploughed his car into a crowd of anti-racist protesters, killing a thirty-two-year-old woman and injuring at least nineteen others.

An ultra-nationalist group called Unite the Right had organized the rally, which was described in the media as one of the largest white supremacist events in recent US history (Strickland 2017). Gangs of white supremacists marched across the campus of the University of Virginia carrying torches and yelling slogans such as 'white lives matter' and 'blood and soil'. Another set of chants went 'You will not replace us', followed by; 'Jews will not replace us'. When he was asked to condemn the violence, President Trump said that there were good people on both sides of the dispute.

Research has shown that violence by far-right actors has spiked in America since Trump emerged as a prominent political force. Historian Kathleen Belew points out that the violence of political extremists often increases when their views are more tolerated by the national political leadership. She maintains that the election of Trump to the White House has in a way worked to legitimize the use of violence among the far-right extremists groups (see in Tenold 2019). J. M. Berger furthermore states that in the Trump era, many of those formerly on the fringe saw an opening in the national discussion for their politics (ibid.). During the Coronavirus Crisis Trump was prone to pin blame on China, where the virus had originated. According to many Chinese Americans, this led to increased anti-Chinese sentiments and abuse against Chinese people throughout the United States.

White Genocide

The anti-Semitic chant is here quite interesting as Neo-Nationalists in Europe had mostly turned their sights away from Jews and firmly towards Muslims instead. Both paradigms, anti-Semitism and anti-Muslim sentiments, were, however, of the same nature, that is, in casting a specifically defined outgroup as foreign interlopers who were to be expunged. Curiously, the American far-right activists in Charlottesville were still revelling in German Nazi symbolism, such as swastikas and Hitler-quotes. Among slogans on their posters were 'Jews are Satan's children.' At the rally, American white supremacist leader David Duke said that 'the American media, and the American political system, and the American Federal Reserve, is dominated by a tiny minority: the Jewish Zionist cause' (qtd in Rosenberg 2017).

American anti-Semitism and anti-Muslim sentiments in Europe stem from similar fears nurtured by the Neo-Nationalist far-right. The two cases cast a light on an ongoing trepidation on both sides of the Atlantic, the anxiety over the dominant people being replaced by a foreign public, that is, the Great Replacement conspiracy theory of a white genocide being plotted by evil external forces, and even already underway. This is the ongoing fear that Christian identity is under siege by multiculturalism and an infiltration of people of other ethnic origins. During the Coronavirus Crisis, similar fears were rising around Chinese influence in America.

Correspondingly, studies have found that most of Trump's supporters believed that Christian whites were being discriminated against in America (Judis 2018). Organizations of American white nationalist movements have been on the rise in recent years. Their most common discussion theme was indeed that of the White Genocide conspiracy theory. Perhaps unsurprisingly, J. M. Berger (2016) found that most white nationalists in America supported Donald Trump for President. Apart from white genocide, they referred to him more often than to any other topic in 2016. Their most tweeted video on YouTube was a documentary titled *Adolf Hitler: The Greatest Story Never Told*. The collection of footage insists that Hitler was not the monster that the mainstream media and elite academia portrayed him as being, but that he, in fact, was a brave fighter against the world's most evil forces, that is, Zionist bankers and economic elite (Berger 2016).

Numerous violent neo-Nazi movements have existed in the US through history, as I have briefly mentioned in former chapters. One of them was the fast emerging *Atomwaffen* Division (in German, meaning atomic weapon), which was gathering many separated individuals and groupings from diverse neo-Nazi online discussion boards. This movement was growing into a kind of a small-scale terror network, with several killings and other violent acts being carried out in its name, for the protection of the white Christian population in America.

Pizza-Gate

The effect of far-right populism and sinister misinformation tactics for political gains have come in many and often unforeseen forms. The story of Pizza Gate is telling for this turn. In March 2016, the social media newsfeeds of many Americans were suddenly filled with stories indicating that Hillary Clinton and other Democrats were secretly running a paedophile ring out of a pizza parlour in Washington, DC. The gobsmacking revelations were tagged Pizza-Gate. The reporting told of leaked emails from Clinton's campaign chairman, John Podesta, unravelling coded message about human trafficking and the paedophile operation exploiting defenceless children. By the November presidential elections more than one million tweets had been sent with the hashtag #pizzagate (Douglas et al. 2017). The story was spread by the infamous American conspiracy site *InfoWar*, published by Alex Jones.

Among those following the story was one Edgar Welch from North Carolina. On 4 December 2016 Welch travelled to DC on a mission to break up the paedophile kidnapping ring that he had read about online. Upon arriving in the US capital, he stormed with his raised assault rifle into the Comet Ping Pong Pizza parlour to rescue the abused children he thought were being kept there.

After quite a commotion and a few shots fired, Welch was finally faced with the fact that no children were being kept there. It was just a pizza joint. Only after the incident did Welch come to realize that the data he obtained online about the alleged evil operation was inaccurate. He explained to an interviewer that 'the intel on this wasn't 100 percent' (qtd in Hannon and Hannon 2016). In 2017, Welch was sentenced to four years in prison. He, the people in the pizza parlour, Hillary Clinton, and indeed US voters, all fell victim to a fabricated conspiracy theory spread as news online.

Many similar violent events have followed. In October 2018, eleven people were killed in a Pittsburgh synagogue by anti-Semite shooter. In August 2019, another anti-immigrant and far-right shooter opened fire on primarily Latinos in the border city of El Paso, killing twenty-two people and injuring twenty-four others.

The National Rally

One of the effects of nativist populism in the third wave was of undermining traditional politics and in vilifying the establishment. This led to the demise of many rooted political parties and indeed to the breakup of the party system in many countries. This was for instance the case in France. Although nativist populists had failed in finding power in France, they were successful in undermining the traditional parties, both to the left and right. In 2017, the remarkable happened and neither of the two major parties graduated to the second round of the presidential election. Socialist Party leader, François Holland, had fallen so unpopular that he didn't even stand. Two relative political novices ended up competing for the presidency. And even though Emmanuel Macron easily won the race for the Élysée Palace on a fully liberal democratic ticket, Marine Le Pen, leader of the National Rally (formerly the National Front) did remarkably well, grabbing just over one-third of the vote.

It is noteworthy here that Macrons success came on an anti-populist premise. But similar to the populists he was opposing, he himself was also fighting against the establishment. His politics were thus in many ways defined by populism, as his success indeed came by opposing both the populists and the political establishment.

Marine Le Pen's father, Jean Marie, discussed in previous chapters, had always been a marginal, discredited and polarizing figure in French politics, nicknamed the Devil of the Republic. Marine had however systematically set out to de-demonize the party, and in 2015 she expelled her own father—the party's founder—for flirting with Nazism.

Jean-Marie Le Pen had also suggested that the Ebola outbreak in Africa could be a solution to its population explosion. When addressing supporters, the eighty-five-year old political veteran leader said: 'In our country and in all Europe, we have known a cataclysmic phenomenon—a migratory invasion that, my friends, we are seeing only the beginning of today' (qtd in Willsher 2014). With the old guard out, the rebranded party, National Rally, had by the 2017 presidential election come in from the cold and to a position of new prominence in French politics.

No Frexit

On Europe, the National Rally had changed tactics and refrained from campaigning for a so-called Frexit—a French exit from the European Union. Instead, Marine Le Pen emphasized rolling back the integration process, saying that with the electoral victories of populist leaders like Italy's Matteo Salvini and Hungary's Viktor Orbán the tide had turned in favour of nationalists who could reform the EU from within.

The result of the Brexit referendum in 2016 did not reinvigorate anti-EU forces in other countries. Prior to the vote, Geert Wilders had been highly successful in rallying support for Nexit—exit of the Netherlands from the EU. In Denmark similar voices had also been prominent. However—contrary to what many expected—exit movements in other EU member states instead lost momentum after the Brexit vote, at least in the short term.

During the French 2017 elections debate, misinformation tactics that had for example been used by Russian actors to interfere in the Brexit campaign, and in the US Presidential elections in 2016, were put to use once again, now for the benefit of Marine Le Pen against Emmanuel Macron (Snyder 2018).

The Syrian Refugee Crisis had also elevated support for Marine Le Pen. Although she had made many efforts to normalize the party and making it more acceptable in society, at the height of the crisis she still set out to block all new migrants from entering France. Indeed, she rather sought to see the back of many existing immigrants out of the country.

In March 2015, Marine Le Pen catered to the Great Replacement theory when writing on Twitter that France was under migratory submersion. She then invited her followers to read Jean Raspail's novel, *The Camp of the Saints*. As I have already discussed, Raspail's book illustrates the demise of Western civilization through mass immigration from India. Biological race is here a key factor in explaining the fates of societies. Previously, Marine Le Pen had said that the book painted a picture of a Europe being invaded by hordes of 'stinking' dark-skinned migrants and 'rat people' flowing in a 'river of sperm' (qtd in Symons 2017).

This idea of the submersion of the French culture to Islam has also been illustrated in prominent contemporary literature, most famously in Michel Houllebecq's (2016) novel *Submission*. In a non-fiction bestseller titled *The French Suicide*, Eric Zemmour (2014) argued that for forty years France had been gradually moving towards becoming an Islamic country.

A Run on Rome

As I have illustrated in previous chapters, populist politics have a long-standing history in Italy. In the third wave, the double blow of first the Euro Crisis and then mass migration from north Africa served to elevate several actors that upheld nationalist and populist views.

After the April elections of 2008, Silvio Berlusconi was back in the Prime Minister's office. The Euro Crisis was about to bite, and he was blamed for the poor state of Italy, for instance of not managing the country's staggering foreign dept. In 2011 he was ousted and two years later he was sentenced for tax fraud. Berlusconi turned increasingly Eurosceptic, for example blaming his demise on Angela Merkel, Nicolas Sarkozy and Christine Lagarde—as well as blaming global economic powers in general.

The Five Star Movement founded by comedian Beppe Grillo was also rising to new heights in the third wave. Grillo was an interesting blend of a social-liberal anarchist who upheld a rather leftist socio-economic policy. He advocated for direct democracy and free access to an open Internet. His populism was mostly found in his profound discontent for the establishment, including also the European Union. In many ways, the Icelandic Pirate Party resembles the Five Star Movement. In an interview Grillo described politicians as 'parasites', and said, 'We should send them all home!' (qtd in Bartlett 2018).

At the same time, Matteo Salvini was rebranding the neo-racist Northern League as The League (*Lega*). Similar to Donald Trump in America, Salvini ran on the slogan 'Italians First'. The League was much more clearly far-right nationalist than the Five Star Movement.

The 2018 election brought a coalition of the Five Star Movement and Lega to power in Rome. Like in France, the traditional party system in Italy had collapsed from under populist parties piling on, who were able to push the established parties aside. The supporters of these parties were found to be much more sympathetic to Italy's fascist past than people of previous generations had been (Judis 2018). In 2019, Salvini dissolved the government in an attempt to increase his influence in government even further. That attempt backfired when his collaborators in the Five Star Movement instead formed a government with the mainstream Democratic Party.

By the time of the Coronavirus Crisis Italy had for extended periods over the last three decades been governed by several creeds of populists. As populists in power often tend to undermine professionalism in governance, it can thus be argued that Italy was left less prepared to deal with the serious crisis when it hit in early 2020.

Notes

1. *Al Jazeera*. 2019, 16 March. 'New Zealand mosque attacks suspect praised Trump in manifesto'.
2. Pew Research Centre. 2017. 'Europe's Growing Muslim Population'.
3. Vidkun Quisling, leader of the Norwegian interwar nationalist party, National Samling, was a Nazi collaborator and traitor during the German occupation of Norway in WWII. He was executed by firing squad in 1945.
4. *The Local*, 29 August 2017. 'Meeting between Swedish and Norwegian ministers scrapped following "no-go zone" claims'.
5. See Yle Uutiset. 2008. 'Police to Investigate Helsinki City Council Member's Blog'.
6. See mtv.fi. 2010. 'Islamin yhdistäminen pedofiliaan toi Halla-aholle sakot myös hovilta'.
7. 'Sverigedemokraternas principprogram'. 2003.
8. See the Hungarian Prime Ministry official site on Ministerelnok.hu. 2018, 8 February. 'Prime Minister Viktor Orbán's speech at the annual general meeting of the Association of Cities with County Rights'.
9. Dw.com. 2018. 'Poland, Hungary say EU migration policy has failed'.
10. See on euvsdisinfo.eu.
11. Posted on hidfo.ru in 2017.
12. *BBC News*. 2016, November. 'Jo Cox murder: Judge's sentencing remarks to Thomas Mair'.

13. *The New York Times.* 2016, 28 April 2016. 'Transcript 2016: Donald Trump's Foreign Policy Speech.'
14. *The Economist.* 2016, 10 September. 'Art of the lie'.
15. *The Economist.* 2016, 10 September. 'Yes, I'd lie to you'.

References

Aistrope, T. (2016). *Conspiracy Theory and American Foreign Policy* (1st ed.). Manchester: Manchester University Press.

Åkesson, J. (2009). *Muslimerna Är Vårt Största Utländska Hot.* Stockholm: Aftonbladet.

Art of the Lie. (2016). *The Economist.*

Barfield, T. (2015). How German Media Shaped the Greece Crisis. *Thelocal.de.*

Bartlett, J. (2018). Italy's Five Star Movement and the Triumph of Digital Populism. *Coffee House.* Retrieved from Blogs.spectator.co.uk.

Bawer, B. (2012). *The New Quislings: How the International Left Used the Oslo Massacre to Silence Debate About Islam.* Broadside e-books.

Becker, J. (2019). The Global Machine Behind the Rise of Far-Right Nationalism. *The New York Times.*

Becker, S., Fetzer, T., & Novy, D. (2017). Who Voted for Brexit? A Comprehensive District-Level Analysis. *Economic Policy, 32*(92), 601–650.

Bennett, O. (2016). *The Brexit Club: The Inside Story of the Leave Campaign's Shock Victory.* London: Biteback Publishing.

Berger, J. M. (2016). *Nazis vs. ISIS on Twitter: A Comparative Study of White Nationalist and ISIS Online Social Media Networks.* Program on Extremism Report: George Washington University.

Bergmann, E. (2014a). Iceland: A Postimperial Sovereignty Project. *Cooperation and Conflict, 49*(1), 33–54. https://doi.org/10.1177/0010836713514152.

Bergmann, E. (2014b). *Iceland and the International Financial Crisis: Boom, Bust and Recovery.* Basingstoke and New York: Palgrave Macmillan.

Bergmann, E. (2016). The Icesave Dispute: A Case Study into the Crisis of Diplomacy during the Credit Crunch. *Nordicum-Mediterraneum, 12*(1).

Bergmann, E. (2017). *Nordic Nationalism and Right-Wing Populist Politics: Imperial Relationships and National Sentiments.* London and New York: Palgrave Macmillan.

Bloom, D. (2018). *UKIP Speaker Branded 'Disgraceful' after Calling Asian Grooming Gangs a 'Holocaust of Our Daughters'.* London: Mirror Online.

Blumenthal, P., & Rieger, J. M. (2017). This Stunningly Racist French Novel Is How Steve Bannon Explains the World. *HuffPost.*

Booth, M. (2014). *The Almost Nearly Perfect People: The Truth about the Nordic Miracle.* London: Jonathan Cape.

Booth, R., Dodd, V., Rawlinson, K., & Slawson, N. (2016). Jo Cox Murder Suspect Tells Court His Name Is 'Death to Traitors, Freedom for Britain'. *The Guardian*.

Boréus, K. (2010). Including or Excluding Immigrants? The Impact of Right-Wing Populism in Denmark and Sweden. *Diversity, Inclusion and Citizenship in Scandinavia*, 127–158.

Boyer, P. (1995). *When Time Shall Be No More: Prophecy Belief in Modern American Culture* (1st ed.). Harvard University Press.

Byford, J. (2011). *Conspiracy Theories: A Critical Introduction*. Springer.

Chrisafis, A., Connolly, K., & Giuffrida, A. (2019). The New Populism: How the Far-Right Appeals to Women Voters. *The Guardian*.

Cobain, I., & Taylor, M. (2016). Far-Right Terrorist Thomas Mair Jailed for Life for Jo Cox Murder. *The Guardian*.

Cobain, I., Parveen, N., & Taylor, M. (2016). The Slow-Burning Hatred That Led Thomas Mair to Murder Jo Cox. *The Guardian*.

Coll, S. (2017). Donald Trump's 'Fake News' Tactics. *The New Yorker*.

Davey, J., & Ebner, J. (2019). 'The Great Replacement': The Violent Consequences of Mainstreamed Extremism. *ISD Think Tank*.

Douglas, K., Sutton, R., & Cichocka, A. (2017). The Psychology of Conspiracy Theories. *Current Directions in Psychological Science*. Retrieved from Kar.kent.ac.uk.

Drabik, J. (2017). *The Dark Modern Age: A Farewell to the Enlightenment*. Gold Book.

Dunne, D. (2014). Finns Party MP Remains Defiant after Race Hate Conviction. *Helsinki Times*.

Duyvendak, J. W., & Kesic, J. (2018). The Rise of Nativism in Europe. *EuropeNow*.

Elabdi, F. (2019). Dane Who Wants to Deport Muslims, Ban Islam to Run in Election. *Aljazeera*.

Elgenius, G., & Rydgren, J. (2019). Frames of Nostalgia and Belonging: The Resurgence of Ethno-Nationalism in Sweden. *European Societies, 21*(4), 583–602.

Enders, A. M., & Uscinski, J. E. (2019). On Modeling Support for Donald Trump. *Joe Uscinski's Website*.

Ennis, D. (2016). Who's Happy Trump Won? The Klan, Nazis and Anti-Immigrant Activists Worldwide. *LGBTQ Nation*.

Espersen, S. (2015). DF Om Krigen Mod IS: Vi Bliver Nødt Til at Bombe Civile Nu - Også Kvinder Og Børn. Copenhagen. Retrieved from http://politik.tv2.dk.

Europe's Growing Muslim Population. (2017, December 6). *Pew Research Center's Religion & Public Life Project*. Retrieved from http://www.pewforum.org.

Fekete, E. (2018). *Europe's Fault Lines: Racism and the Rise of the Right*. London: Verso Books.

Fredricks, B. (2020, 13.4). 'Roger Stone: Bill Gates may have Created Coronavirus to Microchip People'. *New York Post*.

Gad, U. P. (2010). *(How) Can They Become like Us?: Danish Identity Politics and the Conflicts of 'Muslim Relations'*. Museum Tusculanum. Retrieved from Curis.ku.dk.

Geller, P. (2010). The 9/11 Imam. *Atlas Shrugs*. Retrieved from pamelageller.com.

Goldberg, J. (2018). *Suicide of the West: How the Rebirth of Tribalism, Populism, Nationalism, and Identity Politics Is Destroying American Democracy*. Crown Publishing Group.

Graham-Harrison, E., & Rasmussen, J. E. (2018). Stigmatised, Marginalised: Life inside Denmark's Official Ghettos. *The Observer*.

Hannon, E., & Hannon, E. (2016). Comet Pizzeria Gunman Says 'the Intel on This Wasn't 100 Percent' in First Interview. *Slate*.

Harrison, S. (2018). The Weight of Negativity: The Impact of Immigration Perceptions on the Brexit Vote. In *Trumping the Mainstream* (pp. 185–203). Routledge.

Hellstrom, A. (2016). *Trust Us: Reproducing the Nation and the Scandinavian Nationalist Populist Parties*. Oxford: Berghahn Books.

Henley, J., Roberts, D., Henley, J., & Roberts, D. (2018). 11 Brexit Promises the Government Quietly Dropped. *The Guardian*.

Houellebecq, M. (2016). *Submission* (Trans. ed.). New York: Picador.

Islamin Yhdistäminen Pedofiliaan Toi Halla-Aholle Sakot Myös Hovilta. (2010). *Mtv.fi*.

Ivarsflaten, E. (2006). *Reputational Shields: Why Most Anti-Immigrant Parties Failed in Western Europe, 1980–2005*. Annual Meeting of the American Political Science Association, Philadelphia.

Jo Cox Murder: Judge's Sentencing Remarks to Thomas Mair. (2016). *BBC News*.

Jones, J. (2019). Here's A Running List Of The Women Trump Has Demeaned Using The Word 'Nasty'. *HuffPost*.

Judis, J. B. (2018). *The Nationalist Revival: Trade, Immigration, and the Revolt Against Globalization*. New York, NY: Columbia Global Reports.

Jupskås, A. R. (2015). *The Persistence of Populism. The Norwegian Progress Party 1973–2009*. University of Oslo.

Jupskås, A. R., Ivarsflaten, E., Karlsnes, B., & Aalberg, T. (2016). *Norway: Populism from Anti Tax Movement to Government Party*. Unpublished Working Paper.

Kallestrand, G., Hahne, W., Andersson, P., & Ohlson, J. (2015). Finland, You Do Not Want the Swedish Nightmare.

Kessler, G. (2015). Trump's Outrageous Claim That 'Thousands' of New Jersey Muslims Celebrated the 9/11 Attacks. *Washington Post*.

Klages, E. P. (2019). Who Votes for Germany's Far-Right Party AfD? Not Who You'd Think. *Dw.com*.

Klein, A. (2013). The End of Solidarity? On the Development of Right-Wing Populist Parties in Denmark and Sweden. In *Exposing the Demagogues: Right-Wing and National Populist Parties in Europe*. Berlin: Konrad Adenauer Stiftung.

Krasodomski-Jones, A. (2019). *Suspicious Minds: Conspiracy Theories in the Age of Populism*. Brussels: Martens Centre.

Lacarpia, K. (2016). 'Offended Muslims' Attack Christmas Tree? *Snopes*.

Levitsky, S., & Ziblatt, D. (2018). *How Democracies Die*. New York: Crown.

Lewis, P. (2018). Steve Bannon: I Want to Drive a Stake through the Brussels Vampire. *The Guardian*.

Lister, S. (2016). Vote Leave Faces Criticism over Turkey 'Criminals' Claim. *The Independent*.

Machiavelli, N. (1550). *The Prince*.

Mahony, H. (2014). Orban Wants to Build 'Illiberal State'. *EUobserver*.

Massie, A. (2016). A Day of Infamy. *The Spectator*.

McCarthy, T. (2019). Trump Rally Crowd Chants 'Send Her Back' after President Attacks Ilhan Omar. *The Guardian*.

Meeting between Swedish and Norwegian Ministers Scrapped Following 'No-Go Zone' Claims. (2017). *Thelocal.no*.

Milne, R. (2017). Norway Minister Sparks War of Words with Sweden over Immigration. *Financial Times*.

Moffitt, B. (2017). Liberal Illiberalism? The Reshaping of the Contemporary Populist Radical Right in Northern Europe. *Politics and Governance, 5*(4), 112–122.

Mounk, Y. (2018). *The People Vs. Democracy: Why Our Freedom Is in Danger and How to Save It*. Harvard University Press.

Mudde, C. (2004). The Populist Zeitgeist. *Government and Opposition, 39*(4), 542–563.

New Zealand Mosque Attacks Suspect Praised Trump in Manifesto. (2019). *Aljazeera*.

Nielsen, J. B. (2019). Villy Søvndal: "Det bekræfter, at Donald Trump er en narcissistisk nar". *Berlingske.dk*.

Nordensvard, J., & Ketola, M. (2015). Nationalist Reframing of the Finnish and Swedish Welfare States—The Nexus of Nationalism and Social Policy in Far-Right Populist Parties. *Social Policy & Administration, 49*(3), 356–375.

Norocel, C. (2017). Finland: From Agrarian to Right-Wing Populism. In *Populist Political Communication in Europe*. Routledge.

Nougayrede, N. (2015). The Conspiracy Theories of Extreme Right and Far Left Threaten Democracy. *The Guardian*.

Oliver, J. E., & Rahn, W. M. (2016). Rise of the Trumpenvolk: Populism in the 2016 Election. *The ANNALS of the American Academy of Political and Social Science, 667*(1), 189–206.

Osborne, S. (2019). Polish Newspaper Runs Front Page List on 'How to Spot a Jew'. *The Independent*.

Palma, B. (2017). Are Police in Sweden No Longer Investigating Rapes Since Migrants Arrived? *Snopes.*
Paz, C. (2020). All the President's Lies About the Coronavirus. Politico.com.
Persson, E. (2015). Banning 'Homosexual Propaganda': Belonging and Visibility in Contemporary Russian Media. *Sexuality & Culture, 19*(2), 256–274.
Poland, Hungary Say EU Migration Policy Has Failed. (2018). *Dw.com.*
Police to Investigate Helsinki City Council Member's Blog. (2008). *Yle Uutiset.*
Pomerantsev, P. (2015). *Nothing Is True and Everything Is Possible: The Surreal Heart of the New Russia.* New York: PublicAffairs.
Porter, T. (2017). How the 'Deep State' Conspiracy Theory Went Mainstream. *Newsweek.*
Potok, M. (2017). The Year in Hate and Extremism. *Southern Poverty Law Center.*
Potok, M., & Terry, D. (2015). 10 Right-Wing Conspiracy Theories That Have Slowly Invaded American Politics. *Salon.*
Prime Minister Viktor Orbán's Speech at the Annual General Meeting of the Association of Cities with County Rights. (2018). *Miniszterelnok.hu.*
Pyykkönen, M. (2011). 'Luonnollinen Suomalaisuus' Ja Etnosentrismi Kahdeksan Suurimman Puolueen Eduskuntavaaliohjelmissa 2011. *Politiikka: Valtiotieteellisen yhdistyksen julkaisu, 53*(2).
Rankin, J., & Waterson, J. (2019). How Boris Johnson's Brussels-Bashing Stories Shaped British Politics. *The Guardian.*
Raspail, J. (1973). *Le Camp des Saints.* Paris: Robert Laffont.
Raunio, T. (2013). The Finns: Filling a Cap in the Party System. In *Expoising the Demagogues: Right-Wing and National Populist Parties in Europe.* Berlin: Konrad Adenauer Stiftung.
Rosenberg, Y. (2017). 'Jews Will Not Replace Us': Why White Supremacists Go after Jews. *Washington Post.*
Ross, T. (2016). Boris Johnson: The EU Wants a Superstate, Just as Hitler Did. *The Telegraph.*
Rydgren, J. (2002). Radical Right Populism in Sweden: Still a Failiure. *Scandinavian Political Studies, 25*(1), 27–56.
Rydgren, J. (2010). Radical Right-Wing Populism in Denmark and Sweden: Explaining Party System Change and Stability. *SAIS Review of International Affairs, 30*(1), 57–71.
Sæland, I. (2016). Facebook Post. *Inga Sæland.*
Schaeffer, K. (2020). Nearly three-in-ten Americans Believe COVID-19 was made in a Lab. Pew Research Centre.
Schindler, J. (2017). Not So Great: Britain Grows Increasingly Hostile to EU Citizens. *Spiegel Online.*
Schleifer, T. (2016). Donald Trump: 'I Think Islam Hates Us'. *CNN.*
Scott, M. (2019). Half of European Voters May Have Viewed Russian-Backed 'Fake News'. *Politico.*

Seierstad, A. (2015). *One of Us: The Story of Anders Breivik and the Massacre in Norway*. New York: Farrar, Straus and Giroux.

Serwer, A. (2011). Debunking Sharia Panic, ACLU Edition. *The American Prospect*.

Shields, M. (2019). Austrian Far-Right Leader Urges Fight against 'Population Exchange'. *Reuters*.

Simonnes, K. (2011). *I Stjalne Klær?: En Analyse Av Endringer i Høyres, Arbeiderpartiets Og Fremskrittspartiets Innvandrings-Og Integreringspolitikk Fra 1985 Til 2009*. University of Oslo.

Skarvoy, L. J., & Svendsen, S. H. (2011). *Dansk Partileder Refser Siv Jensen: - Hun Mangler Ryggrad*. Oslo: VG.

Smith, D. (2018). Donald Trump Admits Making up 'Facts' in Trade Meeting with Justin Trudeau. *The Guardian*.

Snyder, T. (2018). *The Road to Unfreedom*. London: Penguin.

Stone, J. (2016). Hitler's Nazis Designed the EU, Ukip MEP Claims. *The Independent*.

Strickland, P. (2017). Unite the Right: White Supremacists Rally in Virginia. *Aljazeera.com*.

Sverigedemokraternas Principprogram. (2003).

Symons, E.-K. (2017). Steve Bannon Loves France. *Politico*.

Tenold, V. (2019). The Neo-Nazi Plot against America Is Much Bigger than We Realize. *The Guardian*.

Toynbee, P. (2019). The Anti-EU Lies Are Back to Exploit Britain's Weak Spot Again | Polly Toynbee. *The Guardian*.

Transcript: Donald Trump's Foreign Policy Speech. (2016). *The New York Times*.

Walters, J. (2015). Trump Ignores UK Critics and Claims Country Has 'a Massive Muslim Problem'. *The Guardian*.

Waterson, J. (2019). Most UK News Coverage of Muslims Is Negative, Major Study Finds. *The Guardian*.

Weaver, M., & Jacobs, B. (2017). Trump Retweets British Far-Right Leader's Anti-Muslim Videos. *The Guardian*.

Wheen, F. (2005). *How Mumbo-Jumbo Conquered the World*. *Publicaffairsbooks.com*.

Widfeldt, A. (2015). *Extreme Right Parties in Scandinavia*. New York: Routledge.

Wilders, G. (2017). Our Population Is Being Replaced. No More. *@geertwilderspvv*. Twitter.com.

Willsher, K. (2014). Jean-Marie Le Pen Suggests Ebola as Solution to Global Population Explosion. *The Guardian*.

Wilson, J. (2019). Australians Are Asking How Did We Get Here? Well, Islamophobia Is Practically Enshrined as Public Policy. *The Guardian*.

Winneker, C. (2015). Finnish Politician Declares War on 'Multiculturalism'. *Politico*.

Wodak, R. (2015). *The Politics of Fear: What Right-Wing Populist Discourses Mean*. New York: Sage.

Wren, K. (2001). Cultural Rajcism: Something Rotten in the State of Denmark? *Social & Cultural Geography, 2*(2), 141–162.

Wright, S. (2016). Reproducing Fear: Islamophobia in the United States. In D. Pratt & R. Woodlock (Eds.), *Fear of Muslims? International Perspectives on Islamophobia* (Boundaries of Religious Freedom: Regulating Religion in Diverse Societies) (pp. 45–65). Cham: Springer International Publishing.

Yablokov, I. (2014). Pussy Riot as Agent Provocateur: Conspiracy Theories and the Media Construction of Nation in Putin's Russia. *Nationalities Papers 42*(4). https://doi.org/10.1080/00905992.2014.923390.

Yablokov, I. (2018). *Fortress Russia: Conspiracy Theories in the Post-Soviet World.* Cambridge: Polity Press.

Yes, I'd Lie to You. (2016). *Economist.*

Zemmour, E. (2014). *Le suicide francais - Ces quarante annees qui ont defait la France* (A. Michel, Ed.). Paris: French and European Publications Inc.

Zúquete, J. P. (2018). *The Identitarians: The Movement against Globalism and Islam in Europe.* Notre Dame: University of Notre Dame Press.

Conclusions: The Neo-Nationalist Order

In the last half century, nativist populist political parties have over three waves moved from the fringe to the mainstream in European and American politics. This has led to a new kind of nationalism thriving, distinct from that of previous eras—emerging into a separate Neo-Nationalism in the post-war era.

The first contemporary nativist populist parties to find significant success emerged in Western Europe in the early 1970s, such as in France, Denmark and Norway. However, earlier populists had already found initial support in the Alpine countries, and an agrarian-populist party was established in Finland in 1959. Far-right populism travelled east in the 2000s, when a promise of prosperity accompanying new-found liberal democracy was failing to materialize in many places. In the wake of the Financial Crisis of 2008, populism snowballed south, often taking a more leftist form. On the canopy of the Refugee Crisis in the wake of the Syrian War, anti-immigrant and far-right populism found foothold even in Germany, where such sentiments had been suppressed after the devastations of Nazism. Whether the Coronavirus Crisis of 2020 will lead to another rise of Neo-Nationalism remains to be seen.

Since the 2014 European Parliament election, Neo-Nationalists have come to dictate much of the political agenda in the West. The year 2016 brought a double shock with the Brexit vote in the UK and the election of Donald Trump to the White House in the US. In 2017 Marine Le Pen easily graduated to the run-off in the presidential elections in France, winning one-third of the vote. In 2018, two populist parties united in a government coalition in Italy. And in the 2019 European Parliament election, populist parties again won a record number of seats.

These parties have progressed in varying ways in the different areas in Europe and in America, and they have taken different forms from north to south. For instance, they have evolved very differently in the former communist countries in Eastern Europe from those in the old Western Europe. Many of the leaders here discussed, the Le Pens, Victor Orbán, Vladimir Putin, Geert Wilders, Jörg Haider and Matteo Salvini were fully far-right nativist populists. Some were rooted in other ideologies and only flirted with these traits, such as Silvio Berlusconi, Beppe Grillo and Donald Trump. The same can be said about Perón in Argentina.

The Neo-Nationalist order of our time culminated when three torrents coincided at a common confluence, fusing into a single channel of much greater velocity: the surge of populist politics, the spread of conspiracy theories and the avalanche of misinformation boosted by changes in the media. As I have illustrated in this book, nativist populist leaders were in the the new digital media environment able to spread conspiracy theories and misinformation much further than before, crafting an especially successful recipe for undermining the political establishment.

In this new media environment, the populists were able to bypass the former gatekeepers of the mainstream media and take their appeal directly to the people. By playing on controversies the populist attracts attention. The scandalous message prompts pushback from the establishment, which the populist can then use to spread his agenda even further. As I discussed in the previous chapter, the mainstream media can then easily be baited to pick up the bogus tale, distributing it much further than was possible on social media alone.

As I have documented throughout in this book, the surge of nativist populism has risen directly in opposition to migration, especially in the third wave. The most powerful conspiracy theory fuelling the extremist versions of nativist populism is that of the Great Replacement. In its essence this is the claim that immigrants were flocking to predominantly white Christian countries for the precise purpose of rendering the native population a minority within their own land, or even causing their extinction.

Fear of subversion is only the first part of the full theory. In its complete form the domestic elite is simultaneously accused of betraying the good ordinary people into the hands of the external evil. The full version of the Great Replacement conspiracy theory is more commonly upheld on the fringes. However, many prominent contemporary nativist populists have also alluded to it. Often times, they would rather hint to it, in a style of dog-whistling, than fully spelling it out.

Europe is a continent of inhered tensions. It has for long been torn between ideas of openness and liberal democracy on the one hand and xenophobia and authoritarian nationalism on the other. For comprehending its political culture, it is important to understand that it is a product of both trends.

After the devastations of the two world wars, nationalism was not only discredited but also widely and firmly held in contempt. Nationalism was equated with racism. However, after having been completely contemned for most of the post-war era, another form of racism was—over the progression of the three waves of nativist populism identified in this book—becoming a new normal in Europe and in America. The new racism was not based on biology as in previous eras, but rather on culture. This is a culturally based ethno-pluralist doctrine of 'equal but separate' where biological racism was replaced with cultural xenophobia.

Vitally for the story told on these pages, descendants of well-integrated migrants with an established history in society are thus not necessarily excluded from the domestic demos. Instead they become part of 'us' against 'other' external migrants.

Although the contemporary nativist populism is fundamentally different to the fascism of former times, many of the populist movements still do tap into similar notions of nationalism, ethno-centrism and ideas of cultural separatism. Like the fascists before, contemporary nativist populists also uphold a *Manichean* worldview when incessantly dividing between good and evil. In doing so they tend to position themselves as outsiders fighting alongside the common man against the malignant elite.

The success of the contemporary nativist populists was indeed based on dressing their scandalous message in more benign clothing than the fascists. This is the process of normalizing previously condemned views, such as racism, by way of coded rather than explicit xenophobia.

Although most nativist populists were primarily focused on conditions within their own native societies, they also tended to strike similar tones. A common theme was to offer a contract with the people, for the benefit of the masses against the elite. In Italy, Silvio Berlusconi offered a contract with Italians. Jörg Haider similarly offered a contract with Austrians, and before the 2019 general election in the UK, Nigel Farage of the Brexit Party tendered a contract with the British public.

Another trope was in putting 'our' people first. The FPÖ in Austria published a programme called 'Austria First', stating that Austria would not become an immigrant country. This is similar to Donald Trump in America who campaigned on the notion of 'America First'. That slogan had often been heard before. In the interwar years, the public face of the America First Movement was aviation legend and Nazi sympathizer, Charles Lindbergh. In Italy Matteo Salvini similarly ran on a slogan of 'Italians First'.

Taking back control was also a common theme of nativist populists, for instance upheld in the Brexit debate in the UK. In America Donald Trump ran on a similar chant: 'Make America Great Again'—a slogan that had previously been used by Ronald Reagan.

Definitions of nationalism and populism are fleeting in the literature, and the specifically nativist populism has been somewhat overlooked. In this book I have attempted to illustrate how populist movements have become increasingly ethno-nationalist, and, indeed, nativist. Their nativism has mainly been sharpened in opposing 'others' in society, primarily in protecting the native population against an influx of immigrants. This is the politics of separating outgroups from 'the people'.

In this book I have identified several common features of post-war nativist populism. These are nationalist parties, nativist and exclusionary, that campaign against multiculturalism and strive to stem flow of immigration. Usually they revolve around a strong charismatic leader. Most often they are anti-intellectual and anti-elitist. Another aspect is their simplicity, often insisting on simple and straightforward solutions to meet complex national interest. Often they are moralistic rather than practical, and they tend to be protectionist of national production from international competition. Also, populist parties are usually authoritarian and social conservatives, they belief in a strictly ordered society and are much rather defined on socio-cultural aspects than on the socio-economic scale. Finally, populists in Europe are most often staunchly Eurosceptic.

As I laid out in the book's second chapter, definitions of specifically nativist populists are here framed through identifying a threefold claim for their support of the people. First, nativist populists tend discursively to create an external threat to the nation. Secondly, they accuse the domestic elite of betraying the people, often even of siding with the external forces. Thirdly, they position themselves as the only true defenders of the pure people they vow to protect against these malignant outsiders.

One of the features separating nativist populists from the fascists of previous times is that they do not necessarily denounce democracy, at least not in name. They are however in opposition to the liberal side of the post-war liberal democratic order.

In addition to increased systemic cross-border state co-operation and pooling of sovereignty, the post-war liberal democratic system rested on shared values, including the rule of law, firm division of power, free trade across borders, respect for human rights, wide reaching civil rights, unbiased and professional administration, and a free and independent media. This was the liberal aspect of the post-war democratic order installed to protect individuals and minorities from oppression by the majority. These basic rules of liberal democracies were respected across the political spectrum and the system indeed celebrated human diversity. It actively and persistently countered collectiveness.

With the collapse of communism many people predicted that this kind of liberal democracy would prevail for the foreseeable future. However, as here has been explored, the picture was not to be so simple. In fact, nativist populists have surged, sometimes precisely due to their disrespect for this shared framework of liberal democracy. It is indeed via their willingness in disposing of these shared democratic values that much of their appeal comes from.

When thinking of fascists coming to power, we can commonly envision violent *coups d'état*, such as in Argentina, Chile, Greece, Thailand and Turkey. However, fascists also emerged through traditional democratic routes. As I discussed in the Introduction to this book, the interwar fascist regimes in both Italy and in Germany, however, came about via mechanisms of parliamentary democracy. Both were elected, and both had to rely on mainstream collaborators to form a government. Only in co-operation with mainstream political partners were Mussolini and Hitler able to reign in Rome and in Berlin. And it was only from that democratic position that they were subsequently able to abandon democratic elections. In other words, democracy was in these cases destroyed from within.

Similar to nationalists more generally, the relationship populists have with democracy can also be quite murky, and, thus, sometimes difficult to predict. Populist leaders often start out as being democratic, or at least pretend to be. They would often champion the use of direct democracy, however commonly in a highly selective way, fitted to their own agenda. Many of them even portrayed themselves as particular protectors of democracy, only revealing their true authoritarian tendencies after resuming power. This was for instance true in Venezuela. Hugo Chávez was democratically elected to office. Only after being elevated to power by way of democratic processes, was he—and later his successor, Nicolás Maduro—able to dismantle the very democratic processes that had brought them to power. As has here been explored, similar processes have been evident in Russia under Vladimir Putin and in Hungary under Victor Orbán. Into this mix, we can also append Perón in Argentina and Fujimori in Peru.

Nativist populists do not usually oppose elections. But some of them have proved prone to controlling their outcomes. When seeing oneself as the interpreter of the will of the people, a populist leader in power might not find it too problematic to diverge from conventional democratic practices rather than always allowing his mainstream opponents—those that he deems being traitors of the people—to compete on a level playing field. Instead, he might offer a rationale for it being more democratic to ensure the will of the people, as interpreted by the populist himself.

Rather than rejecting democracy as such, some nativist populists have instead introduced an illiberal form of democracy, dismissing diversity and removing the emphasis on individual rights and separation of power. Instead of liberal democracy, this is democracy without liberal rights.

The relevant question here is thus not only whether populists denounce democracy in name, but rather whether they respect it in reality.

As already discussed, authoritarian leaders have eroded democracy both via *coups d'état*, and by abandoning democracy after being democratically elected. More often than not, democracies die rather more gradually, often without us even noticing their demise. Democracy is thus much rather circumvented than abolished—gradually being eroded via incremental implementation of slowly evolving authoritarian rule.

History holds many examples when polarization has gone so far that mainstream actors have been tempted to collaborate with the demagogues, rather than reach across the traditional dividing lines in domestic politics. In doing so, there are instances where mainstream actors have unwittingly facilitated the demise of democracy and paved the way for populists coming to power.

Given the right conditions, all democracies can abandon their principles and turn to autocracy. In fact, history tells us this might easily happen. However, history also tells us, as is discussed above, that when the mainstream establishment is able to unite against illiberal forces then they are usually in a position to stem their surge. Populists rarely muster the support of the majority. Thus they often need help from the mainstream to gain control.

Conventional wisdom states that populist political movements do not last, that they have inbuilt difficulties of persistence. The resilience of many of the parties examined here has however proved those predictions to be wrong. Rather, much of their political message has prevailed over many decades. In several cases, as documented here, they have been able to find legitimacy and pull the national discourse in their own direction.

Although populism has been elevated on waves of crises, there are also many examples where such parties have persisted far passed any economic difficulties and have found support even in times of recovery after crisis and relative economic prosperity.

In recent years populism has indeed been immersed into mainstream politics. Contemporary Europe-wide opinion polls have shown that two-thirds of the population think that their country has reached its limit in accepting migrants. Anti-immigrant and authoritarian sentiments are thus not isolated on the fringes of society, they are no longer alien from the ordinary population.

This process of the normalization of populist politics occurs, for example, when mainstream parties follow suit in the wake of the populists, and in their quest for winning back lost supporters start themselves to abandon the once-shared values of Western liberal democracies. On that route, the *Cordon Sanitaire* that the mainstream had in many places encircled around the rough nativist populists was gradually loosening. This is the process of eroding once-shared democratic norms. Progression of this kind has, for example, occurred in Austria, Denmark and in the Netherlands.

In the UK, the Conservative Party was able to suppress first UKIP and then the Brexit Party by more or less adopting their approach on Brexit. This is similar to the move made by Mark Rutte in the Netherlands, and that of the Social Democrats in Denmark.

Denmark is a curious example of this trend. For over almost two decades the nativist populist Danish Peoples Party was continuously finding ever greater authority. By the 2019 general election they had however fallen victim to their own success, after other parties had more or less adopted their policies. This is particularly interesting as it illustrates how the demise of a populist party does not necessarily mean the rejection of its politics. In some instances, like in Denmark, it indeed rather indicates its ultimate success—in making the mainstream following it, and permanently altering existing policies.

Nativist populism has evolved over the past years and decades. When Herbert Kitschelt introduced what he called the 'winning formula' of right-wing populism in the late 1990s, he argued that its success came primarily in combining neo-liberal politics with authoritarianism and a policy of anti-immigration. As I have illustrated on these pages, another aspect has, however, become increasingly important for populist politicians. That is in speaking on behalf of the ordinary man against a corrupt elite while in an aggressive style pointing to an imminent external threat. The winning formula of contemporary nativist populists is thus also found in the dual process of instating fear and scapegoating. First fear is created and then blame is attributed. The fear is used to legitimize their means of protecting the people, of putting up barriers, closing borders, ousting immigrants, exiting international institution, emasculating the elite, and so on.

The relationship between populism and liberalism is precarious. Most obviously, these are usually quite authoritarian actors, emphasizing Christian family values and strongman leadership. However, with increased emphasis on opposing Islamization in the West many of these parties have shifted to position themselves as the protectors of Western liberalism, mainly when it comes to gay rights and gender equality.

Pim Fortuyn in the Netherlands was a pioneer in this regard, positioning himself as an ally of the LGBTQ community. Some of the Scandinavian populist parties have also somewhat followed suit, such as the Danish Peoples Party, the Norwegian Progress Party—both were under female leadership—and the Sweden Democrats. In these instances, the nativist populism was not necessarily anti-liberal, but rather they attempted to realign what liberalism meant.

The socio-liberalism of the Danish Peoples Party revolved around the authoritative nature of Islam. Their liberalism was almost exclusively in opposition to Muslim migrants, who were seen not to share liberal attitudes in northern Europe regarding gender and sexual preferences. This relatively recent commitment to liberalism is thus fuelled by their anti-Islam agenda.

This repositioning of the populist message, in protection of the West's liberalism against authoritarian Islamism, was made by several nativist populists in the third wave. Even some of those who had started out striking a highly masculine tone, turned to claim that they were now the true protector of women's rights. They would pick and choose which aspects of liberalism they would follow, and most often those useful in opposing Islam. In other words, it was an opportunistic move. More generally this was a move from authoritarianism to socio-liberalism aimed against Muslims.

In recent years nativist populists have not necessarily always been right-wing on the socio-economic axis. Many of them have indeed found success in occupying the traditional space of social democratic parties. Even the National Rally (formerly the National Front) in France has travelled from the right end of the socio-economic spectrum towards the centre, and on some issues even all the way over to the left of it.

The Sweden Democrats were never right-wing on the socio-economic spectrum. Instead, they presented a nostalgic backward-looking vision and incorporated the previous ambition of the Social Democrats of transforming Sweden into a genuine People's Home. However, the SD presented immigration as a threat to the People's Home and to the promise of universal welfare for the native population.

Rather than primarily referring to the social-economic situation of the *ordinary* people the emphasis of nativist populist has thus moved over to a socio-cultural notion of *our* people.

As I have discussed on these pages, the rise of nativist populism has had various effects. One is a greater volatility between elections in many Western states and the increased fragmentation of party systems in many countries. Governments now change much more frequently than before. The centrifugal nature of this trend has led to a transformation in European party politics, where centre parties are largely losing to the periphery at both ends.

One side effect of this activity has been an ongoing call for renewal in politics, generally dismissing political experience and instead bringing an increased appetite for inexperienced newcomers. When insisting that the professionalization of politics had turned governance into a trade that ordinary folks were in effect barred from, populists attempt to discredit mainstream professional politicians. This drive for the re-amateurization of politics has brought the political novice to prominence, and dismissed from duty many experienced and skilful politicians. This became evident during the Coronavirus Crisis of 2020. Authorities in several countries under control of populists leaders initially responded by dismissing warnings made by specialists, later finding themselves inept in dealing with the complexity of the calamity.

In undermining traditional politics and in vilifying the establishment the Neo-Nationalist era has indeed brought about the demise of many traditional political parties. This has given way to the populists establishing new party constructs, which, usually stripped of traditional party structures, were turned into vehicles of their leaders to wage a challenge against the establishment.

Populism has often been dismissed by the mainstream as being a pathology, some sort of delusion and deviation from normal politics. That has always been misleading. And after populist politics has infiltrated the mainstream—to the extent that here has been documented—it is apparent that the feeling driving these surges cannot simply be dismissed or marginalized as paranoid and/or delusional. Populism should thus not necessarily always be viewed as being derogative or negative.

Although populism can in many instances be viewed as perilous—at times leading to violence and the erosion of democracy, as here has been established—it can also in some situations be seen as a sensible strategy of the deprived and powerless who are faced with a socio-economic order that is skewed against them.

Over the past decades public authority has clearly been shifting to non-governmental actors, such as specialists, media and financial elites. In many Western countries special interests have become increasingly stronger. It is therefore not an illegitimate claim, upheld by many populist leaders, that politics has become increasingly alien to the common people. In that regard, populism can thus be a practical tool to delegitimize established authority and power relations for the purpose of winning back lost authority from an overtly powerful elite.

Understanding a longing for 'sticking it' to the establishment elite is key to comprehending the rise of nativist populism. This feeling has indeed been brewing among many people who feel left behind. It is, though, equally important to keep in mind, that there are several forces at play here. No single factor can be found driving the populist surge. Economic anxiety is surely one. But cultural backlash is another. To get the full picture it is not sufficient only to look at those left behind in the fast-moving global economy. Neither is it enough to view this trend as solely a nativist cultural backlash against immigration. The two are here intertwined, and they are also entangled with other aspects as well.

Donald Trump proved to be especially skilful in playing on divides in America, on the increasing economic anxiety and fears of cultural replacement. While spurring horror among most of the prosperous educated economic elites on the coasts, many people in the more deprived inland areas were glad to see somebody 'sticking it' to the ruling class.

Many people in these inland areas felt left out in the fast-moving economy of the twenty-first century. On the coasts some people would refer to the Mid-West and more deprived areas in demeaning ways, calling them the Rustbelt or the flyover states. In the more deprived areas that had lost masses of manufacturing jobs, many felt that that trade deals made by Washington benefitted only externals—either foreigners abroad or increasing number of Latino workers flocking over to the US. Keep in mind that absolute level of the economy is not the only driving factor here—no less significant is the sense of one's own situation in society compared to others.

This growing gap has for a long while been somewhat overlooked by the liberal cosmopolitan elite in America. Trump, however, told them what they wanted to hear, and even though he himself was a flamboyant millionaire from Manhattan, deprived whites proved to be happy using him as a kind of a wrecking ball on the Washington establishment.

As already explored, Trump did not just emerge from out of the blue. In fact, as I have discussed over the three previous chapters, the Republican Party had for decades been flirting with notions that Trump was able to play on, of pitting the virtuous people against parasite 'others'.

As I have already examined, the nativist populism of contemporary times has travelled in waves elevated by crises—similar to the fascism of the interwar years, which was largely born out of the Great Depression of 1929. Parties of this kind have ascended to power when successfully playing on polarizations within their respective societies, most often when aided by establishment collaborators. Although history holds many examples of polarization leading to a populist rise, it also teaches—as I discussed above—that when liberal democratic forces unite across traditional political dividing lines, they can commonly curb the surge of illiberal actors.

By the time of the Coronavirus Crisis of 2020 we had, witnessed a new counter-wave emerging, a kind of anti-populist pushback against the nativists and their populist gale. However, with the new crisis nationalist sentiments were mounting once again. Although Covid-19 was a global outbreak, it still prompted a highly nationalist response in many places. In

Hungary, Viktor Orbán and the Fidesz government went for a quick power grab, almost completing the transformation to authoritarianism. In Brazil, Jair Bolsonaro scorned scientific warnings around the decease. In America, Donald Trump started out dismissing most concerns raised by specialists, even those coming from within his own administration. Numerous examples like these existed of populists in power undermining proper and professional administration when dealing with the crisis. Erratic decisions and a lack of coherent and coordinated policymaking served to deepen the crisis.

The Coronavirus Crisis also illuminated the importance of science and professional governance. The crisis clearly revealed an ongoing conflict between nativist populist politics on the one hand and governance based on established knowledge on the other. With conspiracy theories and misinformation blazing, nationalist populism was once again on the rise. It however remains to be seen whether the Coronavirus Crisis will amount to the rise of a fourth wave of Neo-Nationalism.

Index[1]

NUMBER AND SYMBOLS
11 September 2001 (9/11), 26, 47, 83–126, 171, 192, 193

A
ABC News, 139, 193
Afghanistan, 103, 105
Africa, 5, 16, 58, 169, 198
African, vii, 7, 124
Aino Freyja Järvelä, viii
Aistrope, Tim, 103, 187
Åkesson, Per Jimmie, 160–165
Alabama, 79
Al Arabiya, 149
Albania, 181
Albertazzi, Daniele, 37
Alexander Platz, 1, 2
Algerian, 58
Algerian War, 65
Al-Jazeera, 149
Allah, 177
Allen, Chris, 106
Allende, Salvador, 17
Allenza Nazionale, 94
Alp countries, 8
Alpine region, 70
Alps, 89
Al Qaeda, 103, 104
Alsatian, 69
Alternative for Germany (AfD, Alternative für Deutschland), 11, 25, 134, 143–146, 148
Alt-Right, 104
Amaudruz, Gaston-Armand, 70
America, 25, 38, 42
American, 2, 11, 12, 16, 29, 38, 39, 41, 56, 59, 68, 78–80, 103, 105, 106, 109, 125–126, 131, 139, 154, 174, 186, 188–190, 192, 194–196, 209
American Nazi Party, 79
Americanness, 187
American Revolution, 124

---

[1] Note: Page numbers followed by 'n' refer to notes.

Amsterdam, 41, 106, 116, 140
Amsterdam Treaty, 99
Anderson, Benedict, 30, 32
Anglin, Andrew, 194
Anning, Fraser, 141
Antichrist, 102, 126, 138
Anti-Semitic, 142, 195
Anti-Semitism, 65, 97, 170, 195
Anti-Semitist, 113
Apartheid, 64, 99
Arab, 97, 103, 107, 117, 165, 192, 193
Arab League, 107
Araujo, Ernesto, 17
Area 51, 101
Argentina, 17, 210, 213, 214
Argentinian, 16
Ascoli, Max, 33
Asia, 80
Athens, 133
Atlantic, 141
Attack Party, 135
Attlee, Clement, 60
Australia, 141
Australian, 141
Austria, 1, 10, 14, 21, 24, 26, 47, 49, 53, 70, 71, 83, 87, 95–98, 105, 112, 131, 135, 139, 140, 146, 147, 212, 215
Austrian, 71, 96, 98, 146, 147, 211
Austrian Freedom Party, 95, 161
Austrian Peoples Party (ÖVP, Österreichische Volkspartei), 96, 97, 146, 147
Austro-Hungarian Empire, 55

B
Baader, Andreas, 61
Babis, Andrej, 25, 188
Balkan peninsula, 85
Balkans, 72, 96, 107, 182

Baltics, 59, 134, 176
Bannon, Steve, 133, 185, 190, 191, 193
Basque, 30, 134
Batten, Gerard, 180
Bawer, Bruce, 106, 154
Belarus, 117
Belew, Kathleen, 195
Belgium, 18, 86, 90, 91, 140, 150
Bellen, Van der, 147
Berger, J.M., 195, 196
Bergmann, Ægir, viii
Bergmann, Eirikur, 10, 38, 105, 115, 124, 165, 166
Bergseth, Irina, 176
Berlin, 1, 11, 25, 133, 145, 176, 213
Berlin Wall, 1, 2, 6, 8, 26, 47, 55, 67, 83, 84, 86, 103, 110, 167
Berlusconi, Silvio, 9, 26, 37, 86, 92–94, 112, 116–118, 188, 199, 210, 211
Bernardino, San, 193
Bertelsmann Stiftung, 9
Betz, Hans Georg, 38
Bible, 125
Bild, 144
Bilderberg group, 171, 180
Billig, Michael, 40
Bin Laden, Osama, 103, 105
Birmingham, 69
Birther movement, 137, 187
Blair, Tony, 88, 105
Blocher, Christoph, 70
Bobba, Giuliano, 118
Bolivarian revolution, 17, 19, 89
Bolivia, 17
Bolsonaro, Jair, 17, 220
Bonikowski, Bart, 11
Bosnia and Herzegovina, 85
Bosniaks, 86
Bossi, Umberto, 47, 94, 95
Boston, 124
Branch Davidians, 102

Brandenburg, 146
Brazil, 9, 17, 131
Breitbart, 190
Breivik, Anders Behring, 135, 141, 154–155, 182, 183
Bretton Woods, 3, 56
Brexit, 10, 14, 22, 24, 26, 41, 42, 131, 137, 143, 146, 174, 177–181, 183–185, 198, 209, 212, 215
Brexit Party, 22, 133, 180, 184, 185, 211, 215
Britain, 15, 18, 24, 41, 54, 57, 114, 146, 178, 180, 183, 184
British, 9, 12, 60, 89, 113, 124, 177, 178, 181, 182, 184, 193, 211
British National Party (BNP), 113, 114, 133, 181
Brussels, 89, 90, 133, 138, 159, 178, 180, 184
Buchanan, Pat, 125
Budapest, 14, 109
Bulgaria, 135
Bundestag, 11
Bush, George W., 80, 104, 105, 117
Butter, Michael, viii
Byford, Jovan, 137, 171

C
Caesar, Julius, 89
California, 102
Cambridge Analytica, 137, 178
Cambridge Dictionary, 14
Camre, Mogens, 118
Camus, Renaud, 139
Canada, 7, 30, 80
Canadian, 187
Canovan, Margaret, 12, 36
Capitalism, 17, 56, 60, 62, 68, 85, 110, 132
Caracas, 19

Caribbean, 5, 80
Carinthia, 95
Carnation revolution, 55
Castro, Fidel, 17
Catalonia, 30, 134
Catholic, 65, 92
Catholicism, 91
Cedroni, Lorella, 95
Central European University, 109
Charlottesville, 141, 194, 195
Chávez, Hugo, 17, 19, 37, 89, 134, 214
Chávismo, 88–89, 134, 190
Chechen War, 110
Chicago, 25, 71
Chile, 17, 213
China, 29
Chinese, 187, 195
Chirac, Jacques, 111, 112
Christchurch, 135, 141, 182
Christian, 8, 13, 64, 75, 80, 85, 96, 100, 102, 103, 115, 121, 124, 125, 139–141, 146, 148, 153, 154, 158–159, 168, 177, 188, 195, 196, 210, 216
Christian Democrats, 144
Christmas, 177
Churchill, Winston, 56, 57, 179
Clinton, Bill, 101
Clinton, Hillary, 126, 174, 188, 189, 191, 196, 197
CNN, 137, 189
Cold War, 2, 3, 17, 55, 56, 77, 83, 85, 86, 110
Coll, Steve, 189
Colombia, 190
Colonialization, 4, 126n1, 179
Combat 18, 113
Comet Ping Pong Pizza, 197
Communist, 2, 6, 7, 17, 37, 55, 56, 67, 78, 85–87, 103, 107, 117, 126, 210

Conservative Party, 22, 69, 119, 153, 154, 177, 179, 181, 182, 184, 215
Conspiracy theories, 42, 48, 66, 69, 76, 101, 102, 105, 106, 109, 125, 126, 135–142, 146, 147, 153, 165, 166, 170–172, 176, 182, 185, 190, 195–197, 210
Continuation War, 77
Cooper, Milton William, 102
Copenhagen, 114, 118, 170
Cordon Sanitaire, 90, 97, 160–162, 164, 165, 215
Coronavirus, 11, 17, 19, 24, 27, 47, 125, 132, 137, 139, 169, 174, 177, 179, 187, 191–192, 195, 200, 209, 218–220
Correa, Rafael, 37
Costa Rica, 18
Cotton, Tom, 139
Cox, Jo, 135, 141, 182, 183
Craig, Alan, 183
Credit Crunch, 132–133
Crimea, 176
Critical Discourse Analysis (CDA), 25
Croatia, 85
Croatian, 85
Cuba, 17, 29
Cuminal, Isabelle, 66
Cummings, Dominic, 178
Czech Republic, 25, 167, 174, 188

D
Dagný Birna, viii
Daily Stormer, 194
Daily Telegraph, 180
Danes, 118, 120, 148, 189
Danish, 8, 53, 72–75, 98, 99, 118–121, 148–152, 189
Danish Association (DDR, *Den Danske Forening*), 121
Danish People's Party (DF, *Dansk Folkeparti*), 72, 74, 87, 98, 99, 118–121, 123, 148–154, 158, 161–163, 184, 215, 216
de Benoist, Alain, 67
De Cock, Christian, viii
de Gaulle, Charles, 65
Deep State, 42, 138, 139, 185
Delors, Jacques, 180
Delrieux, Arnaud, 132
Denmark, 8, 13, 21, 24, 49, 53, 63, 65, 72–76, 78, 87, 92, 98–100, 110, 118–121, 124, 133, 139, 143, 147–154, 157, 165, 175, 184, 189, 198, 209, 215, 216
Denmark's National Socialist Movement, 114
Dewinter, Filip, 91
Document.no, 155
Douglas, Karen, 137, 196
Drabik, Janos, 138
Dresden, 1
Dreyfus affair, 69, 70
Dreyfus, Alfred, 69, 70
Dugin, Alexander, 174
Duke, David, 195
Dunkirk, 89
Duprat, Francois, 69
Dutch Freedom Party, 24, 116

E
East Germans, 1, 144
East StratCom, 175
Ebola epidemic, 142
Eco, Umberto, 35, 45
Economist, 117
Ecuador, 37
Egypt, 103
Eika, Jonas, 152
El Paso, 135, 182, 197
Élysée Palace, 111, 112, 197

Enders, Adam, 186, 190
England, 109, 113
English Defence League, 114, 183
Enlightenment, 29, 33, 34, 136, 138
Erdoğan, Recep Tayyip, 37, 116
Erixon, Louise, 164
Espersen, Søren, 150
Eurabia, 76, 107, 139, 146, 155
Euro, 66, 99, 111, 132, 184
Euro Crisis, 78, 85, 134, 143, 145, 156, 159, 199
Europe, vii, 3, 5–9, 12, 13, 16, 21, 23–26, 29, 30, 33, 35, 38, 40, 48, 50, 54–59, 64, 65, 67–72, 75, 76, 80, 85–88, 90, 92, 95, 96, 100, 101, 105–107, 109, 111–114, 116, 124, 131, 132, 136, 139, 140, 142–144, 146, 150, 158, 160, 165, 169, 174–177, 180, 184, 191, 193–195, 198, 199, 210–212
European, 13, 54
European Central Bank, 156
European Commission, 180
European Economic Community, 73, 75
European Free Trade Association (EFTA), 75
European Parliament (EP), 10, 15, 65, 113, 116, 133, 146, 149, 156, 170, 174, 209, 210
Europeans, vii, 4, 5, 8, 9, 14, 21, 22, 29, 33, 36, 39, 40, 48, 54, 56–59, 64, 68, 69, 71, 75, 84–87, 89, 92, 106, 107, 111–113, 118, 126n1, 131–135, 138, 139, 142, 143, 145, 149, 155, 169, 180, 182, 184, 209, 217
European Union (EU), 3, 11, 15, 41, 50, 56, 66, 70, 71, 84, 86, 90, 97, 107, 108, 110, 111, 138, 140, 143, 169, 170, 174, 175, 177, 178, 181, 185, 187, 198, 199
Evangelic, 80, 81
Evangelic-Lutheran Church, 148

F
Fallaci, Oriana, 107
Farage, Nigel, 36, 41, 179–182, 185, 211
Fascism, 5, 14, 16, 30, 33–35, 39, 44–47, 55, 59, 61, 65, 87, 92, 94, 141, 211, 219
Fatherland League, 99
Faye, Guillaume, 112
Feiler, Arthur, 33
Feminism, 30, 80, 165
Fidesz, 20, 108, 167–169
Fields, James Alex, 194
Financial Crisis, 10, 15, 23, 26, 39, 47, 72, 131–200, 209
Finchelstein, Federico, 17, 44
Fini, Gianfranco, 94
Finland, 8, 18, 24, 53, 72, 77, 78, 123, 131, 143, 156–160, 165, 209
Finnish, 77, 156–159
Finnish Agrarian Party, 77
Finnishness, 158
Finns, 77, 156–159
Finns Party, 156–160, 165
First World War, 33
Five Star Movement (M5S), 93, 94, 132, 199, 200
Fjordman, 155
Flanders, 89–91
Flemish, 89–91
Flemish Block, 86, 90, 140
Florida, 190, 193
Flynn, Michael, 194
Fortuyn, Pim, 91, 92, 106, 115, 116, 216

Forza Italia, 9, 93
Fox News, 193
France, 7, 8, 13, 21, 26, 31, 32, 41, 45, 47, 49, 53, 58, 63, 65–67, 69, 70, 81n1, 92, 95, 104, 110–112, 114, 121, 124, 131, 133, 143, 150, 161, 171, 174, 191, 197–200, 209, 217
Francisco, San, 62
Franco, Francisco, 16, 55, 134
Frankfurt, 184
Fransen, Jayda, 193
Fredriksen, Mette, 151, 152
Freedom House, 9, 117
Freedom Party of Austria (FPO, *Freiheitliche Partei Österreichs*), 71, 95–98, 212
Freedom Party of the Netherlands (VVD, *Partij voor de Vrijheied*), 116
Fremskridtspartiet (FrP), 73, 99, 100, 122–124, 153–156
Fremskrittspartiet (FrP), 72, 100, 122–124, 153–156
French, 3, 9, 11, 15, 29, 31, 40, 57, 65–70, 89, 90, 104, 111, 112, 114, 139, 141, 153, 175, 185, 198, 199
French Revolution, 3, 29, 33, 34, 68
Front National (FN), 8, 65–67, 111, 112
FrP, *see Fremskridtspartiet; Fremskrittspartiet*
Fujimori, Alberto, 17, 19, 37, 88, 89, 214
Fukuyama, Francis, 2, 3, 6, 8, 10, 83

G
Gates, Bill, 139
Gates of Vienna, 155
Gaul, 89
Gauland, Alexander, 41, 146
Gayropa, 176–177
Geller, Pamela, 192
Gellner, Ernest, 32
German, 1, 6, 11, 31, 35, 38, 69, 71, 77, 90, 144–146, 148, 149, 176, 194–196, 200n3
German Democratic Republic (DDR), 1, 2, 146
Germanic, 71, 146–147
Germany, 9, 11, 13, 16, 18, 21, 25, 31–33, 41, 45, 47, 54, 55, 61, 62, 64, 65, 77, 86, 114, 132, 134, 139, 143–147, 171, 176, 180, 209, 213
Gidron, Noam, 11
Gingrich, Newt, 81, 125, 188, 192
Glistrup, Mogens, 73–76, 92, 98, 151
Globalism, 17, 132
Globalization, 6, 22–24, 49, 60, 66, 146, 148
God, 78, 101–103, 194
Golden Dawn, 134
Goodwin, Matthew, 38, 113
Gorbachev, Mikhail, 11
Gove, Michael, 179, 183
Great Depression of 1929, 33, 46, 56, 219
Great War, 4, 34
Greece, 15, 17, 55, 131, 133, 134, 156, 213
Greeks, 144
Greenland, 189
Griffin, David Ray, 105, 113
Griffin, Nick, 113, 114
Griffin, Roger, 68, 94
Grillo, Beppe, 199, 210
Guardian, 10, 141, 171
Guland, O., 66
Gulf War, 103
Gunnlaugsson, Sigmundur Davíð, 166
Gypsy, 158

H

Habermas, Jürgen, 6, 85
Hagelund, Anniken, 122
Hagen, Carl I., 76–77, 100, 121, 122, 124, 153
Haider, Jörg, 10, 14, 26, 35, 47, 71, 86–87, 95–98, 105, 112, 135, 210, 211
Haiderization, 96
Halla-aho, Jussi, 156, 158, 159
Hansen, Jonni, 114
Hegel, Friedrich, 3
Heinisch, Reinhard, 96
Hélin, Willy, 180
Hellstrom, Anders, 123, 160, 161, 163
Helsinki, 157
Henriksen, Martin, 150
Herderian, 91
Higham, John, 38, 39
Hitler, Adolf, 18, 34, 35, 60, 89, 113–115, 117, 175, 180, 195, 196, 213
Hobbesian, 63, 186
Hobsbawm, Eric, 32, 55
Hocke, Björn, 145
Hodge, Steve, 101
Hofer, Norbert, 147
Hofstadter, Richard, 11, 12
Holland, François, 197
Holocaust, 70, 97, 145, 183
Hörchst, Nicole, 144
Houllebecq, Michel, 199
Hrafnhildur, viii
Human rights, 5, 17, 72, 80, 84, 89, 97, 110, 170, 213
Hungarian, 1, 108, 109, 114, 138, 167–169
Hungary, 1, 11, 18, 20, 25, 26, 42, 87, 98, 108–110, 131, 135, 143, 167–170, 174, 198, 214
Huntington, Samuel, 83, 103
Hussain, Saddam, 97, 112
Hutaree, 102

I

Iceland, 72, 132, 165, 166
Identitarian movement, 68, 69, 112, 139, 141
Identitarians, 68, 69, 84, 139, 141
Ignatieff, Michael, 7
Immigration, 6, 8, 24, 25, 41, 47, 49, 53, 54, 59, 64–66, 69, 70, 72, 73, 77, 96, 100, 107, 111, 113, 116, 118–126, 132, 139, 143, 144, 147–155, 157, 159, 160, 163–165, 169, 175, 181, 184, 187, 199, 212, 217, 219
Independence Party, 166
India, 5, 9, 131, 199
Indonesia, 9, 125, 131
International financial crisis starting in 2008, 47
International Monetary Fund (IMF), 3, 56, 138
Internet Research Agency, 175
Iran, 140
Iraq, 29, 97, 103–105, 112, 116, 191
Iraqis, 104
Iron Curtain, 5, 47, 55, 56, 83, 84, 86, 96, 107
Isis, 181, 191, 193
Islamism, 24, 116, 217
Islamist, 101, 103, 106, 114, 139, 142
Islamization, 92, 106, 152–153, 193, 216
Islamophobic, 105, 121, 154
Israel, 117
Italians, 33, 35, 57, 70, 92–95, 114, 116, 117, 180, 211
Italian Social Movement (MSI), 94
Italy, 7, 18, 21, 26, 27, 33, 35, 37, 47, 54, 57, 61, 63, 65, 86, 92–94, 98, 112, 116, 117, 131, 133, 139, 180, 188, 198–200, 210–213
Ivarsflaten, Elisabeth, 162

J

Jagers, Jan, 91
Japan, 17, 89
Jensen, Siv, 13, 76, 100, 122, 153, 154
Jerusalem, 192
Jews, 39, 49, 59, 69, 117, 170, 194, 195
Jobbik movement, 108, 114, 135
Jones, Alex, 171, 189, 193, 196
Jospin, Lionel, 111
Judis, John B., 78, 108, 125, 143, 145, 156, 168, 169, 196, 200
Jupskås, Anders, 40, 100, 119, 123, 124, 153
Jyllands-Posten, 120

K

Kaczynski brothers, 107
Kaczynski, Jaroslav, 169
Kaltwasser, Cristóbal, 7
Karelia, 77
Karlsson, Mattias, 115
Kazan, 20
Kennan, George, 16
Kennedy, John F., 105
Kenya, 137, 179, 187
Keynesian economic model, 60
Khodorkovsky, Mikhail, 110
Kiev, 176
King, Steve, 126
Kitschelt, Herbert, 46, 74, 122, 150, 216
Kjærsgaard, Pia, 13, 74, 87, 98, 99, 110, 118, 149, 151, 154
Klarström, Anders, 115
Knight, Peter, viii
Knight Templars, 154
Koch brothers, Charles and David, 124
Kohn, Hans, 78
Koran, 41
Koresh, David, 102
Krarup, Søren, 121
Kremlin, 14, 19, 109–110, 171–174, 176
Kronen Zeitung, 95
Kuk Klux Klan, 101
Kurz, Sebastian, 147
Kyle, Jordan, 9

L

Labour Party, 60, 88, 121, 141, 153, 154, 156, 177, 182
Lagarde, Christine, 199
Laissez-faire, 94, 109
Lane, David, 117
Lange, Anders, 75, 76, 99, 100, 124
Langenhove, Dries Van, 140
Lapua movement, 77
Latin America, 16, 17, 80, 88, 126n1
Law and order, 50, 69, 91, 96, 100, 111, 148, 153, 158, 162, 169
Le Figaro, 68
Le Pen, Jean-Marie, 8, 45, 47, 53, 65–67, 92, 111, 112, 114, 124, 133, 134, 174, 198
Le Pen, Marine, 11, 13, 45, 112, 131, 133, 134, 191, 197–199, 209, 210
Lebanon, 103
Lee, Robert E., 194
Leefbaarheid, 92, 115
Lega, 14, 93, 94, 132, 135, 200
Lega Nord (LN), 92, 94
Legnante, Guido, 118
Lehman Brothers, 132
Leipzig, 1
Le-Pen, Marion Maréchal, 24
Levitsky, Steven, 16, 18, 79, 81, 104, 168, 188
Lewis, Bernhard, 103

INDEX 229

Liberal democracy, 2–3, 5–9, 11, 21, 26, 33, 34, 55, 56, 58, 68, 71, 83, 85, 107–110, 167, 169–171, 174, 176, 209, 211, 213–215
Liberalism, 7, 30, 33, 36, 49, 62, 63, 72, 80, 91, 92, 106, 108, 109, 115–116, 148, 164, 165, 216, 217
Libertarians, 54, 98, 100, 124, 158
Libya, 7, 97, 116
Limbaugh, Ross, 104
Lindbergh, Charles, 16, 186, 212
Lipset, Seymour Martin, 79
Lisbon, 133
Lithuania, 29, 107, 175
Littman, Giséle, 107
Liveable Netherlands, 92
London Stock Exchange, 184
Lucardie, Paul, 92, 116
Lukashenko, Alexander, 117

M
Maastricht Treaty, 84, 111
Macedonia, 85, 181
Machiavelli, N., 135
Macron, Emmanuel, 11, 112, 175, 176, 197, 198
Madrid, 133
Maduro, Nicolas, 19, 134, 190, 214
Mafia, 117
Magyar, 109
Mair, Thomas, 135, 182, 183
Manhattan, 192, 219
Manichean, 37, 126, 211
Marseillaise, 29
Marshall, George, 56
Marshall Aid Plan, 56, 61
Marx, Karl, 3
Marxism, 33, 154
Marxists, 39
Massie, Alex, 183

Mazower, Mark, 60, 64
Mazzini, Giuseppe, 33
McCarthy, Joseph, 78, 79
McCarthyism, 47, 78–80
McDonnel, Duncan, 37
McRobbie, Heather, viii
McVeigh, Timothy, 101, 102
Mecklenburg, 146
Medellin, 190
Mediterranean, 57
Meinecke, Friedrich, 31, 91
Meinhof, Ulrike, 61
Merkel, Angela, 144, 175, 199
Mexican, 41, 190
Mexico, 11, 190
Michigan, 186
Middle East, 16, 24, 72, 103, 104, 142, 169, 192, 193
Middle Eastern, 68, 104
Migrants, 5, 7, 10, 24, 38, 40, 42, 50, 58–60, 63, 64, 66–69, 96, 98, 100, 106, 109, 111, 121, 135, 139, 142, 144–146, 150, 152, 159, 163–165, 168, 169, 172, 177, 181, 189–191, 198, 199, 211, 215, 216
Migration, 4–6, 11, 16, 24, 25, 58, 59, 63, 64, 69, 96, 99–100, 107, 113, 119, 120, 122, 139–142, 144, 145, 147, 152, 164, 169, 177, 180–182, 199, 200n9, 210
Milan, 61
Milosevic, Slobodan, 85
Mitterrand, François, 66
Moffit, Benjamin, 47, 164
Mohammed, 120
Monet, Jean, 57
Mongols, 108
Montenegro, 181
Mordaunt, Penny, 181
Moroccans, 92
Morocco, vii

Moscow, 14, 172, 173
Moscow State Institute of International Relations, 171
Mounk, Yascha, 6, 7, 9, 25, 41, 143, 189
Movimento Sociale Italiano (MSI), 94
Mudde, Cas, 7, 13, 14, 35, 36, 106, 132
Mueller, Robert, 175
Multicultural, 5, 6, 58, 73, 78, 100, 115, 144, 148, 160, 163, 182
Multiculturalism, 7, 8, 26, 47, 49, 53, 68, 72, 91, 92, 106, 116, 132, 140, 145, 154, 157, 159, 164, 195, 212
Munster, 4
Muslims, 14, 24, 25, 39, 44, 47, 49, 53, 67, 69, 70, 73, 74, 76, 85, 91, 96, 97, 103–107, 111, 114, 116, 118, 120, 124–126, 135, 137, 139–146, 148–153, 155, 159, 160, 163–166, 177, 180–183, 190–195, 216, 217
Mussolini, Benito, 14, 18, 34, 35, 57, 94, 117, 135, 213

N
Napoleon, 89, 180
National Health Service (NHS), 178, 181
Nationalism, vii, viii, 4–6, 10, 16, 22, 24–26, 29–34, 36, 38–40, 47, 48, 56, 57, 61, 64, 65, 68, 69, 71–73, 78, 84, 85, 87, 90, 91, 96, 107, 108, 131, 134, 142, 143, 145, 148, 157, 165, 183, 185, 186, 188, 189, 194, 209, 211, 212
National Rally, 9, 65, 133, 153, 174, 185, 197–198, 217
National Security Agency (NSA), 104
Nativism, 4, 38–41, 185, 189, 212
Nativist, vii, 1–27, 29–50, 53, 54, 61, 63–65, 67, 69, 71, 72, 77, 78, 83, 84, 86, 90, 92, 94, 95, 98, 100, 101, 107–110, 113, 115–117, 124, 131–133, 135, 139, 140, 142–147, 150–151, 153–155, 163–166, 172, 177, 180, 181, 188, 197, 209–219
Nazism, 5, 11, 34, 59–61, 70, 183, 198, 209
Neoconservatives, 8, 11, 54, 80–81, 104, 125, 126
Neo-liberalism, 62, 63, 111, 157, 167
Neo-Nazis, 46, 62, 64, 65, 70, 87, 113–115, 134, 135, 145, 159, 161, 162, 194, 196
Netanyahu, Benjamin, 117
Netherlands, 21, 24, 41, 43, 49, 86, 90–92, 106, 115, 139, 140, 163, 184, 198, 215, 216
New Jersey, 105, 193
New Right, 40, 67, 151, 152
New World Order, 3, 4, 102, 137, 138
New York City, 102, 142
New Yorker, 189
New York Times, 189
New Zealand, 135, 141
Nice, 24
Nolte, Ernst, 33
Nordic, 8, 48, 53, 54, 72–73, 91, 115, 116, 147, 152, 157, 163
Nordic Council, 152
Norse, 161
North America, 2
North Atlantic Treaty Organization (NATO), 3, 56, 67, 75, 110, 189
North Carolina, 196
Norway, 8, 13, 53, 63, 65, 72, 75–76, 78, 99, 100, 106, 121–124, 131, 141, 152–155, 157, 158, 176, 182, 200n3, 209

Norwegian, 8, 40, 75, 76, 100, 121–124, 141, 153, 155, 156, 176, 200n3, 200n4
Norwegian Progress Party, 72, 99–101, 121, 124, 162, 216
Nougayrede, Natalie, 171
Nouvelle Droite (ND), 40, 67, 68, 70, 84, 114, 121

O
Obama, Barack, 124–126, 137, 179, 187, 191
Ohio, 186, 194
Oil Crisis, 3, 8, 24, 53–81, 83, 107
Oklahoma, 101
Oligarchs, 109
Oliver, J. Eric, 185
OPEC crisis, 47
OPEC Oil Crisis, 53
Open Society Foundation, 109
Orbán, Viktor, 20, 36, 108–110, 134, 167–170, 198, 200n8, 210, 214
Organization for Economic Cooperation in Europe (OEEC), 3
Organization for Security and Co-operation in Europe (OSCE), 20
Orlando, 190
Oslo, 154, 155
Osnabruck, 4
Österreichische Volkspartei (OVP), 96, 97, 146, 147
Ottoman Empire, 55
Ottomans, 108, 155

P
Pakistan, 5, 140
Palestine, 29
Palin, Sarah, 192
Palme, Olof, 163
Paludan, Rasmus, 152
Panama Papers, 166
Paris, 25, 61, 62, 66, 112, 133, 150, 193
Parisian, 67
Park51, 192
Patriot Act, 104
Patriotic Europeans against the Islamization of the Occident (PEDIGA), 144, 146
Paul, Ron, 125
Pauwels, Teun, 91
Paxton, Robert, 35
Pegida, 45
Pence, Mike, 185
Pennsylvania, 102, 186
Pentagon, 102
Peoples Party, 118, 120, 166, 183
Peoples Party of Switzerland, 8, 70, 95
Peron, Juan, 16, 17
Peronism, 17
Perry, Frauke, 13, 145
Peru, 17, 37, 88, 214
Peruvian, 19, 88
Pew Research Centre, 200n2
Pim Fortuyn's List, 86, 115, 116
Pinochet, Augusto, 17
Pirate Party, 166, 199
Pittsburgh, 197
Pizzagate, 196
Podemos, 15, 134
Poland, 18, 20, 25, 26, 87, 98, 107, 131, 134, 167, 169, 170, 174
PolitiFact, 187
Pomerantsev, Peter, 171
Populism, vii, viii, 27–50, 53, 54, 61, 64–67, 70, 71, 77–78, 83–86, 90, 92, 94–96, 98, 100, 101, 107, 109, 110, 113, 115, 122, 124, 131–135, 140, 142, 143, 147, 154, 157, 163, 181, 185, 188, 196, 197, 199, 209–212, 215–219

Portugal, 16, 55
Post-war order, 3, 5, 6, 54–55, 61
Pots-and-Pans Revolution, 166
Potsdam, 144
Poujade movement, 65
Poujade, Pierre, 65
Powell, Enoch, 69, 152
Progress Party, 26, 73, 74, 76, 118, 123, 152, 154
Prussia, 55
Prussian, 29
Punk-rock, 64
Pussy Riot, 172, 173
Putin, Vladimir, 14, 20, 31, 109, 110, 117, 134, 135, 170–173, 176, 210, 214

Q
Quebec, 30
Quisling, 154
Quran, 125

R
Racism, 4, 39, 40, 48, 59, 64, 68, 71, 73, 87, 96, 99, 104, 113, 118, 120, 122, 141, 148, 152, 155, 161, 175, 179, 182, 184, 211
Rahn, Wendy, 185
Rakete, Carola, 7
Raspail, Jean, 69, 191, 199
Reagan, Ronald, 11, 63, 66, 81, 186, 188, 212
Reinthaller, Anton, 71
Renan, Ernest, 31, 32, 41
Republican Party, 8, 54, 79–81, 87, 104, 124, 185, 188, 219
Reykjavik, 2, 167
Riess-Passer, Susanne, 97
Robinson, Tommy, 114

Rockwell, George Lincoln, 79
Roe vs Wade, 81
Roemer, J. E., 119
Roman Empire, 138
Romania, 168
Romanticism, 29
Roma people, 39, 49, 155
Rome, 9, 11, 35, 45, 61, 93, 94, 133, 199–200, 213
Roosevelt, Theodore, 16
Rothschild family, 176
Russians, 20, 31, 109, 170–173, 175–177, 198
Russia Today (RT), 171
Rutte, Mark, 140, 184, 215
Rydgren, Jens, 39, 40, 123, 148, 160, 162

S
Sæland, Inga, 166
St. Nicholas church, 1
St Petersburg, 175, 176
St Stephano, 57
Salazar, António de Oliveira, 16, 55
Salvini, Matteo, 7, 14, 35, 36, 133–135, 198, 200, 210, 212
Sami population, 100, 123, 158
Sarkozy, Nicolas, 199
Saudi Arabia, 103
Saxony, 146
Scandinavia, 15, 26, 54, 86, 88, 98, 176
Scandinavian, 35, 75, 134, 216
Schabowski, Gunther, 1, 2
Schedler, Andreas, 37
Schengen border scheme, 66, 184
Schumann, Robert, 57
Schussel, Wolfgang, 97
Scmidt, Helle Thorning, 151
Scott, Peter Dale, 105, 174
Scottish, 30

INDEX   233

Second World War, 3, 4, 13, 14, 16, 22, 25, 30, 34, 53, 55, 58, 67, 73, 75, 77, 78, 85, 97, 99, 142, 145, 147, 160, 165, 170
Serbia, 85, 181
Serbian, 85
Serwer, Adam, 141
Sex Pistols, 64
Sharia laws, 124, 141–142, 160, 165, 192
Shining Path, 88
Sigurður, Einar, viii
Slovak National Party, 107
Slovenia, 85
Smith, Adam, 63
Smith, Anthony, 32
Smith, Ian Duncan, 181
Social democratic, 8, 21, 22, 53, 87, 88, 150, 152, 162, 164, 217
Social Democrats, 21, 87–88, 97, 146, 150, 151, 160, 162–165, 184, 215, 217
Socialism, 30, 33, 36, 110, 157
Socialist Unity Party, 1
Soini, Timo, 156, 157, 159
Soldiers of Odin, 159
Solidarnosc, 169
Sorensen, Lone, viii, 43
Soros, George, 109, 166, 168, 169
South Africa, 64, 99
Soviets, 86, 101, 170
Soviet Union, 11, 55, 60, 77, 86, 103, 109, 110
Søvndal, Villy, 189
Spain, vii, 15, 16, 30, 55, 133, 134
Spencer, Richard, 194
Spencer, Robert, 167
Spinelli, Altiero, 57
Stalin, Joseph, 14, 60, 135
Stephanopoulos, George, 193
Stephen, Magyar King Saint, 108
Stoltenberg, Jens, 154

Stone, Roger, 139, 180
Strache, Heinz-Christian, 96, 140, 147
Straeten, Van der, 119
Suomen Maasedun Puolue (SMP), 77, 78, 157
Suomi, 77–78, 158
Sverigedemocraterna (SD), 72, 217
Sweden, 15, 65, 72, 74, 115, 123, 149, 155, 160–162, 164, 165, 175, 177, 193, 217
Sweden Democrats (SD), 72, 115, 145, 160–165, 216, 217
Swedish, 40, 72, 115, 148, 158, 160–165, 175, 177
Switzerland, 53, 70, 83, 131
Sydsvenskan, 177
Syria, 142, 150, 173, 181
Syrian, 144, 149, 169, 181, 191
Syriza, 15, 134

T
Taguieff, Pierre-André, 68
Tambroni, Fernando, 61
Tatarstan, 20
Tea Party, 11, 124–126, 138, 188
Texas, 102
Thailand, 17, 213
Thatcher, Margaret, 63, 81
Thatcherian, 63
Thatcherism, 63
Thatcherite, 86
Third Reich, 55, 71, 89, 97
Thirty Years War, 30
Thulessen Dahl, Kristian, 149
Thuringia, 146
Time magazine, 144
Tito, Josip Broz, 85
Tory, 182
Trianon, 108
Trudeau, Justin, 187

True Finns Party (PS, Perussuomalaiset), 24, 72, 78, 143, 156–157
Trump, Donald, 9–11, 14, 16, 25, 26, 36, 37, 41–43, 45, 56, 66, 79–81, 93, 105, 125, 126, 131, 138, 139, 141, 145, 168, 172, 174, 175, 185–196, 200, 209, 210, 212, 219
Turkey, 5, 17, 20, 37, 96, 116, 138, 180, 181, 213
Turkish, 181
Turks, 181
Twin Towers, 105

U
Ukraine, 176
Unidentified Flying Object (UFOs), 101
United Arab Emirates, 103
United Kingdom (UK), 10, 14, 22, 41, 58, 59, 63, 65, 69, 75, 81, 88, 113, 114, 131, 133, 135, 139, 141, 143, 171, 174, 177–182, 184, 185, 193, 209, 211, 212, 215
United Kingdom Independence Party (UKIP), 15, 22, 177, 179, 180, 183, 184, 215
United Nations (UN), 3, 56, 67, 138
United States (US), vii, 6, 8, 9, 11, 14, 16, 26, 35, 41, 47, 48, 54–57, 59, 61, 63, 66, 78–81, 87, 93, 99, 101–105, 109, 116, 118, 124–126, 131–139, 141, 143–145, 167, 168, 171, 172, 174, 175, 178, 179, 185–188, 190–192, 194–197, 200, 209–212, 219
University of Virginia, 194
Uruguay, 17
Uscinski, Joe, 186, 190
Utøya, 154

V
VB, 90, 91
Venezuela, 17, 19, 37, 42, 89, 134, 190, 214
Venezuelans, 17, 19, 190
Vennamo, Veikko, 78
Venner, Dominique, 68
Venstre, 119, 149, 151
Ventotene, 57
Ventotene manifesto, 57
Vienna, 71, 97, 147, 155
Vietnam War, 61, 62, 80
Villiers, Theresa, 181
Virginia, 141, 194
Visegrád countries, 167
Vlaams Belang, 90
Vlaams Blok, 90
Voeman, Gerrit, 92
Von Beyme, Klaus, 46
Von Herder, Johann Gottfried, 31, 32, 68
Vox party, 134

W
Waco, 102
Waffen-SS, 97
Wallace, George, 79
Wallonia, 89, 90
Wallonians, 90
Walloons, 91
Wallström, Margot, 175
War on Terror, 103, 104
Washington DC, 10, 14, 42, 56, 81, 102, 173, 179, 185–187, 196, 219
Watch, Jihad, 167
Watergate, 62
Waterloo, 89

Welch, Edgar, 196, 197
Welch, Joseph, 79
Westminster, 183
Westphalia, 4, 30
Wheen, Francis, 136
White, 13, 25, 59, 69, 80, 89, 101, 114, 140, 141, 146, 147, 175, 182, 183, 186, 190, 194–196, 210, 219
White Genocide, 69, 106, 139, 141, 195–196
Whitehall, 63
White House, 10, 195, 209
Widfeldt, Anders, 75, 120, 121, 148, 161
Wikileaks, 166
Wilders, G., 36, 41, 43, 116, 139, 140, 163, 198, 210
Willoch, Kaare, 122
Wilson, Jason, 141
Winston Churchill, 56
Winter War, 77
Wisconsin, 186
Wodak, Ruth, 22, 25, 32, 36, 42, 44, 96, 147
World Bank (WB), 3, 56, 138
World Trade Centre, 102
World War I (WWI), 55, 56, 89
World War II (WWII), 30, 53–55, 67, 85, 200n3
Wren, Karen, 40, 73, 74, 120, 121, 148

X
Xenophobia, 39, 48, 68, 74, 84, 87, 92, 96, 133, 141, 162, 186, 211

Y
Yablokov, Ilya, viii, 170, 173
Yakunin, Vladimir, 176
Yeltsin, Boris, 109, 110, 170
YouTube, 152, 196
Ypres, 89
Yugoslavia, 85
Yugoslav War, 85

Z
Zemmour, Eric, 199
Ziblatt, D., 16, 18, 79, 81, 104, 168, 188
Zúquete, José Pedro, 68, 132

Printed by Printforce, the Netherlands